UNGOVERNABLE

UNGOVERNABLE

The Political Diaries of a Chief Whip

SIMON HART

MACMILLAN

First published 2025 by Macmillan
an imprint of Pan Macmillan
The Smithson, 6 Briset Street, London EC1M 5NR
EU representative: Macmillan Publishers Ireland Ltd, 1st Floor,
The Liffey Trust Centre, 117–126 Sheriff Street Upper,
Dublin 1, D01 YC43
Associated companies throughout the world
www.panmacmillan.com

ISBN 978-1-0350-6879-1

1 3 5 7 9 8 6 4 2

A CIP catalogue record for this book is available from the British Library.

Epigraph copyright: Michael Dobbs, *House of Cards* (1989) and Netflix (2013–2028)

Typeset in Janson Text by Palimpsest Book Production Ltd, Falkirk, Stirlingshire
Printed and bound by CPI Group (UK) Ltd, Croydon, CR0 4YY

Visit **www.panmacmillan.com** to read more about all our books
and to buy them. You will also find features, author interviews and
news of any author events, and you can sign up for e-newsletters
so that you're always first to hear about our new releases.

For Abigail, Adam and Nell

'Proximity to power deludes some into thinking
that they wield it'

FRANCIS UNDERWOOD, *HOUSE OF CARDS*

CONTENTS

Preface

I need to get a couple of things straight from the start.

This is a contemporaneous diary written as events happened and as I saw them at the time. The original diaries cover six journals, containing over 200,000 words, all handwritten in illegible scrawl, often late at night, and which, when looking back, with the benefit of hindsight often seem comic. That's why real diaries are a rarity, especially when they cover political events that unfold so quickly: they're hard work, and you sometimes feel like a fool when you reread them several years later.

My initial plan was to note down interesting and amusing anecdotes, partly as a confession and an apology to my family for the prolonged periods of absence, secrecy and fatigue-induced curtness they tolerated with such patience and good humour. Now they serve as a record of what turned out to be an extraordinary time in British politics, and a glimpse behind the curtain of what truly goes on in Westminster and especially what happened during the last four and a half years.

My diaries also cover an aspect of politics that is rarely reported accurately: the Whips' Office. So, it is for whips past and future that I try to put the record straight. Some people will be sceptical about me doing this at all. They may argue either that this is a breach of a long-established custom that 'Chief Whips don't write books' or that, having maintained relative anonymity all

these years, no one will care what I think anyway. Both are valid concerns which I try to address throughout the book.

Where people have stumbled across difficult times it is not my intention to make things worse, or to breach confidences that existed between them and the Whips' Office. As I have often observed, most misdemeanours are the result of normal human frailties rather than intentional malevolence. That said, part of the reason for this book is to record just how problematic government has become (for all parties) and how a relatively small cohort of people, in our case, knowingly made things so hard that what tiny chances we had of a fifth term were extinguished. I believe that shining a light on that, and the reasons for it, is an essential step in minimising the risk of it happening again.

In addition, much of what is written about the role of the Whips' Office is wrong. What it does, how it does it, how we recruit its occupants and the influence it has are frequently exaggerated or fabricated. I jokingly blame the author and politician Michael Dobbs. In creating the mythical Chief Whip Francis Urquhart in his 1989 novel *House of Cards* and its 1990 TV adaptation, and later Frank Underwood in the Netflix version, he subjected all subsequent Chiefs to unfavourable comparisons. For this reason, Michael and I have become good friends, and have spent many happy hours laughing together about the almost invisible line between his 1970s imaginary vision of the Whips' Office, and my twenty-first-century real one.

As Chief Whip I met my opposite number, as well as representatives of the other parties, every week. We talked in complete confidence about the week's business, the pinch points and, of course, had a good gossip about the latest pickle that some of our members had got themselves into. The relationship is so important, and so discreet, that there are things I shared with my opposite number, Alan Campbell, that I would never have dared to share with my own side. But as he put it: 'We operate to a

political equivalent of the Geneva Convention.' In other words, it's all-out war, conducted to a set of rules.

And rather worryingly, I was one of the few recent Chiefs to have survived an entire premiership. The fact that there have been eleven of us since 2010 demonstrates the pace at which we burn through what political capital we have.

I have kept a diary since I was elected in 2010 as the MP for one of the UK's most westerly seats, Carmarthen West and South Pembrokeshire, representing it until 2024. Back then, my ambitions stretched only as far as serving two four-year terms (as was the normal term-length) but politics being so unpredictable I was re-elected on three further occasions before the boundary changes (and the voters) eventually caught up with me. In that time, I served on four Select Committees, as well as completing a stint on the executive board of the 1922 Committee, the back-benchers' trade union.

Following Theresa May's election as Prime Minister in 2017, I became her representative on the Committee for Standards in Public Life, during which time we undertook formal inquiries into intimidation in public life and MPs' second jobs. As this was a committee of mainly lay members, the three politicians (myself, Margaret Beckett for Labour and Andrew Stunell for the Lib Dems) were at the vanguard of protecting the interests of MPs and maintaining public expectation too.

And then, to widespread surprise, I was appointed treasurer for Boris Johnson's successful leadership campaign, following which Boris made me Minister for Implementation in the Cabinet Office. As Boris said in the appointment interview: 'Before you ask, I don't know what that is either.'

During the 2019 election campaign the then Secretary of State for Wales, Alun Cairns, was forced to stand down, leaving a vacancy that I was asked to fill. I occupied the position between 2019 and 2022, sitting in Cabinet during arguably the most volatile years in recent political history. All periods of political

history can be described as unique, but compared with our early years of coalition with the Lib Dems, the next bit was off the scale.

And it is with the BBC exit poll of December 2019 that this book begins. I am one of a small number of Cabinet members who made it through (almost all of) Boris Johnson's premiership, before a brief hiatus from the Cabinet was followed by my becoming Chief Whip under Rishi Sunak. As a result, I've had a front-seat view of everything from negotiations around Brexit to Covid and its political fallout; from the impact of Liz Truss's extraordinary forty-nine-day premiership to the Russian invasion of Ukraine.

What I witnessed, from inside the rooms in which these successive dramas unfolded, was less a story of scandal and incompetence (of which there was still plenty) and much more the opposite. In other words, if you look behind the curtain you will – more often than not – find people driven by solid values, who are doing their best in increasingly intolerable circumstances. However, politicians and those around them are flawed people too, at the mercy of all the pressures that modern life presents, and are constantly in the full glare of an ever-more merciless media. Decision-making is forced into ever shorter timescales; the only reaction permitted is one of outrage to any government or human failing, however trivial. Whatever happened to 'mildly disappointed' as a reaction to a political event? At the same time, there has emerged an irrational public expectation that politicians should be simultaneously unexceptional and exceptional; that we should be an exact replication of society yet above some of the flaws from which we all suffer.

So what started as a daily résumé of 'funny things that happened at work today' for my then very young children has become my version of a 'rise and fall' account, which concludes (with some sadness) that governing Britain in a kind, empathetic

and effective way is becoming increasingly impossible. What started as a comedy, ended as a tragedy.

The big question that these recollections raise is this: how on earth have we reached a position where we can win an 81-seat majority in December 2019, yet burn through three very different Prime Ministers, concluding with a thorough beating at the hands of an unproven Labour alternative less than five years later?

So, in publishing these accounts it is not my intention to embarrass, humiliate or destroy people. Rather, it is to reveal my fear that the state of our politics and government is harming our ability to attract, and retain, leaders of the future.

The book also seeks to be a discreet tribute to the nameless, especially special advisers. 'What do those SpAds in No. 10 know about anything?' is a phrase I heard many times. In fact, they know quite a bit, work incredibly hard and strive to achieve much the same outcomes as the MPs and ministers they serve. And, of course, there is plenty of comedy too, dark and tragic though some of it may be.

———

In order to showcase the breadth of the events that I cover – from Covid to the 2024 election, via whipping and the machinations of Cabinet – and reveal the full complexities of life in, and around, government, I have edited the contents of certain entries slightly to avoid references to events that are not pertinent and which may confuse when read out of context. As a result, some days are skipped. In the original diaries, I also refer often to my family* and personal life but I have chosen not to reference this too much in the book.

---

*   My wife, Abigail, and my two children, Adam and Elinor (Nell for short).

1

JUBILATION

December 2019–May 2020

For those with long memories, the 2019 election was a huge gamble. Parliament and the Government had been paralysed by Brexit stand-offs and our majority was far too slender to get any legislation passed, let alone a Brexit deal. For months, Boris had challenged Labour to an election to resolve the issue once and for all. Yet Corbyn's Labour Party, divided and stubborn in itself, could see the trap and remained wary of falling into it. However, sustained pressure and mounting public exasperation forced his eventual capitulation. We knew too that a contest between Johnson and Corbyn was one we could win. Momentum – the electoral machine Corbyn was so heavily reliant on – spectacularly misjudged the public mood. Boris was determined to 'own the future', and to consign Momentum to the past.

That Boris is unique goes without saying, but it is not always to his advantage. I remember once thinking it would be hard for me to remain in a Party led by him, but then quickly finding myself happy to serve in two ministerial positions under him and to go out on the airwaves defending him. He was a hypnotist like that, and I became the total opportunist. I loved our occasional chats, although we were never really friends as such. In fact, I often wondered if Prime Ministers ever really have any true friends.

In the first part of *Ungovernable*, I reveal the many sides of this political enigma, starting with the day of the remarkable election and the subsequent euphoria, which lasted just a few

weeks before Covid hoved into view. As a 'territorial SoS' (the Secretary of State for Wales) I was embedded in the process from the start – when ministers and officials were grappling to understand the meaning of pandemic, what an R number was and whether the 'reasonable worst-case scenario' really would mean inflatable mortuaries on your local football pitch.

It also exposed me to the thankless challenge of trying to work with a highly politicised Labour Welsh Government under Mark Drakeford, who was determined to undermine the UK Conservative Government. His ambition was made much easier by the nature of the devolution settlement. In short, it grants devolved government the power to spend taxpayers' money with none of the responsibilities. I was never a great fan of devolution in its current form (I voted against but it went through on a paltry turnout in 1998) and my time in the Wales Office reinforced my scepticism. Almost every area of public service under Welsh Government control – health, education, transport, for example – performed worse than its UK equivalent, despite 20% more funding. But this was the model I had to work with, being held to account every six weeks at Wales Oral Questions in the Chamber.

I reflect on how Johnson's Government took shape, who were the winners (me, for one) and who were losers, all interspersed with the battle of Brexit and the demise of Jeremy Corbyn as Labour leader. The Court of Boris Johnson had its fair share of characters and jokers. Many were surprisingly mainstream and centrist. They (our MPs) could see a match-winner in Boris even if it came with a less disciplined side. What mattered was winning not governing. That was for later. But to win both the leadership and the election, he needed a team to support him, which was more complicated. There were scores to be settled, promises to be fulfilled. The Party knew this was where the cracks could appear but was happy to take the risk. Installing Dominic Cummings as chief adviser was one such appointment. To those who didn't know him, myself included, he was a bit

of a caricature; he seemed like a character straight out of *The Thick of It* and was determined to deploy his formidable intellect in the least empathetic way. Boris's partner Carrie Symonds was an experienced media operator with years of Conservative Campaign Headquarters [CCHQ] experience under her belt, especially in populist policy areas like animal welfare – she would be bending Boris's ear too (and why not?).

And then there were the factions. To the right was the ERG (European Research Group), noisy but well organised. To the left the 'One Nation' group, pursuing a more centrist approach, convinced, rightly in my view, that 'elections are won from the centre not the fringes'. What were the realistic prospects of ever establishing consensus between Suella Braverman on the one hand and Damian Green on the other?

Boris often claimed to 'get the big calls right'. This is true, but it turned out the small calls mattered too, and despite its numerous dark corners No. 10 is a hard place to find somewhere to hide.

———— • ————

Thursday, 12 December 2019

ELECTION DAY.

The polls say our lead has been squeezed to just 5%. It's enough to win but it's also worryingly close to hung-parliament territory. Please not that again. The pressure is intense. If I'm feeling it, then God knows what the centre must be experiencing. Momentum is pulling out all the stops here. Can they smell something we can't? We have done all we can, though. We have knocked, Facebooked, argued, notified, lobbied, but even all that combined probably has little impact on the outcome. This is about Brexit and Corbyn, not me. If we lose it's because the nation is happy to have a flirt with socialism.

We watch *Mission Impossible* to while away the time until the exit poll is announced at ten. It is with disbelief that the BBC's Huw Edwards predicts a Conservative majority of 81 seats, substantially better than anything we could have dreamed of. It's a 'fuck me' moment. I keep looking at my watch, but everyone is completely stunned. As the night wears on, one by one Labour heartlands fall – Blythe, Hartlepool, Bridgend; even Sedgefield, Blair's old seat, turns blue.

Ynys Mon and even Bolsover fall to the Conservatives. It is a rout. News from my own count in Haverfordwest is that I have won the box counts in Pennar and Monkton, once no-go zones for Conservatives. For the first time ever, I get more than 50% of the vote and a majority of 7,745. To some that may not seem many, but to us it is an all-time record.

Almost all our seats are returned with bigger majorities. Andrew Percy [Goole] now sits on a 22,500 advantage, a far cry from the 5,000 Labour majority he first fought in 2010.

There is euphoria and surprise at the 80-seat margin. On paper it should give me two more terms. It is genuinely extraordinary. Even odder is Corbyn's refusal to go further than saying he won't fight the next general election. So Labour is now divided between those who blame the voters and those who realise that the Party must change. A familiar scenario where parties are overpopulated with idealogues and underpopulated with pragmatists. The problem with the hard left, and the hard right for that matter, is they always believe that the voters are stupid, or deaf, and that any future success is dependent on just shouting the same message, only louder.

Monday, 16 December

The Private Office suggests that I report to the Cabinet Office to 'resume' my role [as a minister in that department]. Until otherwise informed, the Government continues to be the Government, but an unrealistic hope lingers on all our minds that we might get a 'top job'. I meet up with Permanent Secretary John Manzoni, ostensibly to pick up where we left off. I have been hanging around the Cabinet Office all day, just in case. I had received no guarantees, and we all know Boris functions differently to most people.

At 5.15 p.m. I get the classic 'number withheld' on my phone screen. It's either Mark Garnier [Wyre Forest] taking the piss, or the No. 10 switchboard.

The PM would like to see me.

'Great,' I said, 'when have you in mind?'

'5.20,' comes the reply.

Just as well I was next door, so I cut off Manzoni (who I suspect knew more than he was letting on) and legged it through the access pod into the back of No. 10 and checked in. The place was buzzing with activity, smiling people with clipboards and cameras, explaining the process that was about to unfold. Secretary of State [SoS] Wales seems to be on the cards.

I am ushered into the Cabinet Room where a fired-up and energetic PM greets me with classic Boris charm. The burly figure of Mark Spencer [Chief Whip] sits quietly at the far end taking notes. Boris opens with 'I've been thinking about Wales, Simon, and I want you to take on the Secretary of State role.'

Then a short chat about the battles ahead and getting David 'TC' Davies [Monmouth] as my deputy, and then straight back out into a side room for a final chance for the system to verify my appropriateness for the role.

I wasn't quite sure of the level of detail to confess or deny.

Either way, I calculated that anything I had to say would be mild compared to what Boris might have fessed up.

Spencer then explained that the whole process had not been as straightforward as I first thought. Boris and he were content with my nomination, but some in No. 10 had put forward David Jones [Clwyd West] for the role. He had done it before, was a keen Brexiteer and Welsh-speaking. Spencer objected, but it took the personal intervention of the PM to make my appointment happen.

Then, like magic, it's a photo, a social media post from No. 10 to confirm my appointment, and then across the road to the Wales Office where the team is ready and waiting. Gwydyr House is an inconspicuous building tucked into the shadow of the MoD and dead opposite the Cabinet Office at 70 Whitehall. It's the building used for the arrival of Jim Hacker as Minister for the Department of Administrative Affairs in the first episode of my favourite programme, *Yes Minister*. I am therefore in the very best of company.

I speak to the new team of civil servants. We host an MPs' reception, speak to the First Minister [FM] Mark Drakeford in Cardiff, and generally get our heads around an 'agenda'. It feels like I have actual power or, failing that, at least influence.

Then it's off to the Palace in a black Jaguar to be sworn in as a Privy Councillor [PC]* and receive the Seal of Office. This feels like something that happens to other people.

I am accompanied in the Palace anteroom by Jacob Rees-Mogg who is Chairman of the Council, Thérèse Coffey [SoS Work and Pensions], Ben Wallace [SoS Defence] and Alister Jack [SoS Scotland]. We receive strict instructions from Richard

---

* The Privy Council was originally the executive arm of English government from as early as the thirteenth century, although its powers declined as political authority shifted to the Cabinet in the late seventeenth and early eighteenth centuries. Formally, it remains an advisory body to the monarch and its members are known as Privy Counsellors.

Tilbrook (who runs the Privy Council) on the process. We are to wait in line, the Queen will be announced and we await her taking her position standing at one end of the room. We are to take one step forward, bow, two steps forward, kneel. Take the Queen's hand when indicated, don't slobber on it as the kissing takes place, say a few words, retreat. It sounds easy.

Dress rehearsal complete, it's time for the real deal, something she has done many thousands of times and something we will only ever do once. Someone announces her arrival. We all stand to attention as the door opens and in she comes, probably the most famous woman in the world and definitely much smaller than I anticipated. We do our stuff, I don't think I mess it up, we exchange some formalities and then relax. Jack is the first to engage, carefully pushing the Queen to the limit of 'banter' with which she is comfortable. This time it was to celebrate the absence of any damaging animal welfare references in the Government's plans. 'You will have seen all that animal welfare stuff has disappeared,' he said. Jack knows exactly what he's doing, as of course does she.

Tuesday, 7 January 2020

To my first ever Cabinet. It was hard being cool about it, to give the impression that this was all just a normal Tuesday morning meeting and not to be starstruck or overwhelmed as the fleet of Government limos unloaded their occupants outside the black front door. The knack was to look like you were born to this. It reminded me of school. I think I failed on all counts. The Cabinet Room is laid out as if for a dinner party. The PM's chair is the only one with arms and each place on the green baize table had a name card with your full name and title. There was clearly a pecking order. Chancellor is on the PM's left, Cabinet Secretary on the right, Home and Foreign Secretaries opposite, and so on. Down our end were the junior ranks. I had Gavin Williamson

[SoS Education] on my left, Kit Malthouse [Policing Minister] opposite and Lord Goldsmith [Defra Minister] alongside, and a few officials and the secretariat. Our phones had to be left in a varnished wooden box outside, meaning this was supposed to be one of the few rooms in the whole government operation, apart from COBR,* where private discussions would not leak.

The PM was on great form as expected, full of Boris chutzpah. There wasn't much business to be done, but there were lots of motivational contributions (and some strange ones too) from the old hands whilst us virgins looked on mesmerised by it all. It feels like we are well set for five years, and that Labour will struggle to recover any time soon from such a pounding.

Parliament too was awash with bewildered-looking newbies. I barely recognised anyone. As before, we gravitate towards year groups, defined by our length of service rather than the quality of it. Anybody described by the media in the run-up to all this as a 'rising star' is immediately marked out for a future kicking. How we hate a cocky upstart.

Wednesday, 8 January

COBR – chaired by Michael Gove [Chancellor of the Duchy of Lancaster] to discuss (Br)exit planning. 'Brexit', Michael explains, 'is now a dirty word.' Hereinafter we must refer to it as an 'historic event'.

I am assigned my new office on the Upper Ministerial Corridor. The UMC is just behind the Speaker's Chair and up a scruffy-looking staircase. It is made up of old, but grand, oak-panelled offices with the usual selection of Commons-branded furniture

---

* COBR or COBRA is shorthand for the Civil Contingencies Committee that is convened to handle matters of national emergency or major disruption.

– except mine, which is ridiculously small, cold and quite obviously once a storeroom. It will do as I won't be here much, I guess.

Friday, 10 January

It's a long day in Cardiff for some 'inter-governmental relations', starting with meeting FM Mark Drakeford. My hope is that we can at least generate some cooperation between us but my expectation is more realistic. Alun Cairns was unfairly criticised for being too aggressive and confrontational so I might try a more emollient approach. Drakeford's public persona is one of a dull academic, the sort of lefty philosophy lecturer you used to find at Luton Polytechnic in the 1970s. Disappointingly, that seems to be the case in private too. He is a Welsh Jeremy Corbyn, although to be fair he is noticeably more polite.

Saturday, 11 January

Much excitement as my first 'Red Box' arrives at home. It is delivered by a courier who claimed to be part of the SAS assault team that liberated the Iranian Embassy in 1981, so having been talked through the entire episode I had almost run out of time to open the box and study its contents. I have met so many people who were part of that Special Forces triumph that I'm left wondering how they all fitted in the building.

Monday, 13 January

The Wales Office Mercedes whisks me to Cardiff. All very comfortable and easy to get used to. Everyone wants to meet, mainly to resurrect crazy or unaffordable ideas that were rightly closed by Cairns in the past. But the civil service knows that by dusting them all off again they can keep me fully occupied

until my replacement comes along. Sir Humphrey Appleby lives on . . .

We practise endlessly for Welsh Orals on Wednesday. TC is very good and loves it, I am the opposite . . . maybe the combination will work? The greatest joy is knowing TC has no ulterior motives, at least none that I can see.

Tuesday, 14 January

It's only my second one but Cabinet was dull. Boris chaired it professionally but was clearly keen for it to end. Apparently, Home Sec Priti Patel's excellent crime presentation got leaked to *The Times* prompting a Cabinet Office leak inquiry. I had seen the story and assumed it was put out on purpose as it was remarkably warm about the new Government's determination. I feel guilty even though I haven't talked to anyone!

Wednesday, 15 January

So, the big day and my expectations of nervousness are easily met. Welsh Orals is probably the least-watched political occasion of the week, but a single cock-up can soon change all that. I try to be cool but when Percy tells me he 'won't miss this car crash for anything', I start to fret a little. Colleagues chatter and gossip as we await the Speaker's procession, a few say good luck, others offer deliberately contrary advice whilst TC and I try to give the impression that we have done all this before. We haven't. The Labour benches fill up too, polite but ready to draw blood if any opportunity arises. There is no mercy in the Chamber especially from your own colleagues. Mess up and you are dead. Nothing is more fun than a ministerial disaster at the dispatch box. It's even more fun than a batsman getting a direct hit in the balls in cricket.

Off we go. Mr Speaker: 'Questions to the Secretary of State for Wales – number one.'

What a blur. I take the first 15 minutes and I think it goes okay. Welsh Language, shared prosperity, steel, growth funds, etc. Bit shaky to start and worry that I am a bit long-winded, but the new Speaker is very different to the awful Bercow. No sneering or vindictiveness, he reads the situation well and lets us both find our feet. By 11.55 the Chamber is packed and noisy in readiness for PMQs and we are going well. A huge roar goes up as Boris shuffles in, messy hair, papers all over the shop and shirt hanging out. For someone so untidy he always wears an expensive tie though.

Thursday, 16 January

Catch up with Cleo Watson and Ben Gascoigne (Gazza) from No. 10. Cleo is a SpAd close to Cummings and Boris and tasked, amongst numerous other things, in helping Shelley (Boris's brilliant fixer) get Boris to the right place at the right time, with the right brief and, being Boris, the right jokes. Gazza is the Political Secretary [PolSec]. He's been with Boris since the London Mayor days and seen by MPs as totally sound. He is also fun, and more important than that, unusually normal. They are already talking of a 'Feb reshuffle'. We have only just got going and already there is something to worry about. I imagine the plan is to keep everyone on their toes.

Monday, 20 January

Two flunkeys from the Cabinet Office came to interview me for the Cabinet leak inquiry. Both were in their twenties, clad in jeans and T-shirts and not especially engaged (is this a ploy . . .?). The interview went like this:

'Did you leak the crime doc to the press?'

'No,' said I.

'Do you know Steve Swinford or James Forsyth?' (Two outstanding lobby journalists.)

'Yes,' said I. Eyes light up a little.

A brief explanation of the one conversation I had with them in the last twelve months, and they thanked me and left. Inquiry over, I am a free man once more.

Tuesday, 21 January

Cabinet is now into a rhythm of being thankfully short, sweet and uncontentious. Andrea Leadsom [Leader of the House] dominates and there is no mention of the leak.

Wednesday, 22 January

Meeting with my Scotland equivalent Alister Jack. He's definitely 'one of us' and there is a wicked side to him too. We talk mainly about grouse and salmon, about which he is the Government's leading expert.

Spectator dinner and awards evening, traditionally a rather hardcore drinking challenge. I am placed between two BBC stalwarts – Carolyn Quinn and Emily Maitlis. Not really knowing either, I am on my guard (well . . . a bit). Both are enormous fun. I can't resist asking a very patient Emily about her recent Prince Andrew bombshell but also about her very middle-class background in Shropshire. We agree to meet again. All the journos seem strangely concerned about the No. 10 attitude to them. Since the coronation of Boris they feel No. 10 has cut them out of everything, preferring to just 'supply content' rather than entertain discussion. They blame Cummings and warn that if we don't fill the usual voids, then someone else will and we may not like them. I promise to feed it in, which I probably won't.

Thursday, 23 January

It seems the coronavirus, originally in China, is spreading but no cases yet in the UK. Chief Medical Officer [CMO] Whitty and Matt Hancock [SoS Health] doing a good job it seems.

Tuesday, 28 January

There is a mass exodus to Cardiff, led by Michael Gove.

I have the first group meeting with Conservative Assembly Members [AMs] then Gove and I visit a medi-tech company in Cardiff before a joint ministerial meeting with other Devolved Administrations [DAs] (chaired drearily by the FM).

For some odd reason we all then fly back to Northolt on the Queen's Flight, which Gove has purloined for the day. By the time we flog out of Cardiff city centre to the airport and then drive another hour from Northolt to No. 10, the people who had opted for a train from Cardiff had already arrived. The flight was so short we just about managed to cram in a biscuit and a cup of tea.

Wednesday, 29 January

Yet another COBR meeting on the EU exit. There are too many people present and it all seems rather formulaic. Much more entertaining, despite having a cold, is dinner in Skylon at the Festival Hall with Guto Bebb [Aberconwy], journalist Guto Harri and journo-turned-PR man Ben Brogan. GH has been advising the centre on the strange case of Jennifer Arcuri* but infuriatingly reveals nothing.

---

* A former colleague of Boris Johnson's at County Hall about whom rumours of a relationship abounded.

Thursday, 30 January

COBR, this time on coronavirus. It seems more serious now. Expectation is that we will get it here in the UK and that it spreads fast, but that it's less fatal than SARS. Hancock chaired the meeting well and the CMO was excellent and reassuring, given this is all rather medical for most of us in the room.

Friday, 31 January

'Brexit Day'. Who would ever have believed it?

It's finished numerous PMs and split the country and the Party, but we are leaving the EU. Despite 'respecting the will of the people' I still question whether the political price is one worth paying. I voted remain not because of ideology but because unpicking this fifty-year relationship is an expensive nightmare for which no one will thank us.

To recognise this occasion the Cabinet decamps to Sunderland (yes . . .) via trains, planes and automobiles and I guess vast associated expense.

We meet some apprentices, who find the whole thing reassuringly amusing and don't recognise any of us 'B' listers at all. Then to a standard Cabinet meeting where we are gifted a Brexit 50p coin. That makes it all so worthwhile. More reshuffle talk ensues.

Trains back to London – mild guilt as the Chancellor [CX] and Foreign Secretary go standard class and I go first! And then straight to the No. 10 drinkies. A mixture of the sensible and not so sensible who are wearing Union Jack ties and waistcoats. Boris on good form and lots of fist pumping. We even talked and I feel we could get on well in the right conditions. Anyway, I'm glad I went as it suggests I'm 'with the programme'.

Weirdly, no Carrie – she's almost totally disappeared.

Home at 3 a.m.

Tuesday, 4 February

Cabinet postponed until Monday sparking reshuffle rumours but nothing concrete. Meet Manzoni for procurement catch-up. He's leaving which is a shame as he is really very good.

Thursday, 6 February

Visit to Toyota and Airbus in North Wales. Two vast and important businesses. If ever there was an example of the dangers of [Welsh] independence, it's here in Deeside. Something like half the workforce commutes in from England every day and the business owners see this as their UK base, European even, not just Welsh. Imagine the chaos of an alternative tax regime?

Tuesday, 11 February

Cabinet is delayed but no one tells me, so I turn up 90 minutes early. I leave via the Cabinet Office, so the mistake goes unnoticed. When it did happen, there were uncharacteristically aggressive contributions from Esther McVey [Housing Minister], Theresa Villiers [Defra Secretary] and Andrea Leadsom. All presumably concerned that this would be their last moment in the sun before the reshuffle.

Wednesday, 12 February

At their request I meet with Plaid Cymru MPs – who are keen to find 'common ground'. The trouble is there is no common ground in a world where independence remains their principal reason for existence. Ben Lake [Ceredigion] is the best of them mainly because he is the least institutionalised. He also understands that there is life beyond Offa's Dyke. I suspect that were he to live in England he would most likely be a Conservative.

Jonathan Edwards [Carmarthen East] is very sharp but wedded to the cause, and Surrey-born leader Liz Saville Roberts [Dwyfor Meirionnydd] polite and engaging.

Thursday, 13 February

Thank God it's reshuffle day so we can end the relentless nervousness and speculation. We all sit by our phones pretending not to care.

It starts at 07.45 with the sackings – [Julian] Smith [SoS Northern Ireland], McVey, Villiers, and various others. The big shock comes mid-morning when No. 10 offers Sajid Javid the chance to remain as CX but only if he fires various advisers. Apparently, No. 10 (Cummings) wants to blend the No. 10 and 11 SpAd teams to try and de-risk the endless competition between the two machines. After a lengthy row, he refuses and then honourably resigns.

In one move the reshuffle goes from restoring authority to creating chaos and disorder.

No. 10 moves quickly to restore order by installing the competent Rishi Sunak in his place. He was lined up for the Chief Secretary to the Treasury [CST] job so his day has taken an interesting and unexpected turn.

To move the story on they accelerate the other appointments ASAP.

No startling newbies other than Anne-Marie Trevelyan getting SoS for International Development and Suella Braverman (over-promoted to DFID [Department for International Development] and now even more so as Attorney General) and who is now presumably unsackable.*

My turn came mid-afternoon when I 'get the call'. By now

---

* Having leveraged various Government positions, No. 10 felt Braverman's removal could be more trouble than it was worth.

it was all a well-oiled process of reappointment with Boris, the new Chief Whip and a few others in the room. It was all very boisterous and public school.

However, it is a relief, as up until now the Government has felt very probationary, after today it will resume the air of something more permanent and real.

Friday, 14 February

Fun and games at the 6.30 p.m. Cummings meeting for SpAds. These have become a bit legendary for their silliness. Cummings likes to project the image of some kind of pound-shop hard man, but nobody really takes him seriously any more, especially it seems one of the MoD SpAds who gives him a telling off in public for bullying. An overdue, good and brave move leading to an especially riotous SpAd drinking session afterwards. You can't run a team based on fear and hatred, however brainy you are.

Cabinet and political cabinet were happy affairs, despite the rather odd Boris habit of asking members to shout out answers to questions like: 'How many hospitals are we going to build?', 'How many police officers are we going to hire?'

I assume they did that at Eton (they definitely did at Radley) but the Cabinet is not so well trained in these techniques, so it looks a little awkward and is all on camera.

Wednesday, 19 February

Call with the FM on flooding issues which the Welsh Government [WG] then unhelpfully leaks to the press. As ever with the WG they want money when it suits them but never the responsibility.

The most worrying aspect of the torrential rain is that certain coal tips across South Wales are showing signs of instability. Nobody seems sure about the level of risk but there is no way we can drag our feet and risk an 'Aberfan Two'. I'm insisting on

instant reaction to that and No. 10 and the Treasury are being engaged and helpful.

To St Athan to see the Prince of Wales unveil the new £158k Aston Martin DBX. I get a spin around the tarmac. PoW arrives in his own bioethanol fifty-year-old Aston.

Apparently 98% of the Astons ever made are still on the road and average 12,000 miles a year, making them incredibly climate friendly compared with other modern vehicles. I was reprimanded for describing their engine 'sound' as 'noise'. 'Maybe', I suggested forlornly to the civil servants, 'the Wales Office car could be made in Wales and could be a DBX?'

Then off to Pontypridd with HRH to visit flood sites and victims. The water was up and down so quickly that the alarms were pointless. Businesses and dreams washed away in a matter of hours. The Prince of Wales does this sort of thing so well and it was appreciated by the thousands who turned up to see him. The town is out in force, waving flags (Union Jacks as well as the Dragon). There are even selfies, something I imagine could worry the royal household. But it works because he is authentic. The empathy is real not contrived and the warmth can be felt. Importantly, he doesn't 'dumb down' as a politician might. He is the Prince of Wales and not afraid to wear that title with pride.

At my insistence, urgent meetings are held in Cardiff re coal tips and movement. I forced the FM into agreeing a joint statement and taking urgent action, whatever that means. Astonishingly, it seems that we don't really know who owns what and where the liability lies. Some are owned by the Coal Board, some by private landowners, who claim that, at the point of sale, the liability

was never transferred (sensibly if you were the purchaser). We agreed to create a risk register and start the process of costing all this out. It is devolved, but there was still no sense of urgency and I sensed that WG loathed being leant on by UKG on this.

Wednesday, 26 February

'Wales in London' dinner at the Guildhall with BBC's Huw Edwards in charge. Charming, clever and very good company. He rings his mum in Llanelli every day and speaks to her in Welsh to keep his language skills up. Lord 'Mervyn' Davies on the other hand was a little too long-winded. With the image of John Redwood [former Minister and SoS] firmly engraved in my mind I had rehearsed the National Anthem as I knew the 'top table' would be facing the 600 guests – one word out of place and I was toast. I got through, well enough for Manon Antoniazzi to notice and comment. (She is William Hague's sister-in-law and the most senior civil servant in the Senedd.)

Thursday, 27 February

St David's Day 'General Debate'. It sounds grand but we get squeezed into a couple of spare hours on a one-line whip Thursday so it's hardly a sell-out. However, I get to 'open' for the Government and TC 'closes'.

It went quite well, and I think I have just about perfected 'authoritative' with 'affable' for occasions like this. Had to slip away to the No. 10 reception where (despite chaotic build-up!) Boris gave a spot-on speech full of humour and optimism. There was a spattering of the well-known including bizarrely Carol Vorderman, who is no friend of ours. The explanation (rumour) was that she was fronting up the kids' charity who were guests of honour. Given her antipathy for politicians generally, and ours in particular, she seemed remarkably comfortable accepting our

hospitality. For some reason she had mistakenly wandered into the Wales Office on her way to No. 10, but Eric the security guy hadn't recognised her so summoned Jack Sellers (my Wales Office SpAd) down from upstairs to vouch for her.

Friday, 28 February

Yet more rain and more flood/mud slide warnings.

Early start to get to Tata in Port Talbot. Great people but what a dump of a site. It doesn't look like any serious money has been spent on it since the 1960s.

It now appears that the Home Secretary Priti Patel is at war with her Permanent Secretary [Sir Philip Rutnam]. Not sure that will end well. In fact, within hours, it clearly doesn't.

Sir Philip has resigned and will sue the government for constructive dismissal. If this gets to tribunal all hell will break loose. Priti can have an abrasive and demanding style, but he is the senior civil servant in one of the biggest government departments so he should be able to handle things. The PM orders us to 'form a circle round the Pritster'.

Coronavirus has gone from 'Reasonable Worst-Case Scenario' [RWCS] to the 'actual' scenario. Probably still hysteria but a massive economic hit could be just what we don't need.

And then, Boris and Carrie announce her pregnancy (that explains why she wasn't at the Brexit celebrations perhaps) and their engagement. How the hell does he find the time and energy?

Monday, 2 March

COBR, this time with the PM. Numbers still low but the RWCS talks of many thousands of potential victims. There is talk about whether the handling should be conducted under the auspices of the Civil Contingencies Act, a measure that would need quite

frequent Parliamentary approval but is UK-wide, compared with Public Health legislation which is less onerous but fully devolved. Hancock favoured the latter, Rees-Mogg the former adding that, 'if this isn't a civil contingencies emergency then I don't know what is'.

Wednesday, 4 March

Lunch with Kate Ferguson and Lizzy Buchan (from the *Sun* and *Independent*) at the Blue Boar. Cummings would be livid and immediately suspect mischief if he knew. In fact, the whole purpose of private chats with journos is not to spill the beans but to provide some factual context.

Continuing the theme, it's dinner with Laura Kuenssberg [BBC] at Cafe Murano in St James's (she's paying). For all the years I have known her, I would have no more clue now how she votes than on the day we first met. Anyway, I rather tactlessly suggested that she looked knackered, so we finished at 10.30.

Friday, 6 March

Long drive to Llangollen for the Welsh Conservative Party Conference. Paul Davies [Leader of Welsh Conservatives] spoke well, Byron Davies [Welsh Chairman] was fine but I think my speech went even better and people were kind about it. Certainly, Jack Sellers and I were on about draft ten by the time we got there. The key thing is to keep it short and funny.

Then the main gig was Boris. There was a lively introduction video, big entrance, shout-out, and he was funny, irreverent and compelling. The punters loved it even if the speech contained little by way of actual content. Then I had 20 mins face to face with him – we talked about Goldie Looking Chain [Welsh comedy hip-hop group] and some other frivolities (like a North–South cable car). I find him incredibly hard to fathom.

Saturday, 7 March

To Holyhead and Colwyn Bay with Priti Patel. She's permanently annoyed about something but gave a 7/10 speech after dinner. Her battle with Sir Philip is going to get bloody.

Left at 10.45 and got home at 2.30 a.m.

Wednesday, 11 March

Early start with Steve Barclay [CST] at the Treasury. A good brief as to what's in the budget for Wales. Sort of okay without being mind-blowing. Quite a lot of 'Barnett'* but some other stuff also. Then a quick Cabinet where it is confirmed that Covid-19 is turning quite nasty, so to COBR where that and more is confirmed. We are four weeks behind Italy and numbers are starting to accelerate.

Finished with a round of media and a drink with the BBC's Vicki Young.

Thursday, 12 March

COBR chaired by the PM. Coronavirus is now officially a crisis, and we move to the next stage. The mood has entirely changed. Even the PM has cut back on the jokes. Excellent contributions as ever from the CMO, CSA [Chief Scientific Adviser Patrick Vallance] and even Dominic Cummings makes a pertinent intervention. Shame he was dressed like he had just come back from a week at Glastonbury. The PM was statesmanlike and clearly much more worried than previously.

We are told by Hancock that the aim is to 'flatten the curve',

---

* The formula by which UK Government calculates the money it provides devolved Governments for the purposes of delivering public services. In Wales it is 20% more per capita than in England.

to prevent the NHS becoming overwhelmed at any one time. This means we should peak in June and develop something Vallance describes as 'herd immunity' thus mainly protecting the over-seventies who he thinks are the most vulnerable to this thing. There is NO evidence that closing schools helps but the public is not really listening. We are making good progress, but it is marred by Nicola Sturgeon [FM Scotland] (and Drakeford) racing off to the media to get their word in first and reveal our decision.

Then there was a ministerial spat on a range of things that some participants thought should have been planned for but haven't been, tactfully resolved by the PM before it got too spiky. I was sat close to No. 10 Director of Communications Lee Cain and we both agreed that the row will end up in the papers as there were multiple leakers in the room or dialled in.

Despite this, the PM and scientists were excellent at the press briefing.

Friday, 13 March

All plans are cancelled so that I can accompany Matt Hancock to Cardiff to see their Health Secretary Vaughan Gething, and Senedd members Angela Burns and Adam Price. Matt is tired but doing a really good job. Welsh Government is suddenly behaving more responsibly. However, the numbers look grim. I ask Matt what single thing is keeping him awake at night. 'Ventilators. However many ventilators we have it won't be enough,' he replies. 'We need to buy as many as we can, from wherever we can get them.'

The big race meeting at the Cheltenham Festival goes ahead but the Wales vs Scotland rugby in Cardiff is postponed. It's a shame as a strong No. 10 contingent was planning on coming. The scientific view is whilst the events may be open air, the trains and hotels needed to house everyone would be overcrowded.

Sunday, 15 March

It seems that Covid-19 has seized control across the globe and is accelerating faster here in the UK than expected. Every possible measure is now in play. Clearing hospital beds, buying ventilators, accessing drugs, and keeping the nation informed.

Boris and the experts now conducting a daily 5 p.m. press conference from No. 10 and COBR also meets at least daily, complete with TOs [the Territorial Offices, Wales, Scotland and Northern Ireland] in attendance.

Tuesday, 17 March

At a very sombre Cabinet, we are told by the PM that this is the 'last time we will meet like this for some time'. It's now a war cabinet, handled accordingly by the PM.

Wednesday, 18 March

At COBR we agree to close schools from Friday – against our own advice and mainly because Scotland and Wales won't hold the line. Privately, Gavin [Williamson] thinks this is a big mistake and will trap some kids in more enclosed spaces at home than they have at school and in the more extreme cases put them in danger of abusive parents. But he is cornered.

However, we will keep them open for the children of 'key workers' which turns out to be between 20–40% of the population.

Thursday, 19 March

I spend all day calling stakeholders, trying to reassure and explain what we have in mind. The economy is panicking. Big businesses like Brains, Folly Farm and Bluestone could go under in days if

business collapses. Multiple thousands of jobs are instantly at risk. It is hard to picture a more serious situation.

Friday, 20 March

5 p.m. The PM and Chancellor join to give the most extraordinary press brief I think we are ever likely to experience. All four of us sit glued to the TV in the kitchen as they set out what we do next.

In short, we are about to nationalise the economy with what amounts to £300 billion of aid. Although to some this is 'deeply unconservative' it is also exactly how a serious government should act in a moment of international crisis.

We are throwing the kitchen sink at this and will pay for it for years. None of us has really appreciated that we are even capable of such drastic action, but it is enthusiastically received, and Boris and Rishi are hailed as heroes (despite there being a long way to go yet).

Somehow Brexit is a sideshow. 'This', as Blackadder would say; 'is a crisis.'

During the GE and before, the big question was whether Boris was capable of the big stuff. Well, we are about to find out.

Sunday, 22 March to Sunday, 29 March

The sense that Covid has no boundaries deepens as Prince Charles tests positive (not so funny as an over-seventies bloke). Does this mean the Queen is at risk? Still no sign of Prince Philip.

The Cabinet meets remotely for the first time ever as we are told to stay away. Zoom is the chosen method and works remarkably well and provides amazing insights into colleagues' houses and dress sense. Behind each Cabinet member is a bookcase, picture or similar artefact, creating a glimpse into their reading habits or sporting prowess. Alister [Jack] clearly transmits from

his estate office in the Borders, but I can't quite make out the size of the fish on the wall behind him. Hancock seems to be in a downstairs loo, Rees-Mogg in a lovely high-backed leather chair (with a spaniel making an occasional entrance) and [Grant] Shapps [SoS Transport] has a collection of high-brow political literature on display. I opted boringly for a 1922 photo of the Chamber.

The numbers are still hard to fathom. We are at around 700 deaths but is the trajectory slowing? Boris sounded more confident.

Monday, 8 p.m. – Boris 'addresses the nation' from No. 10. Basically, it's all but a total lockdown now which the police will be enforcing. 'Essential activity only' we are told, whatever that means. He makes it clear that it is an instruction, not a request, although the usual moaners say, 'it's not clear'. In fact, it is 100% clear.

All the fiscal reassurances are kicking in, but the timescale is crucial for them to avert catastrophe. If this goes on for long, we have a huge and long-term issue to contend with. Already Jaguar, Tata, Airbus and even Aston Martin are just weeks away from running out of cash. What must the SMEs [Small and Medium-sized Enterprises] be feeling?

Supermarkets are invaded by panic buyers and we are still short of PPE and equivalent vital medical equipment.

You couldn't make it up. The PM, Hancock and the CMO go down with the virus. We have little detail, but they are off the pitch. Alister Jack (the only person in Cabinet older than me) also has it – sixteen more and I will be PM.

For now, they all have mild and manageable symptoms. Yet we can see that Gove's daily meetings which we all attend remotely, are packed with officials and advisers sat cheek by jowl in the same room.

It feels like a race against time. There are signs that people are beginning to get the message though. Down here the streets and

roads are empty bar a few essential workers. Although we have almost no cases, we feel that a storm is heading our way but we just aren't sure when it will hit or what its ferocity will be when it does. And it's a lovely sunny spring also.

Tuesday, 31 March

Remote Cabinet via Zoom. PM looked and sounded like crap, really bad and bloated. A few people (Priti Patel and Thérèse Coffey mainly) ploughed on regardless. The crunch point will come over the next few days, but it seems some of the measures are having a positive effect. Chris Whitty explains why it will take a year to create a usable vaccine.

As the PM says: 'the next bit is complicated'. Rishi has added the economy will barely survive a six-month stretch like this. GDP will contract by 20–35% in this quarter, with two million unemployed and borrowing between 10% and 20% – it is World War II levels. Complacency will be our greatest enemy . . .

Lockdown week two

Every day follows a similar pattern. Office conference calls, Welsh office calls, 'daily Gove' or COBR-lite and stakeholder calls.

The 'daily Gove' has between 80 to 90 participants and therefore largely operates not as a discussion forum but as an essential communications device.

Gove has now become so programmed that he responds to every comment identically. Me, Gavin, Brandon Lewis [SoS Northern Ireland] and Thérèse exchange suitably irreverent messages throughout.

Yet the numbers continue to climb. There are an extra 600 to 800 deaths a day (against an average of 2,500 per day who die anyway . . .). There is a problem of PPE and testing that continues

to dog us, made worse by the fact that the PM, Hancock and the CMO are still sick.

It seems our testing regime is falling behind and the PPE picture is at best uneven.

Yet we miraculously manage to build a 4,000-bed hospital at the ExCel Stadium in nine days. Totally remarkable.

In Wales our deaths are in the hundreds still, but we all feel like it's just a matter of time.

Sunday, 5 April

The PM gets admitted to St Thomas's Hospital.

The claim is that it is all fairly routine and down to 'persistent symptoms', yet respiratory experts are quick to suggest that much treatment can be done at home other than the advanced O2 provision for pneumonia. He is exactly the profile the medics keep telling us is the most susceptible. Middle-aged and overweight.

Either way, and serious or not, if the national leader is incapacitated it is hardly ideal. We stop joking.

In a parallel world Sir Keir Starmer is re-elected as leader of the Labour Party. No. 10 astutely ask him immediately to a meeting about Covid-19.

He will be an altogether more reasonable-sounding and therefore more formidable opponent than Corbyn, despite being dull and quite far to the left.

In another first the Queen gives a five-minute address to the Nation, only the fifth that she has ever done. Well-judged, authoritative, reassuring. The sort of thing the Palace does well and helpful in steadying the ship. She has a knack of touching the right notes as she talks about the 'national spirit' and how many are 'feeling a painful sense of separation from their loved ones'.

Monday, 6 April

I get a withheld call around 8 p.m. from the Cabinet Office with startling news. The PM is being moved into intensive care at St Thomas's with immediate effect as his condition has worsened. This is a huge development and sends shockwaves through the nation. Our PM is now in a precarious position. This just shouldn't happen. News is not clear if he is on a ventilator, or if he has pneumonia, but either way he is now incapacitated at a time when we need his style of leadership more than ever.

The phones go wild, but with a sober downcast feel about them. Sam Coates calls (from Sky) sounding genuinely stunned, not because he is a great lover of Boris, but because this is the starkest evidence yet that Covid is a threat to everything. Even the endless noise of social media is softened. Speak to Gav and others agreeing that we must support Dominic Raab who, as Deputy PM, will deputise in the meantime. What will the morning bring?

Tuesday, 7 April

No overnight calls must be a good thing? We hear that he has been 'comfortable' (I doubt that) and in 'good spirits'! They say he is not being ventilated and does not have pneumonia – two very important features. This may end well, but he will be off for a bit. The numbers still look a little better . . .

Sunday, 12 April, Easter Day

Lovely spring day. PM leaves hospital and issues a heartfelt video message. Twitter trolls start to claim that it was all a massive sympathy-seeking hoax. I struggle to accept that such people exist and roam amongst us. Presumably they have jobs and kids

and look normal, yet in some strange corner of their mind there is a lunatic at work.

The PM is lying low at Chequers, rightly. I get a nice message back from Carrie following my note to her. She may be reputed to be tricky, but all of this must be tougher for her than most.

The No. 10 private office issues instruction to ministers to stop messaging him. Fortunately, I haven't been, but I can hazard a guess as to who has been most active in that area.

Thursday, 16 April

Zoom Cabinet with Raab (who was good) where we talked (or listened to be more precise) to the usual suspects explain their take on everything. I am not sure why they do it. They must know that the rest of us are bored. Perhaps it's just to get in the minutes.

Further lockdown is agreed for another three weeks but the signs are improving. Wales expectation running behind though. So much for nice Mr Drakeford's brilliant handling. At this rate we may not even need the new hospitals or the whole range of PPE that we have spent months identifying and buying.

Dear old Jacob Rees-Mogg keeps referring to 'the ancient right of MPs' to attend Parliament but we should probably spare a thought for the ancient right of the staff to stay alive too. As ever with MPs it's a bit too much 'all about us'.

The Cabinet Office has still not quite decided on the format of Wales questions on Wednesday. Remote questions will be a historical first so we will trial the guinea pig sessions on Zoom, or in a van parked (ominously) at the local crematorium, the nearest place that we can get a signal. I hesitantly suggested that satellites don't work too well in my valley. I've also picked up mumps from Adam so will look quite weird under lights.

Wednesday, 22 April

8.30 a.m. A large satellite truck turns up at home for 'Virtual Welsh Questions'. Masked men start rolling out cables, tramping through the house and setting up in my office. I check the shelves and pictures behind me for embarrassing giveaways or revealing artefacts.

Two hours later and it transpires that connecting to the satellite is indeed a challenge in our valley. We can get sound or pictures, but not both. We now have less than half an hour and no means of making contact. The Speaker's Office suggest we revert to good old Zoom. With the seconds ticking away we dig out the iPad, balance it precariously on the Ministerial red box, dial in as per normal and at 11.26 we are off, with four minutes to spare. The questions went well, unsurprisingly as there was none of the aggression and combativeness of a Chamber session.

A rare occasion when I made history, becoming the first person ever to conduct the ancient ritual of oral Parliamentary questions from a remote location.

Thursday, 23 April

It looks like we are now pursuing the 'test and trace' policy that is being rolled out in South Korea.

Monday, 27 April

The Covid numbers fall to the lowest for a while. Exiting lockdown is the new ambition as businesses are really feeling the squeeze. Airbus and Tata tell us that they are 'on the brink'. Their confidence levels seem to have changed in the last week, so I must ask whether this is a bluff call to secure some more Government cash?

The PM returns to work. A moment that has been trailed as

a game changer. I thought he was understandably quite muted at his 9 a.m. statement, the theme of which was 'more of the same'. That said he is at least back and his curious ability to get a message across is much needed.

Wednesday, 29 April

Boris and Carrie announce the birth of their son, Wilfred, as if there weren't enough plot twists already! A few ungracious Labour MPs just can't resist making some venomous observations and add it to the list of conspiracies they believe lie behind everything we do, but the public reaction is quite happy.

Thursday, 30 April

Political cabinet with the impressive pollster Isaac Levido. His polling shows ongoing confidence (which is under pressure now) of the public in the Government's approach to Covid. Hancock gets the prize for Minister most like an unruly Labrador puppy.

Tuesday, 5 May

We move toward some kind of unlocking of lockdown, but it could be very gradual. Welsh Government has warned that the R number* here is 0.9 whereas in England it is in effect 0.7.

One is the number to avoid. So much for the Drakeford approach being so much more effective. All it's done is use up a ton of time and money and ended up with a near identical outcome.

---

* The reproduction number (R) is the average number of secondary infections produced by a single infected person.

Thursday, 7 May

Science brief with Professors Whitty and Vallance, the latter being a lot more cautious than usual. They are basically non-committal about us in Wales but will 'send us what he has' on the data. On to Cabinet at 11 a.m. which becomes a metaphor-laden PM introduction speech followed by a gallop through his assessment for the big 'lockdown relief' statement he will make on Sunday. Although he is keen to avoid divergence with the devolved administrations, he did say that they may just have to 'suck it up'. At last!

(Today is ten years since I was elected as an MP and Abi's 50th birthday.)

Friday, 8 May

The Drakeford press conference turned out quite lame. Apparently, we can now take two sessions of exercise a day, go to a garden centre and bizarrely a library. And that's about it.

It turns out that Prof Neil Ferguson of Imperial College, Sage, etc., has been having a bit on the side with a lady hilariously called Ms Staats. A perfect match for a data scientist I suppose. Anyway, to achieve ongoing relations he broke the distancing roles he himself had recommended and has had to step down. Forever more will he be known as the smutty professor.

Monday, 11 May

Chat with Gove, Cabinet at COBR all with a view to pre-empting the PM's imminent 'address to the nation'. Much of the conversation was about the increasingly annoying and pointless divergence of Welsh Government and UK Government policies.

We are assured this will be dealt with in the speech and in comms. Needless to say, it isn't really. The result, predictably,

is that those who want to be permanently outraged are now outraged. It seems like people in the MoD are also currently briefing the media to the effect that their Sec of State and the Cabinet are also outraged, which of course we are not. The PM's actual broadcast was pretty good. He looks better, and he had a proper suit and tie; he looked and sounded the part. Lockdown was always going to be the easy part though.

Thursday, 14 May

Cabinet. A quickfire 55 minutes in which there was no meaningful discussion about anything at all. Plus, a load of unhelpful contributions about limiting the summer recess to which the PM seems strangely attracted. It's just a gimmick, it won't win any votes, won't really speed up legislation, will piss off the staff and be very difficult to ever revert from. Worst of all, it will make no difference to Covid handling or messaging.

When I described the meeting to Gav as 'almost a complete waste of time', he said I was wrong to use the word almost.

Monday, 18 May

Evening run interrupted by a phone call from Rishi. He's a calm Chancellor, which is just as well, but he thinks Tata Steel will find it very difficult in the current economic climate. I rather sympathise, so we agreed to get Welsh Government in early on the problem and start looking seriously at alternatives. There will be colossal local wipeout (6,000 jobs) and big social and cultural impacts also if they cease operations altogether, so another outcome is vital.

Thursday, 21 May

Zoom call with Labour MPs. They were polite, concise and focused. A lesson for some of our own group.

Cabinet – if last week's meeting was of no relevance to most then this week was even less so. The PM barely disguises the disdain in which he now holds them.

Saturday, 23 May

Shitstorm number one – in a meeting with Wales' Chief Constables there was agreement around the definition of 'local' when it came to Welsh Government Covid guidance on how far you could travel to take exercise. Under questioning they agreed that 'about ten miles' was what they considered reasonable. We tweeted accordingly.

Soon after, the Chief Constables then denied their 10-mile guide (despite there being numerous others on the call) thus landing us in the middle of a 'brave officer versus lying politician' story. I will remember this when they come whingeing about the lack of money.

Shitstorm two – the media reveals that Dominic Cummings and his wife drove to Durham with their kid during lockdown. It seems to be turning into a real drama and there are multiple calls for his head.

Sunday, 24 May

Press conference about the Cummings saga – delayed an hour and Boris 'in the chair'. A disaster to be honest. Boris backs Cummings, uncomfortably it seems, talking of his 'instinct' as a father. It really was a car crash and has put us very much on the back foot. It has triggered a significant backlash, admittedly from quite a few people who haven't ever forgiven him for Brexit. But this has damaged Boris, not Cummings.

Monday, 25 May

The Cummings fire still burns brightly. MPs are now getting hundreds of emails from constituents who have been diligently following the rules and who would love to have visited relatives but couldn't.

The plan is for Cummings to face the press in the rose garden of No. 10 at 4 p.m. to explain the position and hopefully close the whole thing down.

This needs to be good or else it will simply pour petrol on the whole issue. He turns up, half an hour late, with Cleo Watson, Isaac Levido and Lee Cain. He looks like a dog in a vet's waiting room. Bewildered, reluctant, lips curled. He explains the timeline, lacking the charm and contrition that was the bare minimum needed to get out of this alive. There are some glaring anomalies: 1) He went for a 30-mile drive to check if his eyes were okay after he got over Covid; 2) That he and Boris had both forgotten phone calls they had had with each other and in which this was mentioned, as they were both ill at the time.

First question was from Laura Kuenssberg: 'Do you regret the decision?' It's an open goal. All he needed to do was to say that on reflection he would have chosen a different course of action, that he sees that now and realises he put the PM in a tricky spot.

But this is Cummings. He refused to say that he either regretted or was sorry for what had happened despite repeated questions to that effect. Not only that, but his tone suggested that he thought it was impertinent that anyone should question him. All in all, it went badly and certainly has not lanced the boil. Colleagues are pissed off and the public reaction is nuclear, picking the scab off all the old wounds that colleagues think Cummings inflicted on them.

He is basically fucked – at least his authority is. Boris is also damaged by this, as we all are by association. Ministers are also

being pushed to write supportive tweets but I'm not sure that helps him (or me for that matter). Most of us decline.

Thursday, 28 May

Over 800 emails now in to me from constituents about Cummings (a record). However, the PM has told the Liaison Committee that he is sticking by his man so, unless something else emerges, that is that. The damage has been done and, despite attempts to be loyal, we all know that this has been a shitshow in which the shit has been generated by us and poured over our heads by us and us alone.

Sunday, 31 May

The hot drought continues. Death rates fall a bit but progress is still quite slow and we compare badly with the rest of the EU. Nobody quite knows why. Welsh Government's relief statement is thin on 'unnecessary movement' and gives further fuel to the 'pitchforkers' who seem to think we should remain in lockdown for ever. Back to London tomorrow. How strange will that be?

2

TREPIDATION

June 2020–April 2021

Why trepidation? Because we were flying blind in the Covid drama, which had a huge economic and political price tag. This is a blow-by-blow account of Covid from the viewpoint of the Cabinet, the effect it had on our colleagues and our role in handling, with ever-decreasing authority, the Cummings scandal.

As Covid tightened its grip on the country, and the Government, Boris marched on with a mixture of stoicism and good humour. But we were struggling; we could contain the worst of the spread, just, but we knew that the economy would at some stage start to reflect the fact we were spending every pound we had on support measures and interventions. After this, the prospect of large-scale, voter-friendly spending will be just a dream because there won't be any money left.

It was the ultimate test for Rishi Sunak, who was having to deal with one of the greatest threats to the UK economy in recent history. During the pandemic he managed to move the might of the Treasury at breakneck speed (for them) and introduce new concepts such as furlough and 'Eat Out to Help Out'. He was little known before taking on the second biggest job in government, having come in quietly to William Hague's old seat of Richmond and cut his teeth modestly on various committees (he and I bonded over the badger cull on the Defra committee), before moving to the relative obscurity of Chief Secretary to

the Treasury. Rishi was neat in every sense, was good company and offered a very different style to the politics we were used to.

The relationship between UKG and the devolved nations became ever more strained. We clashed over Covid support measures, coal tips and another raft of Welsh Government restrictions which further confuse an already weary nation. The *Daily Mail* latched onto the 'trolley police' story, following the decision by WG to cordon off items in supermarkets they considered unnecessary, giving rise inevitably to examples of shops where you could buy gin, but not nappies.

Boris came to Wales, and there was increasing media fascination in what influence Carrie was having on the running of government.

It was a time of increasing tensions between Cummings and almost everyone, the closing stages (so we thought) of the Brexit saga and the first indication that Boris might not be able to walk on water after all.

———— • ————

Monday, 1 June 2020

The new normal. Drive to London on strangely quiet roads. At Hammersmith the billboards are adorned with 'NHS hero' posters and adverts. It's an eerie and unfamiliar quiet and leaves an uneasy feeling.

We have a four-way call with the PM, Alister and Brandon. Boris was quite upbeat about 'the Union' and dismissive of Sturgeon and Drakeford but for different reasons – Drakeford because Boris feels people will realise that UK Government is a force for good, and Sturgeon because people will realise that independence would have exposed Scotland to significantly greater Covid risk.

Wednesday, 3 June

Welsh oral questions in the House. It is much more choreographed these days, including a bizarre plan requiring us to leave the Chamber between questions – a stunt which was quickly abandoned. I would answer the question, leave by the main door, scurry through the lobby and re-enter behind the Speaker. Lunchtime Zoom with the PM and Conservative MPs in Wales, me in the PM's office, everyone else remote. BoJo was good, having unusually read the brief. Robin Millar [Aberconwy] was first up with a question about Cummings. We knew it was planned and at least this gave BoJo the chance to be direct and slay the dragon. To our surprise he was very forthright and apologetic. 'I knew I shouldn't have agreed to that press conference,' he said. The trouble is that he can be too easily persuaded.

The overall line of questioning was negative, but that is hardly surprising. MPs feel let down.

To add to the whole Covid mystery Alok Sharma [BEIS – Dept Business, Energy and Industrial Strategy] was later taken ill at the dispatch box and is being tested for Covid. He very visibly started to sweat buckets and feel weird so he disappeared, leaving everyone who had been anywhere near him (including me) convinced that we would be struck down. If it turns out to be Covid it will blow a huge hole in Rees-Mogg's credibility as the return to full Chamber activity is entirely his idea.

Friday, 5 June

Alok is fine, which is great at one level and means JR-M is off the hook! Still, there is a widespread view that the whole 'returning to the Chamber' is carnage. Transpires that Andrew Percy's mystery illness was also Covid – his antibody test says so. Perhaps I should test too?

Monday, 8 June

Back to the House of Commons for a drink with Percy who now claims to be immune to Covid and therefore is on very good form. The rest of the place seems to be attracting very little desire to comply with social distancing.

Tuesday, 9 June

It is announced that primary schools are now not to go back as planned. Gavin will be irritated, and presumably blamed. The BLM [Black Lives Matter] protests rage on. Statues (of just about anyone with a colonial past) are being removed or torn down. There is ludicrous violence and vandalism in London too. What next – the Colosseum in Rome destroyed for hosting barbaric acts?

Cabinet and political cabinet. BoJo on the best form I've seen him for ten weeks. Full of vigour again.

Colleague update. Apparently one of our Conservative members has been filmed having sex with a rent boy whilst taking cocaine, dressed as a woman and in contravention of Covid guidelines. Being Britain, it is the lockdown breach that has caused the greatest indignation. Thankfully for our colleague it is not in the papers as the rent boy in question has demanded money, which turns it into a blackmail case so reporting restrictions apply.

Friday, 12 June to Saturday, 13 June

BLM protests get violent as the knuckle draggers from the English Defence League-types get stuck in. The police are now in an impossible position.

Tuesday, 16 June

Cabinet, unremarkable other than the fact that within an hour of its conclusion we announced a U-turn on free school meals, and the merger of the FCDO [Foreign, Commonwealth and Development Office] and DFID [Department for International Development], neither of which had been discussed in the meeting. They would have gone through anyway, but it's galling to be by-passed quite so flagrantly.

The free school meals scenario just shows how terrified we have all become of celebrities taking political positions, in this case footballer Marcus Rashford.

Wednesday, 17 June

PMQs – the PM was on much better form and rather trounced Sir Keir. Although Starmer is polling rather well (and benefiting from the 'anyone other than Corbyn' bounce) he is quite dull and every bit as north London-centric as his predecessor and his Party. It's hard to picture him as an effective and hard-hitting prosecution barrister.

Sunday, 21 June

Tim Shipman in the *Sunday Times* suggests an autumn reshuffle in which Gavin will be axed in favour of Malthouse. One assumes the 'source' is the likely beneficiary.

Tuesday, 23 June

Call with PM and CDL [Chancellor of the Duchy of Lancaster – Gove] and then Cabinet to discuss 'the big unlock' which is now underway. Cinemas, pubs, etc., but all under quite strict caveats.

CMO and Hancock are a bit more reserved as they think the public will see this as 'party time'.

Thursday, 25 June

Starmer sacks Rebecca Long-Bailey [Shadow BEIS] for re-tweeting an anti-Semitic tweet from the annoying leftie actor Maxine Peake. They all love the McDonnell and Corbyn project so I imagine Sir Keir will be more than happy with the reaction.

It also could make BoJo look weak for not sacking Cummings, and more recently Rob Jenrick [SoS Housing]. Jenrick ended up sitting next to pornographer and property tycoon Richard Desmond at some fundraiser and got into far too much detail about a property development he was working on. That triggered a hefty donation from Desmond to Jenrick and accusations of some kind of insider deal. To make matters worse, the PM has expressed his 'full confidence' in Rob which normally means you're totally fucked by the end of the week.

Wednesday, 1 July

6.50 a.m. call with BBC Wales. Why do I do it?

Wednesday, 8 July

At Cabinet Rishi briefs for two big statements at 12.30. As ever with him, there are no half measures, but he is also discreet about anything market sensitive as he clearly and rightly doesn't trust all of us in the room.

12.30 – the place is packed for 'the statement'. Rishi is good at this but handing out cash will always be easier than collecting it. He touches all the right buttons, such as the VAT reduction and introduces a discount voucher for eating out – called 'Eat Out

to Help Out' – and is upfront about the long-term prospects for furlough, that it won't last for ever.

Welsh Government even gets an extra 500 million via Barnett. TC and I hit the afternoon media and are confronted with the usual handwringing of Welsh Government and others. 'It's not enough' – FFS.

Wednesday, 15 July

UKIM White Paper* is out so battle will now officially commence. It's dull as can be but will trigger numerous reactions. To test the water, we Zoom the Labour MPs who are predictably, synthetically enraged. Anna McMorrin [Cardiff North] is the least surprising. She must be a miserable companion to work with. Every single thing is some kind of huge Tory conspiracy, designed to deliberately impact on the lives of vulnerable people. Why does the Left have to live in this state of permanent anger and resentment? It must be so exhausting.

Tuesday, 21 July

Rejoice! After what feels like an eternity, we have an in-person political cabinet over in the FCDO. We are back, and somehow it feels like another staging post along the road to ultimate victory over Covid.

The agenda is a polling presentation on the state of the Union. It was a bit depressing, to be honest, showing solid numbers in favour of Scottish independence. Better news is that the Cabinet can now see the dangers more clearly. There was little debate as no one could really hear anyway.

---

* This is the early stages of a Bill designed to prevent internal trade barriers in the UK following Brexit, and to restrict the powers of devolved administrations in economic policy.

And then, for main Cabinet we move to the grandest of surroundings, the Locarno Suite also in the FCDO. The room is so large (think tennis court) and there is so much marble that acoustics are second-rate and it's barely possible to make out the identity of people the other end of the rectangular table. Despite that Gove gave a blinder of a pro-Union speech, littered with football league analogies and the notion of a rebranded 'Royal NHS'. Being Michael none of this had been discussed with anybody in advance but that didn't really matter. It was what was needed, a fresh start, and BoJo is concentrating.

Wednesday, 22 July

Last day before recess and a huge feeling of relief and exhaustion across the whole estate – MPs, staff, officials and House personnel too. It's hard to explain the sentiment, but there is a feeling that we have come part of the way through a war with an invisible enemy. Add to that a feeling that everyone involved has done a lot better than the press will ever admit. However we look at it, this will be a lost year, even a lost few years.

Friday, 31 July

Some alarming news on new Covid outbreaks and the PM then hastily undertakes 'regional lockdowns' and suspends by two weeks the relief plan for certain areas of the economy. This is not over yet . . .

Monday, 10 August

To a business roundtable with the PM and ten Welsh businesses. He hadn't looked at his brief so started by comparing the Anglesey Sea Salt company Halen Mon with the ancient Greeks. All a bit surreal and the guests spoke for far too long for the 40

minutes we had allocated for the whole thing. But BJ loves that kind of thing and amuses (and bemuses) the guests.

Tuesday, 11 August

To Brecon for an equestrian centre visit with the PM. I concede it went much better than expected, despite 35° temperature. He loves the adoration that comes with public visits and happily helps shoe a horse and meet some pedigree (black) sheep. Luckily no press was invited as he was a bit too vocal about 'Black sheeps matter'. We were treated to a table groaning with cakes and sandwiches which, Boris tells us, Carrie has banned him from eating. That doesn't stop him tucking in though.

August recess

A-level grades turn out to be a political catastrophe, although the truth is that the downgrades (40% in England, 42% in Wales) were simply to correct the equivalent uplift granted by teachers' assessments. Gavin in particular has become public enemy number one – unfairly, I think. No. 10 looks like they are disowning him and have sent him out to take the heat. We all know he had the policy forced on him in the first place. Add to that the ridiculous 'arms race' going on between the DAs and HM Government and you can see how even Gavin might struggle to survive this in the long term.

BoJo and Carrie go on a camping holiday in the west of Scotland, which I imagine is his idea of total hell. What could be worse than being squeezed into a wet, midgy tent with a noisy and demanding infant? And a baby too . . .

On the other hand, I spend a most comfortable few days shooting in Northumberland with the likes of Michael Hintze [Lord], Matt Ridley [Lord Temporal] and others.

Monday, 31 August

Back to school after what has been a messy recess of news and U-turns, and a general question mark over our competence. Government is never easy they say, but we do make it hard for ourselves.

Tuesday, 1 September

Cabinet in the FCDO again and a '2m rule' Cabinet picture in the Atrium to start things off. Hopefully it will be the only one we ever do like this. Boris is smartly turned out (for him) and flanked by Rishi and Raab. Much of the talk is around UKIM and spending policies in which I suggest we should be 'bold' which the PM seemed to suggest was likely.

Wednesday, 2 September

PMQs. If I can, I try to never watch but I did today and to be 100% honest it reminded me why I am right to avoid it. The PM was all over the shop – unusually so – but Starmer failed to seize the moment either. Mystifying, but there is a zero-tolerance approach for making any mistakes at these set-piece events. People are allowed off-days aren't they?

Thursday, 3 September

Various UKIM meetings with Gove on spending powers. A substantial explosion is heading our way, but about time! Amazing how a subject quite so dull can also generate quite so much heat.

Tuesday, 8 September

Cabinet including a detailed breakdown on Covid from the CMO and CSA. Basically, it's going to be very difficult until the

spring with regional lockdowns, and quite a big spike in infections, especially among the 17- to 21-year-olds. Buckle up was the especially depressing message. Will this ever go away?

Almost as soon as this Cabinet was over, we get another called for tomorrow, followed by a press release about further restrictions that were never even discussed in Cabinet. Afterthought, or plan?

UKIM Bill launched and instantly triggered a furore from the DAs over devolution and spending powers.

Thursday, 10 September

A storm is brewing over the Northern Ireland aspect of UKIM. NI Secretary of State Brandon Lewis takes to the dispatch box and delivers a zinger.

'Will he assure us that nothing proposed in this legislation does or potentially might breach international legal arrangements?' he is asked.

Brandon: 'Yes, this does break international law in a very specific and limited way.'

Well, to say everyone is dumbfounded is an understatement. As a country we abide by the 'rule of law' as a very basic tenet of our whole system, so we have now triggered a full-scale constitutional rebellion. The general expectation is that we will have to capitulate at some stage, so poor old Brandon has been chucked straight into a snake pit, we think probably by Cummings. He must have been carefully briefed to say those exact words though, but the surprise is why he agreed to do so.

Friday, 11 September

The PM is trying to quell colleague nerves with a Party Zoom call, but the event was a farce due to internet breakdown, Michael Fabricant [Lichfield] singing 'Rule Britannia' and Steve Baker [Wycombe] offering to take the chair when the PM dropped out.

As all of this is happening, a drama unfolds about the permissibility of shooting and hunting within the new Covid regulations. Even Rishi, Hancock and the Chief Whip are involved, proving that to some of our members these things still matter a lot. The SNP Government in Scotland has a neat and workable solution which permits people to engage in any activity that is lawful and conducted to a set of rules. In other words, there is no need to draw up a massive list of possible exemptions. But this seems well beyond us, so we create a dog's breakfast of proposals involving Defra Ministers Pow and Prentis, DCMS [Department of Culture, Media and Sport] and just about everyone else.

Eventually Cummings gets in on the act, fucks it up still further, meaning that we hit the deadline at almost midnight (as the car with the relevant papers for the [Health] Minister Ed Argar got lost).

We are, at times, simply very bad at politics and make simple situations complicated.

BoJo chastises Alister by claiming that his 'insistence on including grouse shooting resulted in Carrie giving me grief all weekend' to which AJ retorted, 'Well, I'm sorry if you didn't get your oats this weekend, PM, but this is the right decision.'

Dinner with Brandon at Mark's club. We were the only ones there, I think. There is no doubt that his 'lawbreaking' statement in the Chamber was choreographed.

Tuesday, 15 September

Cabinet back in the FCDO. Normal routine, but PM rather too keen to suggest that we should 'hang up' any time a journalist calls us. Totally self-defeating policy of course, as it will just lead to a more hostile and unrewarding relationship. It's also a tad ironic coming from one of the country's most prolific sources of media material.

Wednesday, 16 September

The Penally migrant case gathers pace.* The bloody Home Office has 'jumped' this on us somewhat and as a result it has brought out a whole bunch of the 'anti-migrant' protagonists, most of whom come from away but who stir up the local population. They seem to be led by some annoying racists with local councillor Paul Dowson and the odious Tommy Robinson weighing in also. Not remotely surprising is the fact that one of the most vitriolic contributors came to me for help in getting their Thai bride into the country not that long ago.

Sunday, 20 September

Cabinet call with Whitty and Vallance (this being a Sunday, there was also a special appearance from JR-M's magnificent tweed suit).

It looks like we are sailing headlong into the second spike although the impact of it may be more marginal. The worst-case scenario is that we could end up with five times the deaths of a normal flu epidemic. They know the PM well enough by now to avoid mention of yet another full lockdown, but there is no question that this will be another bumpy ride.

Monday, 21 September

Dinner at Boodles with JR-M, the mighty Jeremy Quin [Horsham] and Alister Jack. Found myself agreeing with JR-M on most things (including Government competence) which was a bit of a worry. It was one of depressingly few opportunities for gossiping indiscreetly these days.

---

* The Home Office had recently decided to house nearly 300 asylum seekers in a disused army base at Penally in Pembrokeshire, but without having notified the council, police, Wales Office or me as the MP.

Tuesday, 22 September

Cabinet – 55 minutes. Covid prospects look like they are worsening, but at the moment the PM is resistant to another lockdown, other than perhaps locally.

The migrant crisis at Penally continues, and the racist knuckle draggers continue to arrive in the area to stir up tensions. Some guy called Nigel Marcham, who masquerades under the title of 'the little veteran' is banned from the site. What an odious and unwelcome specimen he is. Every time there is a migrant issue he turns up with his BNP, EDL, Combat 18 and neo-Nazi mates with the intention of making the situation worse.

Wednesday, 30 September

Cabinet. 45 minutes. At this rate we will stop having them altogether. Then to COBR where Gove (in the chair) harangues the secretariat for not being able to establish communications with colleagues in the next-door room. As Michael put it, 'We are a G7 country handling a world pandemic from the nation's nerve centre in a bunker under Whitehall,' so we should be able to get comms with those we need to speak to, especially if they are in the same building.

Friday, 2 October

The numbers continue to rise. Boris calls a remote Cabinet to tell us what we have already read in the media.

Saturday, 3 October

Paul Davies and I do a remote 'fringe' for the [Conservative Party] Conference but in true *The Thick of It* tradition the audience cannot access the call, so we end up speaking to each

other for 45 minutes. A reliable lobby hack tells me that the 'usual Brexit suspects' are now turning their guns on Whitty and Vallance who they have concluded are closet lefties.

Tuesday, 6 October

Abi feeling awful so I am officially self-isolating whilst she gets tested. It's suddenly very close again. I was down at Canary Wharf with BoJo doing the virtual conference when I heard so legged it back to the flat.

Wednesday, 7 October

Still flat-bound so watch PMQs on the telly. It is so different to being in the Chamber. Things that we think work don't, and vice versa. PM was attacked on data and misses a chance to highlight Wales (again).

In other news, Gove is making a land-grab of all Union matters.

Thursday, 8 October

Abi is officially cleared, straight after which I get an NHS track and trace alert which was actually meant for Adam. God knows how they have confused our data. Worryingly it also says that isolation should have started on 27 September (it's now 8 October). The fog of war . . .

Infection rates are now looking very bleak indeed. The PM imposes localised lockdowns in the North East and North West but the spike is with us although not yet translating into deaths. Whitty, back in worst-case scenario mode, predicts that it will only be a matter of time. Questions are asked again about suspending Parliament, and numbers in Scotland and Wales are no better either.

Tuesday, 13 October

Cabinet. PM is clearly agitated about some growing criticism of the detailed impact of Brexit. To combat this inevitability, he is pushing our entire Brexit strategy in the direction of a simple comms message. 'Repeat after me, we are a great country with a great future.'

There really is nothing else and a 'no deal' final outcome now looks increasingly possible.

Wednesday, 14 October

Covid numbers keep on climbing. The Privy Council meets via Zoom, probably a first for the Council.

JR-M in the Chair, Priti, Thérèse and I in COBRA and HM Queen in the Palace. The process is identical to the real thing.

Thursday, 15 October

Drakeford announces a travel ban into Wales from Covid hotspots which triggers a drama as no one really knows what that means or how it will be enforced. That is followed up with a commitment to an all-round 'circuit breaker', which has a similar confusing effect.

Friday, 16 October

Rows emerge in the North as Mayors Andy Burnham and Steve Rotherham lock horns with Government over lockdown and Covid response plans and the Drakeford 'circuit breaker' is formally put in place. We are now really in the grip of devolution and, because it is so heavily politicised, there is always this nagging doubt that some of the decisions being taken, or challenges issued, by the devolved administrations have as much

to do with damaging the credibility of UK Government as they do resolving the crisis.

Tuesday, 20 October

Political cabinet. Isaac Levido presents new messaging which seems pretty similar to the old messaging. In some ways it's reassuring that we aren't much more unpopular than we were last time he did this. Boris is quite sparky and emits optimistic-sounding noises throughout.

Chat with Tony Abbott [former Australian PM] in the Wales Office about how all governments in the world appear to be pushing a similarly cautious route on Covid. '55,000 lemmings can't be wrong,' was his response. Got to love the Aussies.

Wednesday, 21 October

Opposition debate is unsurprisingly on the subject of extending the free school meals proposal over Christmas. A trap, obviously, but into which we readily walk, voting down the proposal and thus writing Labour's next 'child killer' leaflet for them. Two PPSs resign.

Secret drink in the office with 'someone in the know' who repeats the rumour that, how can I say this, a 'prominent colleague' may have acquired a new lover . . . Remarkable energy if he has.

Monday, 26 October to Tuesday, 27 October

Free School Meals continue to dominate the media. I am required to do some sweeping up on the morning media round, presumably because all the grown-ups have refused to do it. Had an okay interview on BBC Politics, Adam Boulton and TalkRadio.

It is an unwinnable position though, especially when the country's sanctimonious celebrities are lining up to put the boot in. Helpfully, Mark Drakeford is also under fire for the ludicrous Welsh Government supermarket fiasco. They have cooked up a system whereby shops can only sell 'essential items' and are banned from selling 'non-essential' ones. The devil is in the detail. That means alcohol is considered essential (quite right too) but school uniform and baby milk isn't. Cue photos of supermarket aisles with non-essential items behind police tape.

The *Mail* has a field day running 'trolley police' stories and forces the FM into hasty clarification mode, in which he says it's all up to the supermarkets to use discretion. The sub-text though is how enraged Welsh Government is when subject to just a little bit of criticism. They don't like it up 'em.

Friday, 30 October to Sunday, 1 November

The Covid shit continues to hit the fan.

On Friday night private documents of a meeting between the Prime Minister, CDL, Chancellor and Hancock get leaked showing that Covid numbers are more awful than we thought, especially in areas of low infection and unless we act instantly and extensively hospitals will exceed capacity by 4 December.

There is no good news, and no safe areas it seems. The options are limited, so Cabinet is assembled on Saturday for meeting with the CMO, CSA, PM and the DAs. To be honest both the DAs and the Cabinet were a little better than usual as most people are now 100% engaged.

Basically, it's lockdown in all but name but with schools operating as normal (the teachers won't like that . . .). It will be for one month only, with the intention being that Christmas will be a time for more relaxation. There is no guarantee that this will work and the impact on the economy is going from bad to worse. But what can we do? All the Clever Dick Twitter-based alternatives have

huge drawbacks. PM is clear: we must 'save lives and prevent the NHS running out of capacity'. That is the one, and only, priority.

MPs are getting jumpy, and many are annoyed that they have been defending the 'not a lockdown' stance we have taken so far, and even condemning Welsh Government for their equivalent. (More fool them for not leaving any wriggle room.)

The entire weekend is consumed by this now impossible and international problem.

Tuesday, 3 November

Cabinet in the Locarno Suite FCDO as is the norm these days. PM on humorous form as we rattled through the business.

Jacob Rees-Mogg and the PM had an exchange about the future of foie gras and whether the Catholics could attend Mass (or 'Mars' as JR-M pronounces it) and Thérèse Coffey suggested we wheel-clamp people for Covid non-compliance. Even Priti Patel was not up for that. The PM did give Jacob the assurance he needed about foie gras so all is not lost in the world.

The media is reporting the curious story of the SBS [Special Boat Service] weekend rescue mission off the Isle of Wight. The message to trainee ship hijackers is very clearly not to attempt your mission within a five-minute chopper ride of the SBS head-quarters at Poole where the world's finest anti-ship hijacker teams are itching to have a go for real.

Friday 6 November

A depressing Covid 'O' [Covid Operations Committee] with Jonathan Van-Tam [Deputy CMO], Hancock, Gove and others. Turns out that in Denmark there are examples of a new Covid strain emerging from mink, after it mutated. If true and it spreads (JVT reserved the right to be wrong) it could significantly reduce the efficacy of a future vaccine and set us all back even further.

It's too early to say with certainty but at least the Danes have acted swiftly and openly to the problem. We have, as a precautionary measure, banned all travel in and out of Denmark. It's been a long time since I've heard a meeting quite so sombre and there is a long list to choose from.

Sunday, 8 November

To Cardiff for Remembrance Day with just a small handful of dignitaries. Drakeford looks like a scruffy old university lecturer with dirty shoes. It is the one event of the year when a little effort would not have gone amiss, but I can't help thinking, uncharitably maybe, that the whole concept of the armed forces and defence of the realm is something his Corbynite instincts find hard to accommodate.

Monday, 9 November

Amazing news. The prospect of a reliable Pfizer/BioNtech vaccine looks ever better and even as early as December. Huge rollout plans for 2021 could see lockdown replaced by medicine. I recall Nadhim Zahawi's comments as Vaccine Minister when he said it is the one real game-changer that we have all been waiting for.

This is a colossal breakthrough and all the more so as it will have a global impact.

Tuesday, 10 November

For once Cabinet was upbeat, and even Patrick Vallance had a smile on his face.

Later the news leads with the slightly odd 'SW1 story' that No. 10's Lee Cain may become Chief of Staff in Downing Street to follow Eddie Lister. There is significant adverse reaction to this, led by Carrie. All very strange.

At 9 p.m. we get news that Lee Cain has now resigned and is leaving No. 10. It's even being suggested that Cummings may go also. Apparently, Carrie has laid down the law, and all hell broke loose. She is either more powerful than we all thought or there is a huge car crash heading our way. Or even both.

Friday, 13 November

The media is full of stories briefed from one side or another. Time to keep our heads down, I fancy, as this could go anywhere and it will be easy to end up on the wrong side. Cummings leaves too, by the front door, carrying a box of his stuff to make a point and looking ever so slightly weirder than usual. It's always got to be about him, or was this his quite clever way of bringing finality to his controversial presence?

Monday, 16 November

The Covid brief with Vallance and Whitty was unusually upbeat. Vallance more so than Whitty who wisely tempers everything with a big 'but'. That is his role, to be fair to him.

The Pfizer vaccine looks good to go and pretty soon too. The Government Car Service vehicle fails to show up at Paddington – nothing new – but I do wonder at how bad they really are and how entitled I am becoming.

Wednesday, 18 November

PM launches the new '10-point net zero plan'. Quite good and includes possibilities for Wales around offshore wind, nuclear and carbon capture. Less good news for petrol and diesel people who will see new cars phased out in 2030 and hybrids in 2035. That's a big deal for every manufacturer in the UK, including Nissan in Wales.

Call from Rishi when I was in M&S on the way home. Looks like the Comprehensive Spending Review [CSR] will be a rather more modest affair than usual and the much-trailed Shared Prosperity Fund [SPF] could be a one-year event – with not much cash – followed by a three-year proper programme.* The mechanisms are solid though and Welsh Government will melt.

Thursday, 19 November to Friday, 20 November

The much-awaited report into allegations against Priti Patel for bullying are published and find her guilty – but add that it was 'accidental bullying' which is a new one on most of us. The PM adopts the same policy as he has for Cummings, Jenrick, Williamson and others by not sacking her, the result of which is a bigger scandal during which the author of the report resigns. Boris's first instinct, which is not to capitulate to the noise of social media, is admirable but not always politically manageable. Everyone knows Priti is not the easiest to work with, but that's all apparently okay these days. No doubt more will emerge.

Sunday, 22 November

Another weekend, another crisis. We meet via Zoom to hear from the 'two gentlemen of Corona', Whitty and Vallance, followed by Cabinet at five. Although we have no option a Cabinet via Zoom just doesn't work that well. No sense of mood or timing as to when to intervene – and Boris hates that anyway. The nub of it all is that 'we are coming out of lockdown' but that's debatable as we are actually reverting to a tier system – and God knows

---

* This was a big deal at the time. A central plank of the Government's agenda was dependent on large-scale spending commitments in less prosperous areas, with the emphasis on infrastructure. It was also intended to be an annual process rather than a one-off.

what we will have in Wales – and although the vaccine news is really good, he realises the reality is that its full effect won't be felt till March and many will die in the meantime. Added to this are the anti-vaxxers and anti-lockdowners – and the usual bunch of Brexit purists who are generating rising momentum.

Monday, 23 November

However, the story this week will be CSR and the magic act Rishi has to perform to make a shit sandwich taste palatable. Clearly there has been a row between the Treasury and Gove's office, which was so bad that Rishi had to call me twice to verify an SPF detail as he didn't trust Gove's account!

Tuesday, 24 November

There's silence on Brexit. What can this possibly mean? COBR – this time to decide the plan for Christmas with the devolved administrations. Sort of okay in that a UK-wide approach is at least possible. There is some affection in the room, but definitely no kissing.

A niche, tetchy CSR row is brewing. It turns out that the Treasury has slipped a £4.6 billion levelling-up fund into the CSR but for England only, thereby undermining our Union-based narrative. Apparently, it was bounced on Boris who agreed it (surprise, surprise) one assumes when he wasn't concentrating. It will give us a handling problem, that's for sure.

Wednesday, 25 November

The Cabinet meets briefly for CSR brief followed by the ever sound CST [Steve Barclay] briefing of MP colleagues. Then for the Chancellor in the Chamber – polished, upfront, sensible. His assessment of our economic plight is sobering. Cue high

unemployment, a shrunken GDP and at least five years of recovery. He cuts foreign aid from 0.7 to 0.5% to the annoyance of NW1 but to wider public sympathy. The fact is that 0.7 is entirely arbitrary and is seldom met by other measures anyway.

Thursday, 26 November

Hancock announces the new Covid tier system. Lots of fury about how some no-infection areas end up in Tier 3 and vice versa; they fail to realise it's about trends not numbers. It takes Whitty's unlimited patience to walk everyone through the process.

Monday, 30 November

To Wrexham with Boris. That sounds simple enough, but it never quite is. The final destination is Wockhardt, the pharma company which is packing and distributing the Oxford AstraZeneca vaccine – 300 million doses in year one alone.

No. 10 insists on flying which means leaving early from Northolt, boarding the ancient Royal jet – with twenty-eight colleagues and officials no less – and then a convoy from the Airbus landing strip at Hawarden to the factory. The trip was uneventful and short. As the PM took his seat he was passed two serious-looking Ministerial boxes. 'A PM's work is never done,' I thought. So, he opens the first one to reveal three sticks of celery and some carrots. 'Nobody is going to nick your lunch, PM,' I said, to which he replied: 'I know, but Carrie insists.' He then opens the second box in which there is a huge pile of Christmas cards to sign. He would have been better employed having a twenty-minute kip.

We talked quite a bit about devolution, life as we know it and the politics of Wales, yet I never feel close to him and wonder if anyone ever does? It was the same with Cameron. Polite, funny,

clever and charismatic but a tendency to distance. Maybe it's a quality essential to the rigours of high office.

We reach the factory, where Boris starts talking about the wrong vaccine to the confusion of the Indian proprietors. Being BoJo he ploughs on regardless and with style. The visit is nonetheless a success. Then it's the flight back. In he comes, takes his seat and promptly falls fast asleep, pen in hand. With a reshuffle never far from the headlines it's probably a good thing to be in his line of sight when he wakes up.

Tuesday, 1 December

Cabinet. Mercifully brief as the Locarno Suite is bloody cold. There is an unusual sense of optimism and joy in the air. The reality is that the vaccines may be about to change everything.

Wednesday, 2 December

CDL call with FMs. They seem remarkably on-board with the vaccine rollout starting – we hope – next Tuesday. I'm not surprised as the whole programme will be delivered by UK Government. There are some issues re care homes as the vaccines are difficult to move due to the need to maintain ultra-low temperatures. Further along, we will have Oxford/AZ hot on the heels of Pfizer. Whoever took the decision to pursue them, many months ago, is about to see something truly special occur. I don't even know who they are, or whether they will ever get the recognition they deserve.

Monday, 7 December

Covid brief with Whitty and the team, who were back to their gloomiest norm. They are clearly worried about Christmas and

people getting pissed and behaving badly (or normally). The vaccination programme is going well but it is a colossal project.

Wednesday, 9 December

Cabinet – 45 minutes this time. Buckland [SoS Justice and Lord Chancellor] dominates the questions these days and seems impervious to, or unaware of, Alister's audible sighing and grumbling. Brexit hangs on a knife-edge and yet hardly anyone in the wider public cares any more. The PM is of the mind that we are now heading rapidly for either a 'no deal' or an Australian deal (which is in fact WTO [World Trade Organisation rules] in all but name). The EU has at the last minute made an insistence that the 'level playing field' means we have to mimic their legislation or face penalties, in other words not leave at all. Even I find that manipulative and it's a promise that is not required of any other nation with whom they have an FTA [Free Trade Agreement]. It makes literally no sense, unless their purpose is to blow everything up and just see what remains after the explosion.

Thursday, 10 December

Visits to the vaccine centre in the leisure centre in Cwmbran. Amazing how cheery everyone was, both public and medical staff. Not only were they doing a fantastic job but they really do believe, rightly, that they are involved in a world-changing programme.

Cabinet call in the car on the way home which is impossible to conduct properly as we dipped in and out of tunnels and valleys. I think we agreed to sign up to 'no deal' despite no discussion, no challenge, no papers, no analysis of what that actually means. I think we missed an important opportunity to meet in person and at least fully grasp the politics of this, if nothing else.

Sunday, 13 December

Further brief Cabinet call – at one minute's notice. Even with that prep time dear Rob Buckland managed a speech. He is a word machine. The change is that we have now agreed to keep talking. Does this signal progress? I am beginning to wonder if all this no-deal stuff is a clever bluff, partly to wrong foot the EU, and partly because the PM can't trust anyone to keep a secret.

Cabinet and a chance, surprisingly, to say something about Wales and Covid. Matt Hancock has helpfully signed a joint letter to First Ministers offering help from NHS England should the Welsh NHS get overwhelmed. It was a genuine offer, but as expected Welsh Government reacts with hostility accusing us of scoring political points . . . Idiotic and paranoid I thought.

Thursday, 17 December

'Virtually' signed the North Wales growth deal. £120 million of UK Government (taxpayers') cash. The Nationalists want the money, and it so hurts them when we make it happen and force them to be nice to us.

Chris Bryant [Rhondda] apologises to the House for allegedly telling the Speaker to fuck off. As we all enjoy telling him, he can be far too up himself on occasions, so this comeuppance was warmly received. The fact he is always banging on about standards makes it doubly amusing. As ever with Chris he is 75% amusing, gifted and talented but 25% irritating. It just depends which day you get him on.

Brexit hangs by the thinnest of threads, but the nation appears to have completely disengaged. As far as most voters are concerned the whole thing got boring the day after the referendum result.

Friday, 18 December

As if 2020 couldn't get any worse, more shit is now hitting an even bigger fan. It is emerging that a 'mutant strain' of Covid is on the loose and might explain why, especially in Kent, numbers keep going up and up. Covid meeting in No. 10 but it looks like we are heading for an urgent First Ministers' summit and Cabinet tomorrow, after which it looks almost certain that further restrictions are on the way. Morale takes yet another dive.

Saturday, 19 December

It looks like the new mutant is up to 70% more transmissible than the current mutation, but not necessarily more deadly. In capacity terms this is a nightmare scenario. The proposed guideline is that urgent and stringent action is required, and with that in mind, the Christmas 'truce' will be curtailed to one day only.

In other words, and despite everyone's superhuman efforts, Christmas is basically cancelled. Boris is pretty bleak about it too. 'The grimmest decision I've ever had to announce,' he tells us in Cabinet. And he means it. I thought after lockdown one that he would never do another one but look at us now. Drakeford looked and sounded like a broken man too. It has dawned on him that his alternative approach hasn't worked either.

Understandably the PM struggled at the 5 p.m. press conference but Whitty owned it and performed especially well. To heap further misery, the French and others declare an immediate ban on incoming Brits, and freight, triggering an emergency COBR as massive queues build up at Dover.

Wednesday, 23 December

The Brexit tensions heighten as the possibility of a deal now becomes a reality. All the key people are 'in the tunnel'. It even

looks like Christmas Eve could be the moment – as I have been predicting. The Cabinet is 'stood to' for various meetings and briefings. Detailed information is deliberately and wisely withheld. It all comes together at 10.40 p.m. when the Cabinet meets to be told by Boris that a deal is 'nearly there' and 'one more push' should do it.

As the PM warns though, 'none of it is agreed until all of it is agreed,' which he thinks will most likely be by 7 a.m.

7 a.m. comes and goes without any white smoke. In the best traditions of our relationship with the EU it seems these last few hours are, inevitably, an argument about fish! But it's as good as done. By late afternoon we get the agreement, followed by a statement by Boris and various press conferences to bring this whole thing to a head.

After forty years of wrangling and political division and several Prime Ministers later, we can nearly say this chapter is over, even though there are several chapters still to come. It's a triumph for Boris, David Frost [Chief Negotiator of Task Force Europe] and the negotiating team too.

The press said it would never happen. Remainers, and I remind myself I was one, need to accept that at each turn, we have kept our promise. Parliament will be 'virtually' recalled between Christmas and the New Year to fulfil the legislation and then that is it and we are out of the EU on the last day of the month.

Wednesday, 30 December

The strange virtual recall went with relative ease, enabling the Future Relationship Bill to pass with a majority of over 450. After years of opposition the Labour Party supported the final vote, meaning they are now bought into every problem that will inevitably rise to the surface.

Saturday, 2 January 2021

Off we go again. The row about schools is still rumbling on, ensnaring poor Gavin once more. We want to reopen, but needless to say, the unions don't. Gavin questions why we don't just vaccinate teachers and other school staff as a priority but apparently this is not as easy as it sounds.

Monday, 4 January

The numbers are off the clock, but to counter this gloomy reality the AstraZeneca rollout starts today. It's a race to the line. No Cabinet meeting since before Christmas Eve. Have we been reshuffled without even knowing?

With the numbers soaring we get a couple of hours' notice of a First Ministers' call with Gove at 5 p.m., followed by Cabinet at 6 p.m. and a PM political statement at 8 p.m. It can mean only one thing, that we are back in lockdown.

The PM is weary of all this and who can blame him? He is the sort of person who wants to charge ahead on several fronts but Covid has other ideas, blocking every move he makes. He sets out the grim picture methodically and describes how we should have vaccinated the first four cohorts by mid-February.

Until then it's all back to Zoom. Parliament is recalled tomorrow to confirm. At least this time there is a possible end in sight; April or May?

Thursday, 7 January

Trump stirs up aggravation, leading to a full-scale riot on Capitol Hill [Washington, DC]. It is hard to fathom how US democracy has reached this low point. Yet there are colleagues on our side of the water who find him strangely seductive, Farage being one. They seem to think that politics benefits

from mavericks like Trump and that the rank dishonesty and delusion are prices worth paying to liven things up. In fact, it is extraordinarily dangerous. It ridicules established customs, divides communities and demolishes respect for the rule of law.

Friday, 8 January

Alok Sharma steps down from BEIS to concentrate on COP26 [the 2021 United Nations Climate Change Conference] and Kwasi Kwarteng takes over with Anne-Marie Trevelyan going in as Minister of State. Is this the main reshuffle they have been talking about or enough to put that back a bit?

Wednesday, 13 January

Cabinet. Quite upbeat, with the first faintest signs of a levelling off and even a reduction in certain parts of the UK. Rollout continues to be quite good and the 'first four cohorts by 15 February' target could be met. Not sure about Boris's Cabinet battle cry of 'Let's clap for big pharma and capitalism', even though he has a point. Without large, privately owned global institutions with the firepower to invest in the Research and Development needed to get us to this point, none of this would have been possible. So, when people moan about the 'privatisation of the NHS' are they including the equipment and drugs the service relies on, and which are produced by profit-making manufacturers?

Thursday, 14 January

Covid and Brexit meetings to continue with regularity, even if the purpose is not always obvious to us attendees. It's a process we all have to go through, I guess.

Zoom call with Michael Sheen, currently in Saint Lucia (where

else?), on his way to film *Prodigal Son* in New York (following a public online spat between us over his views on the monarchy). The plan was to talk about the role of the Royal Family in Wales, about which he has strong views – but we talked about a whole range of things. As expected, he was well informed, charming, funny and good company. We agreed to see if we could get a three-way chat in with him, the Prime Minister and Prince William!

Tuesday, 26 January to Wednesday, 27 January

The UK tops 100,000 Covid deaths, a grim milestone which some will use to apportion blame. The PM handles the moment delicately and explains how, 'As PM I take responsibility for all government decisions.' Maybe I am wrong, but I hope people will think twice about blaming him for everything.

He confirms that schools won't open until 8 March and travellers may be required to quarantine in hotels, at their own cost, when returning from various parts of the world. It's the latest 'mutant' variant that is giving everyone the jitters.

Talking of which, Desmond Swayne [New Forest], one of our more colourful characters, is reprimanded for encouraging the anti-vaccine movement. There is a bomb scare at Wockhardt in Wrexham, the manufacturers of one of the vaccines. Unbelievable.

Friday, 29 January

Welsh Government (or to be more fair the FM) is testing my patience again, this time over Freeports, a flagship UK Government policy. He wants a full say in the location and more money but no financial responsibilities. I knew that this would happen when we decided to separate the announcement of freeports in England from those in Wales and Scotland,

thus facilitating endless leverage thereafter. This will now take months.

Saturday, 30 January

In a remarkable move, anticipated by no one, the EU triggers a provision within Article 16 to try to prevent the import of vaccine to the UK via Northern Ireland. This is akin to a declaration of war, globally condemned, spiteful and as DUP leader Arlene Foster puts it, 'an act of hostility'. No. 10 reacts with care and diplomacy and within hours the EU retreats, reputation damaged and that of the UK Government enhanced.

Monday, 1 February

Covid brief with the usual team. Better news again – we seem to have peaked. But the South African variant is thought to be in the community and is therefore causing concern. The vaccine people are doing a brilliant job. We should hit 15 million on time. We are a world leader, and the economic implications of this cannot be overstated.

Tuesday, 2 February

Cabinet. Boris full of beans as a new toy has been delivered to the Cabinet Room in the form of a large model of HMS *Elizabeth*, our latest and shiniest aircraft carrier. With Rishi one side and Boris the other, the opportunities for banter were too much for Boris who described the moment as 'like being Leonardo DiCaprio and Kate Winslet in *Titanic*'.

'Be careful with that, PM,' warned Thérèse Coffey, 'it didn't end too well!'

Tuesday, 9 February

Cabinet. Reasonably upbeat. I tried to intervene but failed, not sure that matters much, partially due to Rob Buckland using up all the PM's headspace as usual. We do yet more work on the Senedd election manifesto. The more I read it the more I conclude how bad it is. It needs a lot more work. The trouble with our Party's approach to elections is that we are always refining the last campaign we fought rather than projecting forwards. Nobody reads manifestos, let alone alters their vote because of them, so we might as well try a totally different approach in terms of both content and comms. I continue to fail to be heard.

Wednesday, 10 February

Grant Shapps on the media round. He suggests that we should all desist from fixing holidays at home or abroad, which is contrary to what Hancock said yesterday. Departmental comms avoiding each other again.

Looks like we may have the Prime Minister in Wales again next week. Not sure whether Covid-related or just a jolly to get him out of London.

I am lounging in the bath and see the phone ringing from 'Boris Johnson MP'. That never happens so I lurch into semi-naked action, double-check it's not a video call and concentrate.

It turns out that he was worried about his PMQ comments on a battery factory in Bridgend. Apparently, he implied there was about to be a huge investment, without realising the investors had pulled out a few days earlier. BoJo never normally worries about small matters of fact so I suggested that he could have toughed that out quite easily with the usual bluster. It was the press office who were panicking, he explained, and wanted to

over-correct the comment by describing the Prime Minister as having 'mis-spoken'.

With all that's going on it seems like an odd reason to call. Sometimes BoJo has an attack of insecurity, sometimes he is utterly impervious to such things, you just don't know when.

Wednesday, 17 February

PM in Wales. We start at the Cwmbran vaccine centre. He bounds into the centre, shirt flying, looking to all intents and purposes sufficiently wired that he must have had at least three double espressos on the trot.

He explained, to a somewhat bemused reception party, that he had been learning the words to Goldie Lookin Chain's greatest hit. Off he went: 'I've been from LA to Japan but I've never seen a vaccine centre like the one here in Cwmbran'. And repeat . . .

It's remarkable really and somewhat unusual. The punters all wanted a pic, the staff were buzzing, and the PM was totally relaxed and at home. From there to South Wales Police HQ and then to the new and very smart Wales Office in Cardiff where we did an okay press brief and a chat with Andrew RT Davies [Conservative Leader in the Senedd]. We then stared out of the top floor of our new offices by the station, towards the Principality Stadium. Boris wistfully announced: 'God, I've got properly pissed in there over the years.'

All light-hearted stuff. There is nothing routine about BoJo. As a 'mood indicator' he was anxious to read in the press that his dog Dylan enjoyed 'rogering Cummings's leg' and asked why the word llama isn't pronounced in the literal Welsh way. He has definitely recovered from Covid.

Friday, 19 February

Oliver Lewis, the new Union SpAd who has been in post for all of two weeks, walks out of No. 10, apparently due to a personality clash following the arrival of Baroness Finn and Henry Newman (one of Carrie's best friends).* Needless to say, the press is pointing an accusing finger at Carrie. My moment of optimism has evaporated rather quickly.

Drakeford's much-awaited announcement on relaxing lockdown is a very damp squib, full of 'we might'. People are underwhelmed because all they really need is certainty.

Starmer's 'big speech' lacks much zing too. He's really not that comfortable with moments like this.

Monday, 22 February

Covid brief, then Cabinet to hear the Prime Minister's roadmap plan for post Covid. 'Data not dates' driven, we are told, but then plenty of dates nonetheless. It's all very encouraging for once as the vaccine rollout hits 15 million and numbers around the whole UK keep falling. Are we over the worst? We can but dream.

Monday, 1 March

St David's Day starts with a one-to-one call with Richard Wynne Jones of the Wales Governance Centre on the GE19 polling analysis. In short, Brexit won it. Hardly a surprise but more interesting was the fact that an election with such a clear message, and a sympathetic national mood, is a rare combination

---

* Under new arrangements in No. 10 the PM appointed Simone Finn and Henry Newman to Chief and Deputy Chief of Staffs roles, inevitably raising eyebrows in some quarters.

and highly unusual. He even suggested that any leader could have won it and it wasn't as much down to Boris as we may have thought. I suspect some personal bias being expressed there but it's a thought. The bigger question is for how long we can hang on to it.

Wednesday, 3 March

Cabinet at 8.30 a.m. for Rishi to set out the loose parameters of the budget. It sounds good, plenty of spend but we include tax measures too which will sting a few people. These things always sound sensational until some bean-counter gets stuck in and spoils it all. It's a shame the Cabinet can't get more detail, but the risk of leaks is too high. I wonder if it was always like that or whether we just have a leakier political class these days.

CST then speaks to Alister and me so we are all set. Rishi performs well. It's a slick formula they use at HMT [the Treasury], but it needs to be. Lots on the Union, levelling up and much better numbers (thanks to the vaccine) on unemployment and recovery. Sir Keir Starmer's response was piss-poor and his attempts at humour lamentable. He has to concede that UK Government extension of all the Covid financial interventions is a good thing. Starmer looks relatively civilised and serious. His back-story is less lunatic than most Labour leadership incumbents have been, Corbyn included, but when he opens his mouth he just lacks any real 'sex appeal'. He may have been the Director of Public Prosecutions but as some of our MP lawyers observe, any decent lawyer goes into private practice.

Then my own round of Wales media who are equally lost for anything to beat us with.

Thursday, 4 March

I get my long-awaited meeting with the PM which I was sure would be cancelled. Forty-five minutes of one-to-one but with new SpAds Henry Newman (in a tie) and Baroness Simone Finn in the room. We shall see. It was a cheery and upbeat meeting that had a good 'vibe' throughout, although BoJo was more livid about devolution than I expected.

Saturday, 6 March

Nurses 1% pay rise dispute rumbles on. All a bit messy. BBC interview presses me on it so I helped a bit by talking about this being the 'start of a process' not the end (in Wales at any rate). The trouble with NHS pay disputes is that you can never, ever win. Whatever number we come up with will be greeted by the unions and the opposition as too little, painting us as wanting to force nurses into foodbanks and similarly emotive nonsense. In fact, NHS pay isn't too bad once you factor in all the accompanying benefits, but no one dares say that.

Tuesday, 9 March

Cabinet. Normal. We really need to get back in a room before they end up being of no value at all (down from the 5% value that they are currently worth).

A Covid meeting (with food) with the inner team.

Wednesday, 10 March

Drakeford has declared that 'The Union is dead'. Helpful as ever. He had recently tried to suggest that the UK Government was 'endangering the Union' by not giving him more power and money. He's very disingenuous on this point as he is politically

in bed with Plaid who only have one reason for existence – abolishing the Union.

On cue I also received a moaning letter from Jeremy Miles [Attorney General of Welsh Government] who is slowly waking up to the realities that: 1) we have left the EU; 2) we are not rejoining the EU; 3) UKG governs the whole of the UK; and 4) I don't really care/give a fuck what he thinks about this topic any more.

Monday, 15 March

The PM hosts a ministerial meeting on criminal justice. Rishi, the Lord Chancellor, Gove and, bizarrely, me are the only Cabinet ministers present. BoJo has clearly been wound up by Carrie, which explains why her good friend Nimco Ali was also on the call. There are absolutely no references to FGM [female genital mutilation], the issue that Ali has brought to public attention, so she therefore had nothing to add. The PM was fixated by delays to the whole CJ [criminal justice] system when it comes to rape victims – an entirely reasonable concern.

Tuesday, 16 March

The Home Office [HO] decides to close the Penally camp for asylum seekers by next week. HO Minister Kevin Foster gave me 30 minutes' notice so I could at least lead the comms even though Plaid and others are trying to claim the victory. All-in-all a rather cack-handed operation.

Wednesday, 17 March

News breaks that there will be a reduction in vaccines for April due to global production issues. This seems at odds with the comments we have been making about an imminent 'splurge'. AZ and Pfizer issue strong comments almost to the contrary,

whereas the EU hints at preventing exports of vaccine to countries that are ahead of it in their programmes.

Thursday, 18 March

The BBC announces a further migration of its staff out of London including a large presence in Wales. This will include *Newsnight* and the *Today* programme from time to time. Just like the time they all had to decamp to Salford, the London-centric elite of the BBC will be in a state of despair.

Breaking news . . . Nicola Sturgeon has been found guilty of misleading Parliament in her account of the Alex Salmond affair* but they stop short of saying 'knowingly'. This is a big difference that could save her from resignation, but she is quite significantly damaged.

Monday, 22 March

Covid brief for Cabinet was sort of okay but the medics are still concerned about transmission for the under fifties and the South Africa variant. The truth is that we cannot keep locked down for ever. If we do, why have we invested so much in the vaccine programme? (Which is currently running at 26 jabs per second). The whole point of the programme was to allow us to reopen.

Tuesday, 23 March

Cabinet from the Cardiff office and then to visit Meritor in Cwmbran which has just got £32 million of UK Government

---

* Salmond was the former Leader of the SNP but had been arrested in January 2019 and charged with fourteen offences, including rape and sexual assault. He was later acquitted but the toxicity within the SNP lasts to this day. Nicola Sturgeon was heavily embroiled and was subject to a Ministerial Code investigation herself.

investment to make hydrogen propulsion units for HGVs. Yet another great example of a family-owned business leading the world in green tech. Then a quick visit from Liz Truss [SoS International Trade] who works like a horse but is a little quirky to say the least.

At the visit brief her SpAd said, 'So we all know the mayonnaise situation?'

'No.'

'SoS [Liz] can't abide mayonnaise and will only drink coffee from Pret's.' (Of which there are none between Cardiff and Brecon to speak of.)

Harry Cole [*Sun*] writes a piece about whether we would exclude the DAs in any future pandemic (I suspect gleaned from a casual remark from me when we had a glass in our hand).

Sunday, 28 March

Vaccine day! Into the Archives in Haverfordwest for my jab. Businesslike mood with a steady flow of my age group; it was an especially efficient process to boot. In and out in five minutes. (Only side effect was a feeling of lack of energy but otherwise fine.)

Monday, 29 March

Easter Monday – Cabinet call to discuss what we had already seen in the papers over the weekend, i.e. relaxation of restrictions, return to 'normal', good jab numbers, etc. PM especially delighted that we could 'reopen massage parlours'!

All that said, the EU medical regulation body still looks like getting wobbly over whether AZ could trigger blood clots although only 7 people out of 18 million (i.e. 0%) have died from them. The upsides so emphatically outweigh the risks that we must crack on.

Off to Brecon to do some campaigning around GCORE [Global Centre for Rail Excellence]. As we arrived news emerged that Prince Philip had died aged ninety-seven. Under the terms of 'Operation Forth Bridge', the much-rehearsed protocol used for Royal deaths, all visits and campaigning are now off for the foreseeable future.

Later, we attend a briefing for ministers at which we are given the full low-down on what happens next, the funeral and any further ceremonials for the nation, charities, politicians to follow.

In the tea room, Alister Jack told a story of a student event that the DoE attended involving the usual line-up of guests, and at which the Duke was in his customary forthright form. When he asked a vet student whether he was going to do 'large or small animals', the vet unwisely suggested that 'it doesn't make much difference'.

'You won't say that when you have to stick your hand up a cat's arse,' was the Duke's response.

There is a tangible feeling of this being the end of an era.

3

EXASPERATION

April 2021–January 2022

Despite everything, our poll ratings held up remarkably well, partly down to Labour failing to operate as a decent opposition. We even stood to make gains at the Senedd elections in May 2021, not something we were used to.

The success of the vaccination scheme helped. We ploughed through the population in a way that was reassuring despite the numerous setbacks along the way.

This period also covers the funeral of the Duke of Edinburgh and whether the nation is moving slowly away from its unbreakable association with the House of Windsor. It took the death of the monarch herself to really answer that question.

I meet Sue Gray for the first time – in her role as second Permanent Secretary in the Department for Levelling Up, Housing and Communities (DLUC) – and warmed to her pragmatic approach to some of the levelling-up challenges facing Wales. I detected tensions between No. 10 and 11 over the Australia Trade Deal as Liz Truss jetted around the world signing countries up left, right and centre.

Matt Hancock was caught on a security camera in the Department of Health in an overly warm embrace with a special adviser, triggering a huge story and his demise. Cummings continued to spray venom around in his Select Committee appearances; there was a reshuffle, a dreary Conference in

Manchester with all the scandals that come with it, and then the tragedy of our colleague David Amess being murdered.

The Owen Paterson affair finally boiled over – highlighting the fact that what look like simple dilemmas for the Whips' Office or No. 10 are seldom easy to resolve in real life, often because we overthink our responses. We lost a subsequent by-election in a rock-solid Shropshire seat, following which were the first real stirrings of dissent within the Party. Questions began to be asked about Boris's suitability for the top job, leading to David Davis publicly calling for his resignation in PMQs.

———— • ————

Saturday, 17 April 2021

Beautiful spring day for the funeral of D of E at Windsor. A subdued affair but handled well by all concerned. To comply with Covid regs, HMQ sat alone and in a mask and the Duke's coffin was transported on a converted Land Rover.

The Palace does these things to perfection. Just enough pomp and ceremony to appeal to the nation's patriotism, but never crossing the invisible line into opportunism or mawkishness.

Thursday, 22 April

Rumour number one is that the Electoral Commission is sniffing around the financing situation of Boris and Carrie's flat in No. 10, and asking who pays for the nanny. Is nothing straightforward in the world of the Johnsons?

Rumour number two is that the delightful, emotional and genuine Johnny Mercer [Veterans' Affairs Minister] is going to resign over some provision in the Overseas Service Bill which affects veterans. Unwisely perhaps, he alerts the PM and Gove that he is 'thinking of resigning' whereupon they sack him. His second mistake is to then spend the next day slagging them off on

any TV channel he can get onto. He claims that 'almost nobody' tells the truth in the Johnson Government. They won't forgive him easily.

Rumour three is that Cummings is about to be revealed as the source of the leak of private texts between BJ and others. The story is duly briefed to Harry Cole and others, but has hallmarks of quite a prolonged and bitter process. Sure enough, it emerges that the PM 'believes that Cummings is behind the damaging leaks' although we don't know the juicy detail yet.

Talked to Gavin about it and we agreed that not enough thought is given to the appointment of people (like Cummings) so when the end inevitably comes, it is always messy.

Saturday, 24 April to Sunday, 25 April

Cummings looks like he intends to take everyone down in what is being described as a 'nuclear Dom'. He's fingered top SpAd – and Carrie's best mate – Henry Newman as the 'chatty rat' (the nickname given to the unidentified source who leaked details of the UK's second lockdown). Add to this the private exchanges between the PM and James Dyson over a tax issue and details of the PM's funding of the flat refurb. There is huge weekend media interest in Carrie's role but worryingly it all looks well sourced and is likely to run and run. Cummings has also agreed to spill his guts in front of a Select Committee on 26 May. We might all think BJ can be a bit of a chancer, but it would be helpful not to have it proved beyond all doubt. One thing is for sure: if Newman is the culprit, BoJo knows there is little he can do without creating trouble at home.

Monday, 26 April

Early start to get to Wrexham to meet the PM, his first public appearance after a torrid weekend's press. First up was a visit to

young Alex Lovén at Net World Sports. Alex started the business whilst still at school and now employs over 1,500 local people. He is full of enthusiasm and positivity; he gave the PM a great welcome (as did the workforce). A real boost with some added table tennis photo ops. At the press brief BJ dealt with the more serious topics followed by the actual media discussion.

The questions were hostile but predictable, during which he issued a categoric denial that he had ever used the expression 'let the bodies pile up'. I assume Cummings has no evidence to the contrary.

Then to Prestatyn where he did a walkabout on the High Street. This is where the whole Boris thing shouldn't work but does. It really was wall-to-wall people, cameras, laughter and goodwill. A scrum from top to bottom, culminating in me and him having a pre-orchestrated drink in the street (it's about the first time people can drink in pubs again). It took almost an hour to get from one end of the street to the other, during which he was mobbed by old grannies, kids on bikes as well as young lads sitting in the pub. I have often heard the hype, but I have never seen it, nor can I explain it. There was no mention of anything in the press that his critics are so desperate to land. My only conclusion is that people see in Boris a bit of what they are, or what they want to be.

Monday, 3 May

Today starts in Monmouth with candidate Peter Fox (who should win) and TC then to Cardiff North and Bridgend. We finished with BJ in Barry where he (in a howling gale and wind) spoke well to the press and did the usual 'Gavin and Stacey' ice cream serving in Mario's on the sea front. It was a bit more edgy than last week, but good Facebook content I thought (apparently, he even asked for me to be present which is a first).

Tuesday, 4 May

Back to North Wales, this time via Welshpool where Priti Patel was putting in a shift and was good with the punters. As ever well run by Craig Williams, the local MP, with dinner at the Nags Head and staying at the Royal Oak. She was more humorous than usual, but she does think the world is against her – perhaps it is.

Wednesday, 5 May

Off early to Rhyl to meet Rishi with Andrew RT and others. It was a sharp and professional well-organised visit, the CX is everything that the PM isn't, which is why the contrast works quite well. He was great with the holiday businesses and the timing was good to max out our essential 'Get Out the Vote' effort. Final polls put us on either 17 or 18 seats – an unbelievable result if it came true, but we think nearer 14 is more likely.

Friday, 7 May

Woke early to see that council seats in the N/NE were falling to the Conservatives with large swings. The Hartlepool by-election is a miracle. Conservative for the first time ever – we gain 23%, Labour lose 9% and the rest don't matter. In any normal era we would have been spanked. Is it Labour? Is it Brexit? Is it Boris? We just don't seem to know but it's probably a mixture. The pressure is now on in Wales where we start the counting in an hour.

Drama here too, for the handful of people watching this election. Turns out that the Labour vote has held up well, almost certainly due to Drakeford's enhanced profile and 'Covid handling'. Outrageous but true.

As a result, our much better showing only unseats Labour in the Vale of Clwyd and the LDs [Lib Dems] in Brecon and

Radnor where the incumbent stood down. However, we do well in the regional list, up with 16 in total (an increase of 5) and Labour on 30 (plus 1); Plaid had a bad time, down at 13. UKIP (Neil Hamilton) and the awful Mark Reckless both lose their seats. I spoke twice to BJ who seems quite relaxed although our position in Wales is based mainly on a comparison with the NE where we rule supreme. In Scotland it looks like the SNP might miss out on a majority but will be propped up by the Indie-supporting Greens.

We have to stop all this internal Party navel gazing if we are ever to govern Wales.

Monday, 10 May

My GWR train is taken out of service due to a fault, meaning a 5 a.m. departure for Cabinet at 11ish. I needn't have bothered as the meeting lasted nine minutes and involved no contributions from anyone other than the PM. Even Buckland didn't get a word in.

The purpose of the meeting was to discuss the Covid summit which we had all read about in the weekend media anyway.

Tuesday, 11 May

The Queen's Speech (diet version) goes ahead. Quite a dull selection of Bills including some worrying stuff on Animal Welfare which will almost certainly go badly wrong as it always does. But the great news that John Gardiner has become Deputy Speaker [in the Lords]. It's a Countryside Alliance reunion. One new minister recounts his very funny call with BJ. Apparently, he was happily ensconced in his new, non-government lifestyle when he gets a call to speak to the PM, with whom he has had a chequered relationship. Instead of giving BJ the proper talking-to that he had planned, and rejecting his ministerial offer out of

hand, he said he found himself blathering away and agreeing to take the role. 'We need you back on the team,' BJ was saying, and of course he fell for it, like so many others. 'I felt like I had been violated!' he said.

Wednesday, 12 May

Cabinet by phone, on time, but a cursory 15 minutes on this occasion. I hope that BJ's new-found popularity isn't going to come at the expense of not having any Cabinet meetings at all.

A freezing lunch on the balcony at the Ivy, Victoria, with Anna Mikhailova of the *Mail on Sunday*. We are all warned off these lobby lunches these days but it's helpful to keep a running dialogue going or else they just guess the truth.

Wednesday, 19 May

Met the new Permanent Secretary for the Union, Sue Gray, who came much touted as a Whitehall legend. Civil servants in the Wales Office speak of her in a whisper, others talk of her having buried most of the bodies littering SW1. I thought she was strikingly normal but a little too keen on devolution for my taste, mainly because she opened the chat with some lavish praise for Drakeford and co. Somebody must have told her I was a fan so when I winced, she went into a hasty reverse gear. More concerning is that her views are at odds with what the PM thinks. To quote Thatcher though, 'we can do business'.

Thursday, 20 May

Quite a day. 8 a.m. meeting in the Cabinet Office with PM, CX, Home Sec, Gove, Frost, Kwasi, Alister, Brandon, me and Liz Truss, [George] Eustice [Farming Minister], plus officials (there was no social distancing either).

The agenda was the Oz trade deal. For a start, it was clear that no one much appreciated being dragged into 70 Whitehall this early, especially the PM who looked like he was still asleep 15 minutes earlier. He then made it obvious in his opening remarks that he favours 'full liberalisation' as does Liz, but with Eustice in favour of quotas to protect the sheep and beef sector. Alister and I sit in the middle, physically and metaphorically. It's clear that Eustice and Truss have fallen out so we hedged a bit and agreed to go for full liberalisation over fifteen years 'with safeguards'.

Gove, who was also in a feisty early-morning mood, was right to point out that we will be fully rumbled by the eco and farming lobbies on welfare standards. 'Don't think for a minute they won't see straight through this,' he said, and the CX reminded us that the deal is much better for Oz than it is for us. Rishi described this as having a 'negligible impact on GDP' and warned against the dangers of 'deal fever' – a side-swipe at Liz who seems more obsessed with signing deals rather than driving hard bargains.

The PM (without irony) then gave us a lecture about not leaking. It was evident from the start that he had aligned with Liz so the rest of the room was basically being ignored.

Then straight into car to Cardiff for the 'Big Speech' on the Plan for Wales. Loads of journalists called about the Oz meeting and sure enough it was written up by Harry Cole by 5 p.m., thankfully with no help from me. So much for not leaking.

Tuesday, 25 May

Cabinet – we must surely return to a physical presence soon. As per usual with this format none of the big issues were even on the agenda at all. I had a stab at raising a levelling-up query but as ever felt like the PM is looking at his watch.

Lunch in the rather empty Cinnamon Club with journalists

Matt Chorley and Chris Mason. The lobby has this habit of doubling up their lunches with two rather contrasting hacks, maybe for expensing purposes or maybe for ambush advantage, who knows. Matt is funny but acerbic, Chris penetrating but engaging.

Wednesday, 26 May

The long-awaited Cummings appearance before the Science and Tech select committee – and what a spectacle it was, quite well jointly chaired by the two old pros Greg Clark and Jeremy Hunt. Seven hours of largely unchallenged Cummings vitriol and bile, largely directed at BJ and Hancock for whom it is clear he has a very special level of hate. It was a litany of abuse, lapped up by the very same people in the press who less than a year ago said Cummings couldn't be trusted to lie straight in bed. There was something for everyone, but special interest was shown in his recollection of a single day spent trying to deal with Covid, a 'Trump bombing the Middle East request' and also Carrie's annoyance that the media was being mean about her dog. Weirdly though, there was no mention of Brexit.

He claimed Hancock 'lied' to the Cabinet and Parliament but offered no supporting evidence and said that BJ was not fit to be PM although it seems he was more than happy to have worked for him (and be defended by him when things went wrong). As one observer mentioned, it was like watching your ex-partner 'cut up all your clothes and chuck them out of the window'. And there was no mention of the fact that Cummings is currently held in contempt of Parliament for his failure to give evidence to the DCMS Committee. Starmer then ballsed up his PMQ slot to land a punch on BJ (as usual) and, as before, the public is more than happy to ignore the whole show.

Saturday, 29 May

In Exeter for a few days for Adam's graduation, but astonished to learn that Boris and Carrie got married in a 'secret ceremony' at Westminster Cathedral. Absolutely no one leaked – which is a remarkable achievement in the current climate. Anyway, Carrie was in a dress she hired for £45 and BJ looked as he always does in 'family' pics – ever so slightly awkward.

(The next day Jack [Wales Office SpAd] is drinking in a pub with a prominent lobby hack who left his phone on the table to go to the bar. Who rings? Carrie. Shouldn't she be on honeymoon? Eyes on the paper tomorrow.)

Tuesday, 1 June, recess

The much-awaited, by about six people, 'First Minister summit' – what are they playing at? We give Drakeford and Sturgeon airtime to slag us off and they demand we should have their consent to do anything at all in the devolved nations.

It's getting to the stage where they might as well be in the Cabinet and do away with the Wales/Scotland Office and Welsh/Scottish MPs. It has to be stopped. I think BJ gets all of this but he is surrounded by appeasers who then browbeat him.

Monday, 7 June

Covid Cabinet. For once I think patience with the CMO is getting a bit stretched. Despite the Delta variant being 'at large' there are very few hospitalisations and deaths, prompting JR-M to ask exactly what our new 'position' is? Whitty responded by saying it was a political judgement not a medical one, which annoyed everyone as all our political judgements are based on his medical ones. That has always been the strategy.

Tuesday, 8 June

Cabinet. On the same day that No. 10 is hosting drinks for groups of twenty colleagues, Cabinet is still remote. This needs to change, especially so as the chat about Covid was terminated by the PM without a single member being allowed to speak.

Thursday, 17 June

In other news it transpires that the Bishop of St Davids, Dr Joanna Penberthy, has been on Twitter slagging off the Tories in no uncertain terms. She says she is 'deeply ashamed' of the nation's pro-Tory voting and you should 'never, never, never trust a Tory'. This is brave given that half her flock voted Conservative in the last GE. We leap into action which results in a Zoom call with the Archbishop of York and a grovelling letter from Canterbury himself, who it seems is as ashamed of her as she is of us. 'Bashing the Bishop' headlines cause endless amusement in the tabloids.

Wednesday, 23 June

A happy drink with Ben Gascoigne in the Wales Office – turned into a gin marathon but his contacts and knowledge of life in No. 10 is extensive and his views largely confirm everything we thought would be the case over the road (in other words, it looks like Carrie is tightening her iron grip).

Friday, 25 June

A tornado of shit hits our shores. Matt Hancock is all over the media thanks to a Harry Cole splash in the *Sun*, with pictures of him passionately kissing a female aide in his office. But it gets much worse, as it's during lockdown, breaking the rules that

Matt, himself, set up. It turns out that the lady in question was an old pal recruited by Matt to a position close to him in the Dept of Health. The pictures, including an agonisingly detailed video (reminiscent of a dirty uncle pissed up on the wedding dance floor), seem to have been taken from an internal security camera, or possibly from across the road through the window.

To his credit, BoJo does accept his apology and declines to sack him but the outlook is bleak. Social media goes mad and vile at the same time, raising all sorts of associated questions.

For me the security question is as big as the other issues this all raises. How could an outsider access film of a minister's inner sanctum? Were they paid or bribed, if so who by? Is this legal and is the public interest threshold met? Are all of our offices bugged? Did this story only work because 'Matt made the rules'?

It's gruesome to watch. Matt may have made a serious error but he is not evil. He got caught making a misjudgement and he and his family will pay a much higher price than the millions of other 'offenders' in a similar position.

Saturday, 26 June

In the least surprising development of the year Matt resigns. He had no option really as his credibility is shot. The *Sun* may parade his head on a plate but I can't help wondering about his kids. And yes, of course it's his fault but life is not simple, or black and white. BoJo appoints Sajid Javid into Dept of Health thus settling the debt owed following the Treasury debacle (when Saj resigned) and avoiding a reshuffle at the same time. The Govt announces an inquiry into security at the Dept of Health.

It's things like this that deter people from entering politics and which make those of us in it question why we do it. Matt is resilient, but not everyone has skin as thick as his.

Tuesday, 29 June

Cabinet is in person but is hardly worth a mention these days. It was enlivened by Lord Nick Herbert who gave a good LGBT presentation and announced an event which the PM said he would attend 'in my Stetson and pink vest'. He just can't help himself sometimes.

Lunch with Laura K and Gordon Rayner (*Telegraph*) at the Ivy, Victoria. The agenda, as ever, Hancock but also the complicated (and rumoured) domestic lives of others in the Cabinet.

Wednesday, 30 June

To Swansea Prison with Robert Buckland – he really can talk. The prison was as expected – soul sapping and gloomy. Full of dismal depressed staff and inmates. It hasn't really changed since it was built by the Victorians in 1870. A prisoner had died a few days earlier (hanging) and someone had been violently assaulted in the exercise yard. It was all recorded for the likes of us to watch in gory detail. We also met a warder who (if I remember correctly) went by the name of 'Dai the Shit'. His job was to hang around the loos every time a prisoner was suspected of concealing some drugs or phones 'internally'. Apparently, they can hang on several days but when it happens there is a race between Dai getting his arm into the middle of it all, and the prisoner, who is attempting to flush it. He told me proudly that the largest thing he has ever successfully extracted was: 'a family-size tub of Pringles'. Cheery stuff. I asked Wales Office officials to nominate him for an honour. That's what I call public service.

Thursday, 1 July

My turn on *Any Questions*, this time as close to home as possible, Narberth, which of course makes it worse. Liz Saville Roberts

[Plaid Cymru], Carolyn Harris [Welsh Labour] and economist Patrick Minford were the other panellists, as per normal these days it all felt a little one-sided. Liz was clapped for everything, which was odd in a Labour/Lib Dem area, but I held the line on the Union, Covid and how Starmer can't be both a Corbynite and a Blairite simultaneously. The Australia trade deal question went badly (well, it's a bad deal really) and there was a gratifying lack of post-show Twitter reaction.

Monday, 12 July

Crime meeting with the PM. Normally a dull affair but much spiced up by him having a pop at Police Minister Malthouse for talking management gobbledegook and trying to prevaricate about BoJo's desire to have Blair-like 'targets' for crime. A bit unfair on Kit but it gave the rest of us much-needed entertainment.

Saturday, 17 July to Sunday, 18 July

Sajid Javid gets a positive Covid test, which means that BoJo and Rishi (and others) will need to self-isolate – or does it? No. 10 cook something up whereby they can opt into some niche scheme that allows them to avoid it if they test twice daily – a privilege that the rest of the nation does not enjoy. Jenrick is sent out to bat against a very hostile 'one rule for you and one for us' media attack (which was entirely predictable).

And guess what? By 11 a.m. Sunday the decision has been reversed, and they have now decided that they will now self-isolate which rather blows a hole in: 1) the credibility of the UK Government; 2) the regional Cabinet on Thursday; 3) the so-called 'Freedom Day' tomorrow. The damage is done and how someone in No. 10 ever thought this was a good idea we will never know.

Tuesday, 20 July

Infections (but not hospitalisations or deaths) are still rocketing thanks to the Delta variant.

Had a Covid meeting with Nadhim Zahawi. Always sound, and increasingly tipped as a future leader. The equally ambitious, and compelling, Penny Mordaunt [Paymaster General] is also on manoeuvres. Dinner in Boisdale's with Spencer [Chief Whip] and Brandon whose security people can't believe their luck as they tuck into one of the most expensive menus in London. Spencer is sound and thinks Buckland will get the chop and that BoJo was never consulted about the self-isolation story at the weekend and is livid.

So, with little fun and bother we reach 'recess'. 'Freedom Day' proved to be nothing of the sort, with a fair degree of chaos and confusion, and a little bit of poll tightening which reflects that. The reality is that the No. 10 machine is dysfunctional – and always has been. It lacks high-quality leadership.

Sunday, 15 August

My birthday. A storm gathers over Afghanistan as the US announce an immediate withdrawal. As is normal with Boris, the Cabinet was not convened, although COBR was and Parliament will now be recalled on the 18th by which stage it will be largely all over.

Wednesday, 18 August

Raab was on holiday and these situations do not suit BoJo. His statement was weak and erratic and contributions across the House were largely critical and met with increasing pessimism and vague indications that today's Taliban 'aren't so bad after all'. Starmer was also weak but Theresa May was better and

other veterans emotional. The 'speech of the day' was deemed
to be Tom Tugendhat [Tonbridge and Malling], himself a
veteran of that conflict. For me he just about struck a difficult
balance between his own (unquestionably brave) expedition to
that country as both a civilian and serviceman and the political
challenges of today. At least he is articulate and knowledgeable
though, which will hardly endear him to the Government even if
it does to Parliament.

The reality is that the Government probably couldn't have
done much anyway and is correct to agree to rehome 20,000
refugees. Yet our comms seemed muddled and unconvincing at
a time when we had the support of the House and the country.
What a strange feeling to be back in a full Chamber even though
it's questionable if a full recall was necessary.

Friday, 20 August to Monday, 23 August

It looks like there is a high level briefing against Raab, No.
10 and Rosenfield [No. 10 Chief of Staff] so it's little wonder
we are in a state. It all makes a reshuffle much easier when
it happens. DIT [Dept International Trade] announce a new
bunch of PM's trade envoys, including Ian Botham for Australia
– since when was Ian a UK/Oz trade expert we ask? I suppose
the thinking was that the Aussies are still terrified of him after
Headingley 1981.

Drive to Snilesworth in Yorkshire for two decent grouse days
at which all this is becoming a more frequent conversation.

Wednesday, 25 August to Thursday, 26 August

Afghan rages and the situation looks bleak. An irritating former
Marine ('Pen' Farthing) is kicking up a fuss about his 'dog sanc-
tuary' and the meddlesome animal rights obsessive Dominic
Dyer is lobbying Carrie to get him and his animals evacuated

before women and children (in effect). Because of the press interest we all think BoJo will be easily cajoled but it's an absurdity that this is taking up time. Ben Wallace is handling it encouragingly robustly well.

Sunday, 29 August to Monday, 30 August

The chippy Marine gets his dogs out of Kabul only to jump on the next flight to Oslo to see his partner. Turns out he also abused an MoD official (which is like being rude to waiters – just not done) using the old cliché 'I will destroy you'. What an arse. Colleagues are livid that he has used up precious MoD resources and burnt the reputation of MoD officials in the process.

Tomorrow is the last flight out of Kabul. The Taliban is back in the game so it's easy to raise an awful lot of questions . . .

Wednesday, 1 September

The SMG [Small Ministerial Group] meets to discuss eligibility of Afghan refugees. Priti Patel attempts to explain to us all the unintelligible management-speak that her department has come up with. They can talk and talk in the HO but delivery appears to be a different matter. Jenrick is the more compelling Cabinet contributor. It's all a bit depressing. Now every illegal migrant will claim to be an Afghan.

Friday, 3 September

Surprise call from Rishi. He wanted to know if I'd been consulted by No. 10 about the social care package (answer – no) and various other issues like Covid and Afghan. Unquestionably this is the first sniff of a more public distancing between No. 10

and 11. I need to be both simultaneously on Rishi's side yet not visibly disloyal to BoJo . . .

Sunday, 5 September

The media tells us that there is a row within Cabinet about social care, which given that the Cabinet has not discussed it, seems an exaggeration. No doubt individuals have been out there briefing. The No. 10 response is to resume talks of a reshuffle – even as soon as this Thursday. Is it genuine or just a 'get back in your box' moment?

Tuesday, 7 September

Cabinet is at 8.30 a.m. but we are allowed in at 8 a.m. to read the paper on Social Care – despite the juicy bits being released to the media the night before. We are clearly not trustworthy, but to be honest that's a fair position for No. 10 to take. The content is as trailed – 1.25% on NICs and dividend income.

It's a hell of a lot for everyone to swallow but in the absence of any legitimate alternatives for the completely underwhelming Starmer, it seems to land grudgingly with the public. Yet again we seem to attach too much importance to the contractual nature of manifestos. They are ambitions, not a legally binding commitment, as we learnt in 2010 with the coalition.

I make a token contribution about the 'Union' and get a laugh for pointing out that as there are almost no high-rate tax payers in Wales anyway, the policy is unlikely to cause too much discomfort. Rishi sends me a congratulatory text.

Reshuffle rumours continue to occupy everyone's thoughts. I get mentioned as a potential 'casualty' on Sky's Jon Craig tea-room gossip network but otherwise nothing. It could be No. 10 floating the threat or it could be real. Either way, I wish they would just get on with it or confirm it isn't happening.

Wednesday, 8 September

The draft boundary changes for Wales are out. The overall impact is not brilliant. Cairns [Vale of Glamorgan] and Baynes [Clwyd South] in trouble and Crabb [Preseli Pembrokeshire] and I left with one decent seat to squabble over. At least the battleground is now nearer 50:50 than in the first variation. CCHQ needs to do a deal with candidates to avoid a blue-on-blue battle. The voting public on the other hand will not be giving even a tiny toss.

Thursday, 9 September

With Jacob Rees-Mogg to North Wales for a Party event and a couple of visits. I feel I ought to be more easily riled by JR-M but it's really impossible as he is so well-mannered, well-informed and more reasonable (on the things that matter) than the press ever reports. That's not to say that he's not deeply eccentric too. Taking to the N Wales zipline (the world's fastest) in a three-piece tweed suit is not normal. According to his team, he also demands cotton sheets (no duvets) and a bath not a shower wherever he stays – not easy in hotels these days. I wish I had that level of self-assurance.

Monday, 13 September

There is still a will they/won't they? air about the reshuffle. It does feel like it's created a momentum of its own and will therefore have to happen to avoid BoJo looking like he has bottled it. In the old days, press speculation was a little more thoughtful than today's Twitter equivalent – which seems to be 'let's make up shit'.

Tuesday, 14 September

Cabinet – no 'feel' of an imminent change. Most of the meeting taken up with chat about supply chain and food shortages. BoJo understands the PR risk so Gove is put in charge.

Wednesday, 15 September

Laura K tells me that the reshuffle is 'on' and will start after PMQs later. Having spoken to Alister [Jack] last night he seems confident that the 'TO3' [Territorial Offices of Wales, Scotland and Northern Ireland] will survive but that there are quite a range of other heads on the block. He predicts moves for Gove and Raab, and of course the death sentence for Gavin and possibly Jenrick. How AJ loves the intrigue!

But before that it's Wales Questions once again in a fullish Chamber and no 'call list', making it much more dynamic.

Reshuffle is now official, so we are all on standby.

Sure enough, the sackings start in the PM's Commons office right away. Raab is dropped from FCDO and after a long and awkward meeting ends up with Justice and it seems Deputy Prime Minister, apparently a sop to stop him going altogether and possibly going native with it. Jenrick and Buckland also get the chop. Buckland is a surprise, but he did get a bit too sycophantic and there was the case of some leaked info too.

The rest of us sit by the phone pretending as always not to care . . . Light relief comes when the PM and his team decamp to No. 10, a sign that the sackings are over and it's now appointments and reappointments only. No great surprises other than Nadine Dorries ousting [Oliver 'Olive'] Dowden at DCMS. Olive is good and Nadine is, of course, crazy. Steve Barclay goes from CST to the Cabinet Office and Gove to MHCLG [Ministry of Housing, Communities and Local Government] but retaining, ominously for Alister and I, his Union brief. I get the call at 5.30 inviting

me to be over to No. 10 by 6.20. I slip in through the Cabinet Office internal 'pod' and straight into the Cabinet Room to see a surprisingly knackered-looking PM along with the Chief Whip, Chief of Staff, Declan Lyons [PolSec] and others. We exchange lame jokes and that's it. Upstairs for a pic, Twitter announcement and I'm still the Secretary of State for Wales.

Friday, 17 September

A happy Cabinet, with a few new faces. It's as if the old ones never existed, their name places erased in favour of the successful replacements; their names never mentioned again. They are the equivalent of George Orwell's 'unperson': 'someone who has been vaporised, secretly murdered and erased from society, the present, the universe and existence'. The dirty work is complete, but will it change much?

Sunday, 3 October

To the Conference in Manchester (my first for many years). God how I hate Conferences. A thousand things can go wrong, and almost nothing can go right. The whole city is overwhelmed with young staffers, MP hopefuls, lobbyists with generous credit cards and worst of all, the entire massed ranks of the media anxious to record every embarrassing moment of inappropriate commenting, kissing and vomiting.

At least the Wales Panel event chaired by Guto Harri goes well, as does the Wales reception, where BoJo is on top form. He 'loves the love', of which there is always plenty at events like this.

The bars are a sweaty heaving mass of bright young things but there is an undercurrent of leadership manoeuvres with Truss (complete with new Thatcherite hairdo) and others making the most of it all. It's too early to start the sprint stage yet though.

Monday, 4 October

Breakfast with Laura K and Jack Sellers. She is also picking up Truss-based rumours.

Tuesday, 5 October

Usual Party Conference gossip abounds. Anything seen as light-hearted, like Thérèse Coffey's karaoke, is damned by the Left as being frivolous. They are a humourless bunch and brand 'having a good time' as 'typically Tory'. I know which lifestyle I prefer.

Needless to say, I perform my duties with the minimum enthusiasm permitted at moments like this, including traipsing unwillingly through the whole excitable preparation for BoJo's big moment, 'the' speech.

To ensure our spontaneous expressions of delight and loyalty, we are summoned to the 'Blue Room' at 11 a.m. to get our orders. I have a coffee with Priti Patel and Nigel Adams [Asia Minister] to get me into a marginally better mood. Nigel is worried that the Cabinet awayday in Bristol clashes with a 400-bird partridge day in Yorkshire, which sounds to me like a legitimate 'apology for absence' moment. Given that Nigel has no speaking role in Cabinet, I rather sympathise.

The Speech. BoJo enters the darkened auditorium like Evander Holyfield. The crowd roars its approval, Carrie and Rachel Johnson look on lovingly, whilst a dapper-looking Henry Newman sits adjacent ensuring that the pair never lose sight of the unrelenting cameras that are yearning for the faintest hint of a Meghan/Kate moment.

What follows can only be described as BJ at his alternative best. It was different, loud, irreverent ('Bring back Beaver'). It teased Starmer rather than attacking him. As an after-dinner speech it was a triumph, less so if policy is your thing. But that was never its intention. This was all about King Boris seeing off

the younger stags eyeing up his hinds. It was for the Party, not the country. The Left hated it, just as they hate him, but all of that was to miss the point. Apparently, Boris wrote it all himself, demonstrating that speeches drafted by experts and teams of script writers don't always capture the audience or indeed the person giving them. And then he was off to Spain for a few days' rest. And guess what? The Left hated that too.

Thursday, 14 October

In Cardiff, where the Queen is opening the Senedd. On the face of it Plaid and Labour are meant to hate all that stuff, but underneath it they always soak up every Royal freebie going. I'm in the reception line-up at Central Station where we are told that HRH will definitely NOT be shaking hands, and to refrain from lunging in her general direction.

The train eventually pulls in at about 1 mph, various flunkies leap out arranging steps and umbrellas, checking our names etc. As HRH dismounts from the train, she vigorously shakes hands with us all. Somehow, without a word being proffered, she makes it pretty clear she would rather be watching the racing.

I skip the Senedd bit – partly in protest, and partly to have lunch with Adam.

Friday, 15 October

Visit with Priti Patel to meet cops in Swansea who are pioneering some anti-drugs operation. Despite her rather corporate vocabulary she is good with them and the drug rehab people, and I think her presence was well received. She certainly makes a genuine effort. Whoever plays her in the BBC's *Dead Ringers* gets her delivery spot on. Off to Rolls-Royce in Bristol for regional Cabinet meeting at 2.30 p.m. I do question the value of these awaydays, but RR is a serious player and it's easy to get to.

As we arrived in the anteroom for coffee and cakes, Mark Spencer [Chief Whip] took a call. News is coming in that our colleague Sir David Amess, the MP for Southend for the past thirty-eight years, had been stabbed multiple times whilst holding a surgery in a local church hall. There is something horribly inevitable about these calls. They just never end well, and Mark is clearly extremely troubled.

Home Sec and PM then arrive, and the 2.30 Cabinet start is delayed. 2.45, and Simon Case [Cabinet Secretary] tells us that the PM will make a short statement following which the meeting will be immediately adjourned. The PM then confirms that David has died but that we must wait until this is officially announced by Essex Police before saying anything to anyone.

The PM and others are visibly shaken. It's not that many of us knew David particularly well (he and I were on nodding terms at best), but that it frames the whole sad concept of politics being 'us versus the world'. There was a genuine, two-way, love and respect between him and his community.

Tears are shed, and there is a tangible feeling of despair in the room as people come to terms with what all this means. As the phones buzz and the internet goes wild it becomes clear that a man has attacked him and then waited to be arrested. It again raises the question of MP security, but also the whole issue of political tone and language. If our profession is deemed to be the lowest form of life, then some people will treat its protagonists accordingly.

As long as we are described as a 'sub-species' these things will happen. The news is awash with tributes, and we cancel our weekend appointments so we can reassess the situation. A good man with five kids, killed doing his job.

Monday, 18 October

Today is dedicated to tributes to David Amess. I'm never quite sure that we don't 'overdo' these things, but BoJo was excellent,

catching the mood and adopting exactly the right tone. It's as good as I've heard him. Starmer was also heartfelt and compelling, and even the SNP's Iain Blackford and backbenchers like Mark Francois [Rayleigh and Wickford] and James Duddridge [Rochford and Southend East] judged the moment with sensitivity. Plenty of humbug too, as many of the tears shed were from certain Labour MPs – themselves the architects of much of the online abuse that can lead to this kind of thing.

PM Zoom with the First Ministers. The weirdest half-hour I've had for a bit. PM was totally disengaged. Like everyone else we start by attempting to work collegiately, but soon discover that it takes two to tango and our dancing partners are just never in the mood.

Thursday, 21 October

Gove has stormed out of a Spending Review call with CST over the SPF [Shared Prosperity Fund], then issued a note slamming the HMT. We take this up with Rishi as, if it's true that HMT are about to shaft the devolved nations, we need to sort it.

CX himself hurriedly convenes a meeting, smothers us in love, including a £10 million last-minute 'investment' for Wales, despairs of Gove and reassures us that all our commitments and promises will be honoured.

Tuesday, 26 October

Coal summit. I really am getting frustrated by Welsh Government claiming that UK Government is 'not engaging' given we have contributed £31 million over and above the £250 million we have already committed for the next six years. The FM really does take the piss sometimes.

Wednesday, 27 October

Cabinet in advance of the Spending Review. Their styles are so different, that I've decided that when it comes to politics Boris 'fucks' and Rishi 'makes love'. Both are strangely effective. Wales does well although it will be interesting to see if it is reported that way.

£2.5 billion Barnett (best for twenty-five years) and £120m levelling up which is very, very popular with the Local Authorities. Fuel and booze duty cuts make for a good day.

All Welsh Government has to say, as ever, is that 'it's not enough' (yawn). What matters is it all gets spent on things that impact on people's lives. Quite a lot of follow-up media, but mainly focused on the cost of living.

Wednesday, 3 November

A storm is gathering over the Standards Commissioner report into Owen Paterson [North Shropshire] and lobbying by Randox. After a long inquiry he has been found guilty and is in line to be banned from Parliament for 30 days. This sentence is sufficiently severe to trigger a recall vote and, if that's lost then there will be a by-election. The claim, it seems, is that he used his (paid) position in Randox to gain undue access to policy-making. Owen is an earnest individual but has never struck me as cavalier with the rules.

To make matters more complex, his wife Rose died by suicide a year ago, something which unsurprisingly has caused his family total devastation. As House matters like this are always treated as a priority, it looks like we are going to vote on this tomorrow. They are also almost always taken on a 'free vote' too, so the rumour that No. 10 are minded to whip MPs to vote down the report and acquit Owen (or at least reduce his sentence) is causing some tea-room consternation.

Colleagues and the media are deeply uncomfortable. For a start, Owen is guilty of an act of stupidity, so if nothing else, to force colleagues to support him is madness. It 'smells' very dubious and if past attempts to deploy 'too clever by half' measures are anything to go by, this will fail dismally. It seems too that Owen's team includes rather too many paid-up members of the crazy gang which ought to be another worrying signal. My whip hints that the vote will be close, and suggests that I might miss my appointments in Glasgow and Cardiff. I decline.

Thursday, 4 November

Cardiff for the Remembrance Day service at which my national anthem efforts (in Welsh) appear to go down okay. Then to Glasgow for COP26. As I arrive, the Paterson drama starts to unfold.

The vote was won by HM Government by 18 BUT with a lot of very pissed-off colleagues. We have gifted Labour attack lines, damaged our own credibility, and reignited the sleaze reputation that always seems to haunt us – and all to clear Owen's name. Are we mad?

Friday, 5 November

You seriously 'couldn't make it up'. Labour and SNP boycott the new Paterson Committee that we voted to set up yesterday, in a move which was heavily anticipated. JR-M agrees to pull the proposal and start again. Paterson resigns. The result of this clusterfuck is that we now have a by-election we didn't want or need, a disheartened PM and Whips' Office and an emboldened Standards Committee.

As fuck-ups go, this one goes straight into the charts at Number One. It raises serious judgement questions about how JR-M and Mark Spencer got legged over by No. 10.

Monday, 8 November

The Paterson fall-out continues as the press rakes over every single possible breach they can find. Next up is Geoffrey Cox QC who has earned a £400k fee for a case he is involved in in the Virgin Islands. That's all fine, but it is claimed he used his Commons office to undertake some of the business, which is perhaps not so fine. It's something nobody cared much about but with the current feeding frenzy that is changing.

It also turns out that almost no one even remembers that we addressed all of this when I was on the Committee on Standards in Public Life – yet almost none of the recommendations in our report were ever implemented.

Thursday, 11 November

Another awayday this time for the Cabinet. The plan was Chequers but that was quickly relocated to No. 10 and therefore much more practical. The theme was levelling up and a chance for different Cabinet ministers, Gove, the Chancellor, etc. to woo the room with their commitment to this eye-catching flagship concept. An excitable BoJo was front and centre of each session, animated, untidy, funny, etc. He had clearly read all the info for once. He was also openly apologetic about the Paterson affair.

It was all rather upbeat and positive, focusing on 'delivery'. Lots of cheesy references to long-term sustainability and how this would secure a future for 'our children and our children's children'. Alister and I just about maintained a straight face until I felt obliged to point out that on all the levelling-up maps around the room, Scotland and Wales had been removed altogether. We remain very England-focused.

Sunday, 14 November

A rare weekend in a (busy) London for the Remembrance Day service at the Cenotaph. After breakfast at the Wolseley, made it to the FCDO where we were mustered for our part in proceedings. The organisation by the Cabinet Office was exceptional, all timed to seconds rather than minutes. First was coffee in the VIP room with Tony Blair, Gordon Brown, David Cameron and John Major, amongst many others. I'm there because as SoS Wales we have the chance to represent the country in Whitehall or in Cardiff, so on the basis of the 'a once in a lifetime opportunity' criteria, I choose London. As does the excellent Plaid Cymru MP Ben Lake so we have some shared fun trying to confuse the foreign diplomats into believing we were former PMs.

Then at about 10.45 a.m. we are lined up alongside our name badges Blu-tacked to the marble walls of the FCDO. In an adjacent corridor is the Royal Party, headed this time by the Prince of Wales, the Queen having pulled out a short time before.

At 10.53 precisely we emerged onto Whitehall and took our allotted places in silence. I was just behind the PM by happy fluke so had what seemed like the best position of all. The silence was extraordinary. Then the order to come to attention for the buglers of the Royal Marines to sound the Last Post.

The Prince looked quite emotional during the National Anthem and the two-minute silence. I think we all knew that the Queen may have made her last appearance at what we all know is the most important commitment in her diary.

Tuesday, 16 November

Cabinet. These days we are treated to bacon rolls as well; a fact Laura K found fascinating when I indiscreetly mentioned it later. Despite an increasing population of electoral elephants in the room, no one, including the PM, chose to mention them.

Wednesday, 17 November

Wales Orals went average to well. BoJo followed me with what was described to me by his team as an 'awful PMQs'. Performing to the same standard every single week, and never dropping the ball, is nearly impossible. I remember David Cameron telling me once that the difference between a dazzling performance at the dispatch box and an awful one, was quite often a single word, or a one-liner joke that didn't quite work. It's a minefield out there.

Gove has been rumbled for planning a private meeting with Mark Drakeford in Cardiff tomorrow. He is perfectly entitled to do that, but I do wish he would loop everyone in so we can maintain the illusion of joined-up government. So, it triggered a mini-row between him and me in the lobby, to which TC also cheerfully joined in. He [MG] really can be mischievous when he wants to be, but most irritating of all was when confronted with this cardinal sin, instead of retaliating he just says, 'Of course, Simon, how awful of me. I really don't know how you put up with me,' making me look intemperate and feel churlish for even raising it.

Thursday, 18 November

To Cardiff for the British–Irish Council [BIC], but first lunch with Michael G (which was civil) despite my views having not changed. He swears blind that he will speak to Drakeford only of the Covid inquiry, which he probably won't, so I told him I had no intention of being wheeled in at the end of the meeting, which he has suggested as a compromise, so I have petulantly boycotted my slot altogether.

Friday, 19 November

BIC – what an utter waste of everyone's time and energy (and money). Nothing but a talking shop and, worse still, a platform for Drakeford to create and expand his 'world leader' status. Just awful. And MG did meet him as I anticipated.

Monday, 22 November

Conservative Winter Party at the V&A. All the usual donors and hangers-on getting stuck in, but first the PM's speech to the CBI [Confederation of British Industry].

The speech had been shortened, thank goodness, as a result of the Union Connectivity Review being pulled that day, but that was not all. The PM also badly lost his way, pausing for what seemed like ages and then, unable to find the right page, started ad-libbing about taking his kid to see Peppa Pig. The whole thing was met with incredulity and dismay but as ever BJ was oblivious to the whole saga. To his credit he refused to blame the private office for fucking up and went on to make quite a good speech that evening at the fundraiser. Most of us would be so traumatised that our confidence would have been shot to pieces and we would have hidden away for several days. Not Boris.

Wednesday, 24 November

The *Spectator* 'Parliamentary Awards' dinner. Sort of okay. No one much on my table other than the new mini-Gove, Sebastian Payne of the *FT*, but a jolly crowd in the room. Fraser Nelson is a great compere; Buckland made an adequate speech and prizes went to all the usual suspects including the late David Amess. Truss was swivel-eyed, Rees-Mogg surprisingly religious and Javid considerably funnier than anticipated.

Hitched a lift home with Nadhim Zahawi who I always think

may be worth a bet for the leadership one day. He arrived in the UK from Iraq with no money and no English and is now SoS for Education. As he said, the UK is a great country in which to fulfil your dreams.

Cabinet. The new SA variant, now known as Omicron, is continuing to confuse us as well as the global scientific community. However, the No. 10 view is that we mustn't be caught out, so caution is the byword.

To a CCHQ business dinner at the In and Out club. They all seem quite upbeat and unperturbed by Omicron.

It seems that some helpful soul is alleging that there was a 'party' in No. 10 during last December's lockdown – but no date, room, or evidence on offer as yet.

Dinner with Laura K at Cafe Murano where we decide that a conversation about dogs is more fun than one about politics.

BBC Radio 4 *Any Questions* in Presteigne, mid Wales. As ever a self-selecting, left-leaning, Boris-hating audience (just like in Narberth). They resolutely refused to give me (or local boy Quentin Letts [journalist]) any tolerance at all, instead just blowing smoke up the arse of Adam Price [Plaid Cymru] and Alison McGovan [Labour]. They can say literally anything they like, and nobody ever challenges them. I really don't know why we do these things as they have no discernible benefit.

Tuesday, 7 December

Cabinet. It seems certain that Omicron is now on its way, if not already amongst us. South African experts seem relatively chilled but our people (Whitty, Vallance and others) seem very spooked and are ominously referring to 'a small % of a small % is still a large number'. Very disheartening that Christmas is once again at risk.

Wednesday, 8 December

Coffee with Jess Elgot from the *Guardian* on the few Welsh matters that her readers might be interested in. She speaks a lot of sense, but I dare not admit that to my handlers at No. 10 lest they suspect a weakening on my part. Then a session with Sue Gray of the Cabinet Office to try and broker a more collegiate relationship with MG. Alister is doing likewise but including the use of whisky.

Cabinet call at 4 p.m. Unusually fractious this time as a beleaguered PM announces an Omicron Plan B which went down badly and is doomed to failure as the DAs are already pushing for Plan C. Plan B is the compulsory wearing of masks (deemed to have little effect other than as a visual reminder); a mandatory NHS Covid Pass and a presumption in favour of working from home. Apparently, we have acted 'quickly and with caution'.

Meanwhile the 'Partygate' saga is burning ever brighter. It seems an odd story that I don't think is resonating with the public. Is having a beer with colleagues you have spent all day with really a breach? The PM tackles it head-on with an apology at PMQs, which sort of worked and raised questions as to why Starmer used his full six follow-up questions on the topic. Everyone is now getting massively pissed off with BoJo for every reason under the sun. I stalk the tea rooms to gauge the

mood, which reaffirms this ill feeling. I don't think it's curtains yet but capital is being used up fast. David Frost and JR-M seem especially troubled – will either of them walk?

Sunday, 12 December

Cabinet brief on vaccine booster. There is a huge acceleration project under way. Gove briefs the First Ministers (without us again) and the *Sunday Mirror* runs another BoJo 'scandal' story. This time he apparently hosted a Christmas party for No. 10 staff, online. Whatever next. The media is now massively over-reacting, I think.

Tuesday, 14 December

Back to virtual Cabinet, which optically is a significant moment. PM is clearly edgy and this is not helped by a dispute between him and Ben Wallace about Ukraine. The trouble is that they both know their stuff and are both stubborn. Ben would not let go and it took an intervention from Thérèse Coffey to 'take it outside, boys' to get it back on course, as AJ messaged me 'taxi for Wallace'. This was followed by the Covid item where it looks like things are really hotting up. Backbenchers getting equally restless and today's vote on more Covid restrictions is causing massive whipping headaches.

6.30–7.00 p.m. As predicted the rebellion is 101 but the majority is 243. I just don't understand what they [our MPs] are playing at.

Wednesday, 15 December

COBR with Gove. First Ministers dealt with rather neatly by Simon Clarke [CST] when they moaned about policies being made 'by English Ministers'. Clarke gave them both barrels,

but respectfully, on how devolution works and how the Union operates and basically to stop trying to play political games with everyone, all the time, on every subject. I ditch everything else and got out of London as Covid is everywhere. Sturgeon really is dreadful.

Friday, 17 December

The North Shropshire by-election goes against us and in favour of the Lib Dems with a 5,000 majority. It's the first time this seat has ever been held by a non-Conservative. This is manageable but serious and should probably be reversed at a General Election, but it has opened up the whole question of whether the BoJo electoral 'magic' has lost some of its potency.

Saturday, 18 December

Chaos continues to reign. There are a few more party tales but Omicron is the big story. Various Cabinet meetings and briefings in which it becomes clear that the Cabinet is by NO means persuaded of the need to take stringent action (and the chances of a massive political meltdown seem to be ignored by officials).

In the midst of it all David Frost resigns, citing his concerns about the 'direction of government' including some odd references to the Greens. I always thought of him as nice but dull, so I'm surprised he has timed this to impose more pain on the PM who gave him all his recent career opportunities in the first place. Nothing like believing your own hype, I guess.

It does now feel like we are in the midst of a tornado . . .

Tuesday, 21 December

A record Cabinet – in terms of its length at least. The PM starts by explaining that he wants a 'thorough discussion' and that he

doesn't want to be as 'directive' as he usually is. The meeting therefore lasts two and a half hours and is all the better for it. It's a 'never say die' opening speech from BoJo about there being no need for further restrictions. It seems like we are agreed that we will maintain the policy of watch and wait, with regular reviews. But that was until Whitty weighed in, ably assisted by Simon Clarke, Michael Gove and Health Secretary Javid. Their message: 'If we don't act now, it will be too late.'

However, despite the mood dampener, the Cabinet holds its nerve and agrees there will be no new restrictions this side of Christmas. Shapps was especially assertive on the data question and wanted to know at what stage the peak of the virus would meet a wall of people who had received the vaccine, or were technically immune due to having contracted it already. Both categories amounted to several million, which meant that the maximum number of people at serious risk was much lower than the worst-case scenario figures being bandied about by scientists and the media. Yet the response was, 'we don't really know so we should adopt a precautionary principle' and should therefore impose a national lockdown over Christmas and the New Year.

Talked to the PM's PolSec Declan Lyons afterwards and take a call from Nigel Adams. Both are concerned that as soon as the meeting ended health officials were all over the PM, essentially bullying him into stronger measures than had just been agreed by Cabinet. I am tasked to call the PM later. We have an amicable, and I hope helpful, chat about the political reality of capitulating into another lockdown. In other words, I explain that if he recalls Parliament, which would be unpopular in itself, and triggers a vote, he will burn through even more of his rapidly declining capital and might not win the vote anyway. Labour will scent blood and abstain and we would be in a whole world of shit.

He explains that he thinks he will hold his nerve over Christmas, but that he's not sure he can last until 4 January so

will need to reconvene us, and possibly Parliament, between Christmas and the New Year. We shall see!

Saturday, 25 December to Saturday, 1 January 2022

A bit of recess in which numbers rise but hospitalisations and deaths remain steady enough for us to hold our nerve. Almost everything back to remote (including Cabinet) for the time being. In Wales, large public events are still mainly forbidden. Love and respect for Drakeford is beginning to come under a bit more scrutiny – at last. He's too comfortable imposing restrictions, like all socialists are, especially when someone else is paying for it.

Wednesday, 5 January

Back to the tedious regime of Cabinet via Zoom. It's clear JR-M is troubled by the notion of tax rises to pay for the NHS; instead preferring to look at savings from other departments. I thought the PM was quite curt with him but that's because JR-M rather missed the point. I suspect BJ has already made these commitments elsewhere so can't easily retreat. Will Jacob be the next resignation?

After Welsh Questions I found myself awkwardly wedged on the front bench between Rishi and Boris for PMQs. That gave me a chance to see BoJo's briefing notes and to see how he handles the incoming flak. Unsurprisingly, they were a jumble of chaos, covered with scribbled thoughts in an illegible scrawl. But as you would expect, as soon as the question lands he converts the whole thing into a nice clear, concise and frequently humorous response.

Monday, 10 January

There is growing disquiet (panic even) about Partygate. The media is reporting multiple parties in No. 10 during lockdown

(May 2020) and at which the PM was present. According to reports, his PPS [Parliamentary Private Secretary] Martin Reynolds sent an email inviting people to the garden for drinks along with a 'please bring your own booze' request. It's reported plenty of people replied raising 'is this wise' type questions but were ignored. If any of this is true, it's utter madness and is beginning to paint a picture of a No. 10 operation displaying some of the Machiavellian characteristics of its principal resident.

Dinner with George Hollingbery [former PPS to Theresa May] and others including Theresa and Philip May in Horseferry Road. (George is leaving Parliament to take up a diplomatic posting in Cuba.) Partygate, as it is now going to be for ever known, was the only subject under discussion. Most of the sensible people in the room think the PM is in last-chance saloon.

Wednesday, 12 January

Lobby brief at which I am pressed into, but just about avoid, calling for Boris's resignation. PMQs was bleak. The PM offered what was a sort of minimalist apology but his excuse – he thought the party at the centre of the current revelations was a 'work event' – was greeted with guffaws from the other side, the worst kind of response possible. We have moved from anger to ridicule. Our side sat in stony silence, whilst the opposition could barely contain their joy. They hate Boris more than they hate most of our leaders. For a start they can't understand how a raffish Old Etonian can possibly be popular. The 'Labour user's manual' instructs people to hate anyone who went to public school (except their own), increasing the resentment if the guilty party is also clever and funny. If they are also wicked and unreliable then their patience is stretched well beyond breaking point; roughly where they are now.

BoJo then adjourns to the tea room where he unwisely portrays himself as the victim. We know Labour hates him, but

you can feel the love for him draining away on our side too, partly because the mutual respect has always been somewhat transactional and hence skin-deep. In other words, we are all reminding ourselves of the fact BoJo was only elected for one reason (to deliver Brexit) and if that no longer applies then what is the point of him?

Ben Gascoigne and I decamp to see Nigel Adams and Deputy Chief Whip Chris Pincher, neither of whom has a magic cure either. Conor Burns [Bournemouth West] joins us and asserts Partygate all to be a Remainer plot. I seriously doubt it. I struggle to think of a plot so good that it had its intended effect.

Thursday, 13 January

To Shrewsbury for *Question Time*. When I accepted this some weeks ago, and after several previous refusals, I thought it would be fine. First *QT* of the year, just after the Christmas break, what could go wrong?

Now it is the shittiest of all shitshows. The audience will be angry, some melodramatically so, and I will be the butt of it, egged on by Fiona Bruce, Jess Phillips [Labour] and some Lib Dem, plus the mean-spirited journalist Isabel Oakeshott. I read all the notes from No. 10 and it still worries me they are still largely in denial.

Jack and I stop off in a nearby pub to get the No. 10 brief and we immediately lock horns with the press team over whether the PM is 'frustrated and remorseful' (the phrase I want to use). Apparently, he isn't, so they instruct me not to say so. I suggest perhaps he should be and say I am not risking my reputation to sound like an idiot. We agree to differ.

The show itself is as expected other than the audience being in masks and much depleted due to social distancing. I got one stroke of luck though. In the warm-up question, which is never broadcast, one of the Labour-voting NHS employees in

the audience (of which there were a suspiciously large number) made a point of thanking me for turning up and facing the heat. In an instant, the mood turned from bitter and angry to a feeling of sympathy that I have been trotted out to get a kicking.

After that, rather than anger (except from Oakeshott) the reaction I get was warm. I think I maintained a careful and delicate balancing act. Not a word from No. 10. Thank God I didn't take the line from them, for as we left Shrewsbury a further *Daily Telegraph* story broke about two more No. 10 parties but not including the PM this time. It feels like authority is ebbing with every hour. Liz Truss and Rishi Sunak's people both get in touch to offer congratulations.

Friday, 14 January to Wednesday, 19 January

'Partygate' is now like a bushfire, destroying all in its path. The key facts are these:

BoJo and his coterie are becoming increasingly delusional, rather than evil. They are incapable of recognising the problem is not one of duplicity or stitch-ups but of piss-poor appointments, chaotic leadership and bad decision-making.

Everyone is waiting for Sue Gray to report. She has found herself in the unenviable position of conducting the Partygate inquiry.

MPs will tolerate BoJo unless he looks like a seat loser. He has only one value to them.

Rishi and others are assessing the situation and rightly keeping everything under wraps.

There are numerous possible outcomes.

The press smells blood, and not just his.

As Andrew Percy pointed out, it's so febrile we all 'wake up on Team Rishi and go to sleep on Team Boris'. Our hearts tell us Boris still has the magic touch; our heads tell us voters will never forgive us for taking liberties (literally) and yearn for someone

serious and trustworthy. Every time we conclude BJ has to go, and RS is the only sensible alternative, Boris does something to make us doubt our instincts again. His two PMQs are frankly brilliant Bothamesque takedowns of a lukewarm Starmer – 'You are a lawyer not a leader,' he bellows. If [Graham] Brady [Chair of 1922 Committee] was waiting for fifty-four letters, he has longer to wait yet.*

What else is happening? An unknown Conservative MP called Christian Wakeford from Bury South crosses the floor and is paraded like a prize turkey at the Christmas Fayre. He will now have no friends at all, of course. On cue, David Davis [former SoS] uses his PMQ slot to call on BJ to go. Someone later misquoted Thatcher (who was talking about Heseltine) saying, 'the trouble with DD is he wants to be the bride at every wedding and the corpse at every funeral'. Does DD have a point though?

Thursday, 20 January to Saturday, 22 January

Nusrat Ghani [Sussex Weald] alleges she was sacked by BoJo for being 'too Muslim' – a charge vehemently rejected by No. 10 and Chief Whip Mark Spencer. It's an extraordinary claim. It was only her and Mark in the room. Those who know both of them think it seems implausible. The excitable Lords Minister Theo Agnew resigns at the dispatch box over Covid fraud. Charles Walker [Broxbourne], Graham Brady and I decamp to Islay to chase some woodcock (as we did when Theresa May was holding on by her fingertips). Our primary aim is to keep Graham away from his inbox and buy some precious time.

Both Charles and Graham think Boris is done for.

---

* In order to oust a Party leader, the Chairman of the 1922 Committee has to receive letters of no confidence from 15% of the Party's MPs.

Monday, 24 January

There is a steady stream, not a flood, of hostile emails from constituents about Boris but I am not sure what that tells us. Other party allegations come in, including a birthday party in the Cabinet Room but there's not much of real substance.

Tuesday, 25 January

The bombshell lands. The Met Police say 7 of the 17 (yes) parties have met the threshold and deserve further investigation, totally spannering the Gray report, the publication of which is now delayed again. Views vary from this being helpful (really?) to it being another 'final nail'. BoJo soldiers on into the valley of death. His visit to North Wales with me is agreed and we fly to Anglesey seemingly without a care in the world. In the meantime, Putin gathers his army on the border of Ukraine. Both these issues have a long way to run yet.

Wednesday, 26 January

Nigel Adams, Pincher and others form a shadow whips' operation garnering support for Boris, but they have a forlorn task ahead. As Malthouse said, 'You know the circus is over when they stop laughing at the clown.'

I also have some private time with Rishi. Whatever the outcome, we surmise Boris won't go willingly as he thinks he has done nothing wrong. We also agree we have only two years to restore our credibility.

Monday, 31 January

The PM is to make a statement on the Gray report at which Cabinet presence is required. The Chamber is fairly full but it is

not a great event. BoJo started well with a heartfelt apology, but the content and the mood are now pretty bleak. Even Theresa May sticks the boot in. Starmer was okay (in fact better than usual tbh) but BoJo lost the plot a bit when it came to describing Starmer as having 'failed to prosecute Jimmy Savile'. Technically it's true, but it's unwise to rehash as it reset the whole story. I sat loyally for two hours but feel we are no better off as a result and more likely worse. The Parliamentary meeting afterwards in Portcullis House was packed out and altogether better as the PM rallied the troops a little. But there seems little chance of escape.

4

DESPERATION

February–October 2022

This was the period of Partygate fines – the Met dished out over fifty to No. 10 staff alone – poor local election results, the Gray report and two further by-election defeats; one of which followed the mysterious case of a colleague watching 'tractor porn' on his mobile phone in the Chamber. We were entering the roughest of seas.

When the country emerged from the wreckage of the pandemic, we breathed a collective sigh of relief that we would, at long last, be able to return to normality. Yet within 24 hours of Covid regulations being eased, Vladimir Putin invaded Ukraine.

Boris was impervious to such unforeseen catastrophes: in fact, it looked like he was relishing the moment, the opportunity to provide the kind of Churchillian leadership for which he always thought he was best suited. It was clear he and Zelensky formed an instant bond. Would this be enough?

But then it all came home to roost. I record the long, slow, painful, messy and inevitable end. Forty-seven ministerial resignations in a matter of hours, mine included, meant only one thing. It was over for Boris Johnson. The man who won the election with an 81-seat majority had, in the view of many, frittered it away in the most trivial of manners.

Many colleagues and officials strove to keep the ship afloat but, one by one, they just ran out of road. To me it was a tragic period in politics rather than a scandalous one.

Throughout the rest of his life, Boris had always been able to position himself just far enough from the scene of a crime as to never quite be the prime suspect. As PM no such space exists.

It is the year of the Platinum Jubilee, a moment of unity and patriotism, but also the year the Queen died, triggering international reaction. Her funeral was an extraordinary moment of national reflection and mourning.

It was the time a choice between Sunak and Truss was put to the members of the Conservative Party, following a decisive show of support from MPs for Rishi (he won their endorsement by a huge margin). But the members thought differently, propelling Liz Truss into office for the shortest period on record, but a stay long enough for her to crash the markets and with it our reputation for economic competence.

—— • ——

Tuesday, 1 February 2022

Cabinet was dominated by Ukraine, on which the Chief of the Defence Staff [CDS] opined. He believes Russia may step over the Ukraine border within about two weeks.

Wednesday, 2 February

PMQs. There is a marginally less bitter feel about the place. Have people given up or simply shut up for now? There are rumours circulating of resignations as well as letters into the '22. Ellwood [Bournemouth East], Mitchell [Sutton Coldfield], Magnall [Totnes] and others go public. This cannot end well.

Thursday, 3 February

Munira Mirza [Head of Policy], Dan Rosenfield [Chief of Staff] and Jack Doyle [Director of Comms] all quit over Partygate and

associated mayhem. No. 10 claims it was the PM who sacked them, but nobody really believes that.

Saturday, 5 February to Sunday, 6 February

No. 10 appoints Steve Barclay as Chief of Staff. He is also staying on as CDL [Chancellor of the Duchy of Lancaster]. In a surprise move, Guto Harri has returned as Head of Comms, a job he did for Boris at City Hall. Guto is a familiar face and obviously heavily Wales-focused which I hope is a good thing. He's been a big critic of the PM so we will see where this leads.

Michael Ashcroft's book about Carrie comes out. It contains nothing we didn't already know.

Monday, 7 February to Tuesday, 8 February

The mini-shuffle continues. Chris Heaton-Harris becomes Chief Whip (I prefer him to some of the alternatives suggested), Chris Pincher becomes Deputy Chief Whip (we are told he's not pleased as he felt he was due the top job) and Mark Spencer is Leader of the House. Jacob R-M becomes the Minister for Brexit Opportunity (which I thought we all were supposed to be in our own way).

In the end no one was sacked so I am not sure what it will really achieve. I am summoned to spend another tactical evening with Ben G and Nigel, Chris H-H, Pincher and co. It's clear they are still deeply worried about an imminent coup. This concern was solidified by Shapps ringing and indicating his data – normally pretty good – was that 52 letters had gone into Brady. However, the Ukraine drama is still at a perilous stage so could distract attention.

Wednesday, 9 February

Lunch with Gary Gibbon [Channel 4] and Sam Coates at Corinthia. They think the Boris peace is temporary.

Meeting with Sue Gray who never fails to be very interesting.

Friday, 18 February

Rumours of Putin easing off Ukraine seem premature. Truss is getting overexcited about it, but it does make Downing Street parties appear somewhat trivial in comparison.

Monday, 21 February

Cabinet called for 10 a.m. Monday (which means a 4.30 departure for those of us who don't reside in London) to prep for the 'big' announcement – Covid regulations are to be eased. Much of it is trailed in the press, but the reality is it's still a big deal. People are now just bored of it all, and the desire to comply with the regulations has all but evaporated. The Queen then tests positive. Even the far less lethal Omicron is a worry when you are ninety-five. So BoJo may yet get a war and a Royal funeral to save his bacon. The big Covid announcement sort of goes okay even with the DAs' final whinge about 'wanting to be different'. No one cares much any more.

Tuesday, 22 February

Putin makes his move on Ukraine. This is a full-scale military invasion from air, land and sea. Disbelief spreads amongst the Western world as we witness scenes most of us thought were consigned to history, thanks to Reagan, Thatcher and Gorbachev. Yet here we are, watching the full might of the Russian Army break every agreement in the book in an attempt to demolish its

nearest and pluckiest neighbour. And whatever we all say publicly, the ever-present worry is: does he stop here? The possibilities are terrifying. The West is stunned but almost immediately a sanction package unfolds. The PM catches the mood and rightly argues that any package must be global to have effect. In this ambition he is followed wisely by Keir Starmer and most of Europe.

In the PM's statement – to an unusually hushed Chamber – we spelt out the terms of our sanctions. Financial impositions on oligarchs in the UK. Trade and travel sanctions may not sound much now, but they will develop.

We promise weaponry to Ukraine and the promise of more aid and help with almost all they need. Countries across the world close their doors to Putin and the wider Russian diaspora. Sporting and cultural events (so important to everyday Russians) are cancelled worldwide. The Russian stock market crashes 40% in one day. This is just the beginning.

The PM addresses the House, passionately and with gravitas. The Cabinet meets in No. 10 at 8.30 p.m. Colleagues speculate about the Russian strategy being 'shock and awe' to be followed by a long period of consolidated occupation whilst sanctions bite. Sanctions often wear off with time, as countries find ways around them, so any sanction package will need updating and refreshing to cause any real impact.

The Commons gives a long and emotional standing ovation to the Ukrainian ambassador in the public gallery.

And so, it seems within hours of one of the world's biggest upheavals (Covid) being finally brought under control, a bigger, more evil and more disruptive force is at work. We are all to be put to the test once more.

Monday, 28 February

A tired PM leads a further emergency Cabinet on Monday morning. The news from Ukraine is grim but the resistance,

especially from President Zelensky, is inspirational. Media speculation is that Russia's advance has been slow and their equipment
lacking. However, sheer 'pluck' may not be enough to assure
victory, added to which, PM's increasing fear is the prospect of
a 'catastrophic victory', one in which the public humiliation of
Putin is so complete he lashes out.

Thursday, 3 March

St David's Day debate. Not many there but we plough through
all the usual Labour nonsense. They are so institutionalised it is
almost worrying. They all made the same speech, the only difference being some of them read it out better than others. It is like
they have been pre-programmed to simply hate Conservatives
for no other reason than they are Conservatives. It's a strange
ability to be able to be relatively civil in normal life but then
default to resentment and hatred as soon as they set foot in the
Chamber or in front of a camera. Jack [Wales Office SpAd] and
I have a theory though, which is that the tribal bond in Labour
is far more developed and deep-seated than it is with us. With
Labour the tribe matters more than anything else, including, on
occasions, the truth.

After 90 minutes of this torture my summing-up speech was
spikier than usual, leading both Jessica Morden [Newport East]
and Anna McMorrin [Cardiff North] to take offence. I had
singled them out for a very gentle ribbing and their complaint
rather proved my point: they can dish it out, but don't like
receiving it. Jess in particular is an old friend and thoroughly
decent, so should know that I mean no harm!

Saturday, 5 March to Monday, 7 March

President Zelensky addresses the Commons via video link.
It was all rather moving as this unlikely, unshaven, T-shirted

superhero rallied us with clever references to both Shakespeare and Churchill. He showed extraordinary passion and bravery as he could be dead or captured within days – a crackly connection just made it more real. And we whinge about a late train.

However, multiple MP's have publicly raised the question of a no-fly zone, in order to avoid accusations of direct military intervention, and all of the retribution that might bring.

A cheery rumour circulates claiming that Ukrainian soldiers shout 'God save the Queen!' before firing any UK-made weapons, and that Ukrainian farmers at one stage had more tanks – which they had stolen off the Russians – than the whole of the US Marine Corps. It would be great if it were true.

Sanctions are being applied by governments and private companies everywhere and the rouble is now almost worthless. Abramovich is frozen out of Chelsea FC. There is no way Putin expected this worldwide condemnation, yet talks of peace come and mostly go.

The CX alerts us to dire economic consequences of this war on energy prices which HMT [the Treasury] estimate could cost as much as £4,800 per average household. There will also be food price inflation of an unknown level.

Friday, 11 March

With Adam to Wales vs France at the Principality as guest of the WRU [Welsh Rugby Union], normally a very civilised affair with great seats courtesy of the great Welsh Rugby legend Gerald Davies in the President's Box.

As I left, I was summoned over for a word with a distinguished-looking guest in his seventies who was seated a few rows behind. Thinking he was about to thank me for my strenuous work on behalf of the nation I was a bit surprised when he said, 'You're a lying Tory cunt.'

It was no less than one of Wales' most senior lawyers. If that

had been a Conservative addressing Mark Drakeford then all hell would break loose. To be fair to Gerald and his wife, they were horrified and assured me he would never be asked again but it was further evidence that sections of the 'Left' can be an increasingly hateful movement.

Meanwhile, the Home Office seems to have missed the public mood with their totally tin-eared approach to refugees. Priti needs to grip this or risk being all noise.

Monday, 14 March

I get a grovelling apology from Gerald Davies about the rugby incident but it's the lawyer who should be apologising.

Tuesday, 15 March

Cabinet. Wallace was quite ballsy about the Russian invasion having stalled.

Alexander Temerko [Ukrainian businessman and a personal friend of mine] fixes a slot for a few of us to see the Ukrainian ambassador at the embassy in Holland Park. They are by no means sure the recent Government wheeze of 'Homes for Ukrainians' is wise. For a start they explain they want their people back home, sustainability is an issue and nobody has discussed it with them. On the question of restricted food supplies available in Ukraine, the deputy ambassador cheerfully reminded us, 'we drink from puddle, eat our cat, but still your food is more revolting.'

I gave evidence to the Senedd Constitution Committee, an academic wankfest if ever there was. Highly unlikely much good will come of it, or indeed anything at all.

Met BBC's Tim Davie. He is a good guy and mainly talks a lot of sense, even if much of it is in the corporate language of W1A. But on BBC editorial guidelines I guess they have decided the

likes of Gary Lineker and Chris Packham are too scary to take on. If I was those two, I would use my platform too, especially now it seems the BBC has given up even pretending to enforce the guidelines.

Wednesday, 23 March

Cabinet. It was brief this morning as we were waiting for the spring statement. The CX summary was by design short on detail. Kit Malthouse and JR-M were scathing in their analysis of yet another spending splurge, but the truth is with inflation at 7% we are in a precarious position, politically and economically.

Wales questions and PMQs were gratifyingly dull and mainly a case of Labour attacks on the cost-of-living pressures. Then on to the real thing with CX. As ever, he delivered well, but the measures including the NI threshold rise, fuel duty cut and a rather odd promise of 1p off IT [income tax] in 2024 will barely address the 8.5% inflation expectation on top of all the other energy and fuel horrors. Both hands are now firmly tied behind his back.

Monday, 28 March

Dinner with Laura K was cancelled (Covid) so I ended up in Nigel Adams' office with Ben Gascoigne, the Chief Whip, the Deputy CW, Charlotte Owen [No. 10 political SpAd] and a bottle of gin.

There has been much dismay, triggering a massive row in No. 10, as some of the old key lieutenants feel 'frozen out' by the new team of Barclay, Harri and others. It's all coming to a head over Partygate too as the Met is tomorrow dishing out twenty fixed penalty notices. That won't be the end of it, but they are fairly confident BoJo isn't among them.

There is a sense of 'trouble at mill' so at 10 p.m. I walk back

over the bridge (and via a pub) with Gascoigne who is clearly unsure what he can and should do next. Losing him would be a terrible waste. He is decent and honest, and the MPs trust him. I think I persuade him, or help to persuade him, to stay put.

Tuesday, 29 March

Party dinner at the Park Plaza. These things are traditionally grim, but it was a little better than usual. My table was quite flat and BoJo's speech had the air of someone who would have rather been anywhere else, and who can blame him?

Sunday, 3 April

Got the call to do the Monday morning 'media round', which normally means someone more senior has dropped out, or more likely, refused. The normal routine involves an obscenely early start followed by eleven consecutive opportunities to make a fool of oneself in front of a large public audience. Little good will come of it.

It really is important to do these in person. Trying to gauge the mood of your host, or the tempo of the whole production, is impossible whilst wrestling with Zoom connections. So off I head again to London to confront the latest drama, which this time looks like it could be David Warburton's [Somerton and Frome] attempt to explain the white powder laid out in neat lines next to which he has been photographed. Twitter invented a story that he claimed it was dandruff. Even *Little Britain* didn't go that far.

Monday, 4 April

And we are off, starting at 5.30 for a 7 a.m. start with Sky, then LBC, Times Radio, ITV and GB News. They were much the

same – Partygate, energy and the like. My ambition was to keep it all quite dull, which I managed other than slightly goading the grating Kay Burley [Sky] when she got even more sanctimonious than usual about parties, having clearly forgotten she was photographed at one herself for which she was suspended.

Then straight back home for a quick turnaround to get back to Heathrow for the 'US trip', a much-awaited Wales Office expedition of which we don't get very many.

News breaks in the UK that Rishi Sunak's wife Akshata is the centre of some non-dom tax story. Quite a furore building and I am not sure from whom this may have come (No. 10?). The media is very agitated but (at this stage) no one else really is. Why is this 'in the public interest'?

As we arrive in London news also breaks of BoJo on a walkabout in Kyiv city centre with Zelensky. Loads of positive coverage indicating that despite Russian aggression not going away, BoJo is playing it rather well.

Wednesday, 13 April

We launch the dull-as-it-sounds Conservative Local Government manifesto in Penarth, but the media is much more interested in Partygate and Ukraine. BJ announces an emergency Cabinet along with the commitment we are going to intercept asylum seekers in the Channel, and send them to Rwanda. As ever, no Cabinet consultation, just a fait accompli. It might work of course (a first for the Home Office if it does) but the optics are challenging and provide an excuse for the liberal left (who are already frothing at the mouth about everything) to go totally berserk with claims of colonialism and the like.

And guess what? It's my turn on the media round again.

Thursday, 14 April

As I describe it to Gary Gibbon, today is a shit sandwich, with extra shit on the side starting with Radio Wales, then Sky and the *Today* programme. It centred predictably on Partygate and Rwanda, neither of which am I allowed to say much about. Most of it was okay but I was annoyed with myself for letting the irritating Kay Burley ruffle my feathers. As per last time, it's pretty rich of her to get on her high horse about parties, or are politicians subject to a different set of standards which don't apply to her? I fluffed my lines a bit although I just about stuck to the policy lines. She seemed to get especially enraged when I didn't know how many No. 10 staffers got fined (I still don't). It was described by some as a car crash interview, but it was just about okay. It was an incredibly stressful morning though, with BoJo hanging on in there. I do wonder if the loyalty colleagues are showing will be rewarded or ignored, or even noticed.

Saturday, 16 April to Sunday, 17 April, Easter weekend

For the first time ever the issue of Partygate is producing some anti BoJo reactions with real people not just the media, as we canvass for the LA [Local Authority] elections. Whilst serious, they can be managed with a conversation.

I text Heaton-Harris and say we MUST prep colleagues and the nation for the worst-case scenario (the one where all of the Partygate rumours are true and we blow up spectacularly), as this may well get worse before it gets better (if it ever does). I also text Michael Ellis QC [Northampton North] to make sure they have double-checked the Met is behaving lawfully in how they are handling this case.

Monday, 18 April

The PM is to make a statement in which he will set out 'his version of events' tomorrow or on Wednesday. This hardly bodes well, and I have forgotten how many times the PM has had to come cap in hand to the Commons.

Tuesday, 19 April

We are back to a Cabinet that carefully avoids any subject of real interest, other than a 'no-change' brief on Ukraine. All that matters is Boris's Partygate statement later.

By happy chance I have a routine meeting with Sue Gray on Union matters but she is more focused (understandably) on her inquiry. I get the impression that it is all extremely complicated.

The statement is at 4.30 and we are all required to populate the front bench in a show of unbreakable loyalty. In the end he dwelt as much on Ukraine as he did on parties which was probably quite wise as it made the Labour and the SNP response a little trivial. However, as per legal advice (apparently), No. 10 declined to get all the new material – if there is any – out on the table now.

Finally, a drink with Harry Cole [*Sun*]. He is confident BoJo only has a couple of possible fines heading his way and he can see no reason why he can't win the next election. That's one view I guess, but I am not sure how many MPs or local councillors would agree.

Wednesday, 20 April

Never one to knowingly overlook a chance to be in the thick of it, the Speaker grants an opposition debate on Thursday to refer the PM to the Privileges Committee. The Government therefore prepares an amendment to delay the debate until May/June. It seems innocuous, but colleagues are still feeling the

after-effects of the Paterson saga when the Government interfered with a 'House matter' by imposing a whipped vote. The custom is that 'House matters' are always dealt with on a free vote. Antipathy is growing, made worse by there being sixteen consecutive votes this evening, each of which provides a brief opportunity for colleagues to chat, drink and panic.

Thursday, 21 April

As Nadhim Zahawi concludes his media round defending the proposal for a Government amendment, the plan is junked. There will be no amendment and therefore no vote. We are told the PM didn't want the scale of the problem (up to 60 abstentions) confirmed in public. I mention this to Nadhim assuming he knew what a tit he had been made to look. He said, 'You are fucking joking, aren't you?' It appears he wasn't told either.

There is a view BoJo is now in a worse position. It's still not terminal, but it is getting increasingly borderline.

Monday, 25 April

Into the dying days of this session (rather than of this Govt, I hope).

Thursday, 28 April

Cabinet was preceded by a sneak preview of the Queen's Speech in which there is nothing especially exciting. We are obviously playing safe with twenty Bills, most of which have already been announced to the press.

Cabinet was therefore quite standard, focusing more on the cost of living and how we deal with it. The subsequent media reports suggested a row over Partygate which was 100% not true. I am summoned to see Pincher who, at four hours'

notice, wanted me and Brandon Lewis to host a drinks party for Partygate wobblers, as we await a vote. We can't really say no, but neither of us want to look like idiots either. We oblige and no one of significance turns up anyway.

A story emerges from a female colleague that an unnamed Conservative MP has been watching porn in the Chamber. Two names get mentioned, both issue strong denials and the claims are silenced. It's grossly unfair that either should have been named at all. The story catches fire with the Chief and the PM talking of this as a 'career-ending matter' should it be true.

Then it transpires Durham Police might re-investigate the picture of Keir Starmer drinking beer during lockdown and Angela Rayner [Deputy Labour Leader] could have been there with him, despite it having been denied by the Party. Highly amusing if true, not because the offence is especially serious, but because they so hate being on the receiving end of any sort of criticism.

Rayner then occupied the weekend news agenda with a story that she may have been distracting the PM during PMQs with her legs, or even worse. The story is roundly condemned as a misogynist lie despite reliable witnesses making it known that they heard her making much of it whilst having a drink and a smoke with friends on the Terrace.

Dropped into Harry Cole's fortieth in Mayfair which was reminiscent of an old-fashioned Fleet Street piss-up. I left at 9.30 by which stage at least two guests were being sick on the pavement.

And now it's a short recess for the local elections.

Saturday, 30 April

Oh dear. It emerges my good friend Neil Parish [Tiverton and Honiton] is the MP caught looking at porn in the Chamber. His twenty-three years as an MEP and MP go up in smoke in an instant.

The press has gone nuts and is much more fixated with this than they are with Putin. Labour and Lib Dems are (as ever) brimming with indignation and synthetic outrage, calling for his head. They seem oblivious to the process Parliament has set up to give everyone a fair hearing and to deal with these things 'in the cold light of day'. They also conveniently forget the numerous occasions on which some of their people have been caught in similarly tricky positions.

No one disputes it was stupid and inappropriate – and probably illegal – and wasn't helped by the admission from Neil he was looking for a tractor website when he accidently fell upon the porn in question. As soon as the story becomes too hot, he resigns, not just from the EFRA select committee, but from Parliament, triggering a Lib Dem facing by-election and weeks of anti-Tory sleaze allegations.

None of this helps anyone, least of all the victims, or people who would like a career in Parliament but have been given the false impression of what the place is really like. The Speaker's reaction and that of the Party will no doubt be to implement the wrong measures. In the meantime, I send a message to Neil and Sue. He is being very public about the issue to his credit, and she is being very frank, to hers.

Thursday, 5 May to Saturday, 7 May

The local elections weren't pretty but nor were they fatal for the PM. We took a beating almost everywhere (including Wales) but there was an underlying message it is salvageable so long as we give people good reasons. Critically, none of the other parties did well enough to be able to claim they had done us over either.

Spoke to the PM in the evening who seemed chastened (good) but still optimistic (typical!).

However, we will have some angry/nervous colleagues about

so maximum care will be needed. Did some media on Friday night to keep 'in' with the centre.

Monday, 9 May

To London for a drink with Lynton Crosby [legendary political strategist and pollster] during which we accidentally end up slagging off the entire Cabinet. He's no fan of Gove it seems.

Tuesday, 10 May

Queen's Speech, delivered for only the second time ever by the Prince of Wales as HMQ was still struggling with 'mobility issues'. Despite the reference to a 'big ticket event' it was rather dull. We need to be more innovative.

Thursday, 12 May

Cabinet awayday in Stoke-on-Trent where we homed in on the cost of living and, rather oddly, slashing the size of the civil service. There is something about JR-M presiding over a cull of civil servants which worries me. It's not that he isn't competent, or that the service cannot be made more efficient, it's just that for these things to work there does need to be a degree of consent and I am not sure JR-M can easily secure it.

The Met issues another fifty fines to No. 10 staff for Partygate breaches – seriously? Is No. 10 the only building in the whole of London they give a damn about or where gatherings took place? At least the PM is not included this time.

Monday, 16 May

Then to London, where I hear that on the plane back from India with the PM two well-known lobby hacks reacted so badly to the

local cuisine they blocked the loo, nearly forcing an emergency landing, which was rendered impossible as they were above Iraq at the time! I don't suppose we will read about that (or who) any time soon.

Tuesday, 17 May

Cabinet was fine, although the PM was clearly keen to leave early. We are hearing the Met has concluded Partygate inquiries and there are no further fines for the PM.

It is hilarious how all the lefties see the Starmer inquiry by Durham Police as a right-wing conspiracy but the Met inquiry into Boris as proportionate and justified.

Only Sue Gray to navigate now.

With two by-elections and soaring inflation we are still nowhere near comfortable.

Wednesday, 18 May

Politics Live with Jo Coburn and Vicki Young just after PMQs. No. 10 was happy I got stuck into Michael Fabricant for flippantly making light of the potential rape case involving Andrew Rosindell [Romford]. It really isn't a subject to joke about.

Friday, 20 May

Off to Newtown in mid Wales with the PM for various gigs including the Spring Conference, which we both dread as the audience will be sixty-five people aged on average, sixty-five.

My speech was 'okay' and received marginally better than Andrew RT and even the PM. The latter has lost a bit of zip, which can hardly be a surprise.

Then today it was Rishi's turn, this time to be 'in conversation'

with William Hague. We went to William's home in Berriew first to see the fantastic library where he does all his writing.

Their tête-à-tête was a mini triumph. It was a great interview because they are serious people and Rishi is better in this format than any other. At one stage someone asked what was William's greatest regret in politics. 'Having a career that coincided with Tony Blair' came the rueful reply. It's a good point. In any other era, he would most likely have been PM.

Monday, 23 May

Then to London for a meeting with Raab on the Bill of Rights, about which absolutely nobody in the Welsh judiciary seems keen. Later in a crowded tea room, I asked Buckland for a steer, but he flatly refused, describing Raab as a 'useless cunt'. At least that's more concise than Robert usually is . . .

Tuesday, 24 May

A rather second-rate lunch with Chris Hope [*Telegraph*] in Iberia but he's on good form and the paper is quite pro-Boris at the moment. Boris seems to be floating the notion of a 2023 GE. Oh joy . . .

It sounds like Sue Gray will report tomorrow. All hands on deck.

Wednesday, 25 May

Wales Orals. With PMQs and the Gray report hot on our heels, our slot has never been more irrelevant. But we did our bit and kept out of trouble.

So, after all these months, Sue Gray finally reports and whilst it was a depressing read there were no more startling revelations. The Met has concluded its investigations which means there should be no further police action.

Gray concludes Boris was poorly advised and there had been numerous parties with wall-to-wall vomiting and at one stage the abuse of cleaning staff at No. 10. The latter exposes an unpleasant arrogance we all know exists. Yet still there was not quite enough to kill him.

I did a lunchtime media round which went okay, the press is desperately grappling to prolong the story. The truth is they have been made to look a little foolish and hypocritical by blowing it up out of all proportion.

I have a drink later with Ben G who seems a bit more confident BoJo will survive – although the Standards Committee is still a problem. I am still feeling tired so early night again.

Thursday, 26 May

Test positive for Covid. After all this time . . .

Monday, 30 May

A couple more MPs join the list of those seeking BoJo's removal. Is it enough yet? Who knows?

I wish they would keep their views to themselves though. A letter of no confidence should be a sombre, sad step to take. There is no need to 'make an announcement'. Those who do are generally the egotists and moaners who want every story to be about them. Andrew Bridgen [North West Leicestershire] has now re-submitted his letter to Brady, for example, just to make sure everyone notices.

The PM talks of returning UK measurements back from metric to imperial – talk about rearranging the deckchairs on the deck of the *Titanic*.

Wednesday, 1 June

There are more letters in, apparently, and a lot more of a sense of inevitability about it all. There is still a lingering chance this will run and run and 'something will crop up'. It will have to be good though. We have tried a pandemic and a war after all.

Friday, 3 June

5 a.m. start to get to London for the St Paul's Platinum Jubilee ceremony (minus HMQ who clearly overdid it yesterday). My 1931 vintage morning coat just about survived and it was a grand musical affair. I sat behind BoJo and Carrie, next to Baroness Natalie Evans and in front of Tony and Cherie.

The service went on a little too long and at one stage BoJo clearly got bored and leant over and asked me, 'Where's the Dean?'

I replied he was in the vestry getting ready.

He looked a bit confused at which point I realised he had in fact asked, 'Where's Nadine?' (Dorries was a surprise no show.)

The music started then, so I never got the chance to resolve the confusion.

We all wandered off to the Guildhall for drinks and canapes, where we were entertained by Mike Tindall and others. I complained to Theresa May I thought the hymns were rather dull as no one knew them and got admonished for not going to church enough – and she meant it!

Saturday, 4 June

The big party in The Mall went okay. Lots of ageing rockers wheeled out, a brilliant drone display and an amusing interlude with HMQ and Paddington Bear. Charles and William gave heartfelt speeches. It feels like their turn is imminent.

Sunday, 5 June

Late on Sunday it emerges fifty-four signatures have gone into Brady, so we go to a confidence vote at 6 p.m. on Monday. I suppose it was inevitable. At least we can now try to get it behind us. It's almost a feeling of relief. The temperature is fierce, so Monday is devoted to damage limitation and expectation management. Most of the media speculation is around what would be a comfortable winning margin. We (the Government) are arguing a win is a win (whether under the rules or not) but I'm sure the media with its never-ending taste for blood will disagree.

I muscle in on various huddles around the building, including a session on the floor in PCH [Portcullis House] where I 'spontaneously' brief hacks. We then have a reasonably upbeat meeting with BoJo in the lower Whips' Office once the ballot starts.

At 9 p.m. in a packed Committee Room 14, Brady announces the result. Boris wins by 216 to 148. Totally predictably this is claimed as a victory or a defeat depending on your starting position. I deploy to Central Lobby where I do eight or nine identical back-to-back interviews with all the usual channels. The place is alive with journos and politicians trying to understand quite how we have ended up like this.

Boris has won but he is damaged. He can probably rebuild if he keeps his nerve, sacks a few people and sucks up to some others. The result was probably 20 or 30 more than comfortable but he did get support from 60% of the Party.

What a day . . . I call Nigel Adams and suggest an urgent plan for the 148 who voted against Boris. It needs to become 147 quite soon to indicate recovery rather than an ebbing of power. Either way, we have some tough times ahead. History has generally been unkind to anyone subject to a confidence motion, whether they won it or not.

Tuesday, 7 June

Cabinet discusses the NHS although the PM briefly stops to acknowledge the support given last night, the first time he has ever raised his own challenges in Cabinet. Is it business as usual? Off to Toulouse with Airbus. Thank goodness.

Wednesday, 8 June

Although I wasn't present, I'm told Starmer totally fucks up PMQs. How he can do that in a week when we publicly blow ourselves up is beyond me.

Monday, 13 June

Three-way meeting with Shapps and Clarke. Shapps is a better operator than most people think. Dinner with Ione Wells [BBC] and Jack but I learn nothing I didn't already know. The trouble is no one really knows what is going to happen next, least of all the PM, who swings from high to low and back again depending on who he is speaking and listening to.

Tuesday, 14 June

Cabinet – what can I say? When Liz Truss and I met on the street outside afterwards we both agree they serve no real purpose at all any more.

Wednesday, 15 June

Media reception in the Wales Office. They turn up and drink the place dry. BBC, ITV, C4, *Daily Telegraph* and *The Times*, plus Guto Harri with Dylan Jones [*GQ*] and the new 'cost of living

Tzar' David Buttress who appeared from nowhere. At least the Wales Office can show we have friends in high places.

Harry Cole even asked if I wanted to be on the *Sun* list of the 'up and coming' but I declined. At the moment the most attractive place to hang out is in the shadows.

Monday, 20 June

News Corp summer party at the Hyde Park Gallery. Charlie Brooks [husband of Rebekah] made sure I met Rupert Murdoch himself although he seemed totally bemused by the concept of the SoS Wales. I don't think he had ever heard of Wales. Apart from Rebekah Brooks [CEO News UK] and Charlie, the guests included Grayson Perry, Gordon Ramsay and inevitably Piers Morgan. BoJo appeared although we were told he had a 'minor' medical procedure that morning. No. 10 says it was a nasal polyp removal, but Twitter prefers the notion of a vasectomy.

Thursday, 23 June

Tiverton and Wakefield by-elections. The former is the result of Neil 'tractor porn' Parish and the latter because Imran Khan was convicted for child sexual assault, hardly good starting points. We are on course to lose both, despite a huge majority in Tiverton. It will cause further jitters.

Friday, 24 June

We lose both and Olive Dowden resigns. He is the first Cabinet member (and a sensible one) to do so. He went gracefully but there are clearly some nerves about. He hated his chairman's job but conducted himself with class. He was also a tad pissed off with BoJo for moving him there from DCMS. The whips are out in force to steady the ship. Leaving aside BoJo, mid-term

by-election defeats are nothing new. We lost Brecon to the Lib Dems in August 2019 and won it back easily that December. However, there is a last-chance-saloon feel about things.

Thursday, 30 June

To the Business Club dinner at the Household Cavalry Museum in Horseguards, a great venue if you like the snorting of cavalry horses and the sweet smell of ammonia accompanying your meal – which to be fair most of us do.

Guest speaker Sunak was engaging and handled one boorish question about Brexit with dexterity. He is compelling and will be a contender for PM one day.

As we start dinner the ominous news emerges that the Deputy Chief Whip Chris Pincher has resigned following allegations he groped two men at the Carlton Club last night. (Jack the SpAd was there and described him as 'utterly wankered'.)

And guess who's down to do tomorrow's media round? Oh great . . . why do these dramas follow me around like a bloody shadow? We rehearse a few lines and retire to the pub.

Friday, 1 July

5.30 a.m. Pret's on Horseferry Road. Grumpy.

As expected, the only story is Pincher. The No. 10 line is that 'he has fallen on his sword and therefore there is nothing further to say'. This clearly won't hold. Chris has been battling these rumours for years and the press is already asking how much all of this was known by BJ when he appointed him.

So, I adopt a position of 'let's establish the facts' and 'I'm sure the Chief Whip will be speaking to lots of people as the day unfolds', thinking it's inevitable the whip will be withdrawn at some stage.

Guto Harri goes a bit tonto, accusing me of 'prolonging the

story', at which point I offer to hand over the media round to any other minister with an appetite for early-morning masochism.

Most colleagues take my side, but No. 10 doubles down, insisting BJ knew nothing of the rumours surrounding Chris – which sounds implausible to be honest.

The fire burns fiercely all day. I speak to CH-H and CDL [Steve Barclay] in the meantime. By 5 p.m. the official line changes (who would have guessed . . .?), and the whip is suspended 24 hours too late. The upshot? We have failed the victims, the public, the Government, the voters and, to a great extent, Chris Pincher himself. For the first time I have grave doubts we can turn this around . . .

Monday, 4 July

Pinchergate rumbles on noisily. The No. 10 line has gone from 'we knew nothing' to 'we knew stuff but forgot'. It feels unbearably awful.

Tuesday, 5 July

Cabinet is a subdued affair with no mention of this week's elephant in the room. BoJo maintains an air of exaggerated optimism and good humour but it's not looking good. I have rehearsals for Welsh Orals, so TC and I decide we should announce the abolition of the Senedd on the basis no one will notice and it might make us smile.

We are cut short by breaking news – Sajid Javid and Rishi Sunak both resign within minutes of one another, citing the issue of trust. The dam has burst. It's now just a question of whether BoJo bleeds slowly to death or swallows the cyanide pill.

Numerous ministers start following suit, PPSs go in droves and No. 10 adopts full bunker mentality. Colleagues huddle in

corners, mystified, angry, confused. Even if BoJo holds out, the '22 will surely get him now. Buckland accosts me and TC outside the Speaker's office. He is incandescent, demanding that the Cabinet 'show some balls and resign'.

Wednesday, 6 July

Wales Oral Questions in the House. TC and I feel even more irrelevant than usual as we valiantly hold the Government line. The thing about Orals is they always come in the Wednesday slot just before PMQs. Hence, unlike most departmental questions, the Chamber, public and press galleries fill rapidly, as we are performing. The chatter becomes louder and more distracting by the minute. The Ministerial team files in also, being ushered to prominent positions by the Speaker's Chair.

The Welsh questions are invariably dull and very niche. 'Does the Secretary of State agree with me,' Virginia Crosby (Ynys Mon) asks, 'that Wylfa on Anglesey is a world-leading site for new nuclear production?' Well of course I do. Virginia gets another hit before we move to Tata Steel, the Welsh language, or independence. But whatever the question, the opportunity for cock-up looms large. TC always wants a big climactic moment – the money shot, as he calls it – whereas I just want to get through 25 mins without falling over. We know that, as we resume our seats, BoJo will give what the media is predicting is his last PMQs. This will be followed by Javid's 'personal statement'.

Javid's comments are nowhere near as vindictive as these things can be. They were measured but painful, delivered under duress rather than with any sense of revenge. We listen in stony, depressed silence.

Forty-seven ministers have now resigned. An earthquake is in progress.

I contact Chris Heaton-Harris and implore him to persuade BoJo to read the tea leaves and go with dignity but I get told (and

I don't blame CH-H here, he's just doing his job) that the plan is to 'fight on'. But why? What is the plan, or indeed the point?

My team, too, is urging me to go, not to be the last man standing with only Nadine Dorries for company. They have a point. The line between remaining loyal for as long as possible, but not being reputationally damaged in the process is a narrow one.

But Boris being Boris, an elegant and well-timed exit doesn't seem likely. My mind is made up. I go back to my office on the Upper Ministerial Corridor, grab a piece of paper, write a short and heartfelt letter of disappointment and resignation, and ring CH-H. He is calm, invites me to No. 10 where he says the team is gathering to speak to the PM direct. Our task: to tell Boris the game is up.

In the oak-panelled state dining room upstairs are Nadhim Zahawi, Priti Patel, Anne-Marie Trevelyan, Michelle Donelan [Minister for Higher Education], Kit Malthouse and Grant Shapps. (David Canzini [Deputy Chief of Staff] comes and goes, as do the battle-worn duo of Nigel Adams and Guto Harri.) Gazza [Ben Gascoigne] is there too, his very welcome humour masking the emerging trauma of the moment, which was by now enveloping every room in the building. Andrew Griffith [Policy Minister] looks in, and Party Chairman Ben Elliot is determined there is a way to survive this.

Nadhim is the most adamant that the 'herd is stampeding', it will trample everything in its path and Boris must go now. Other opinions vary, but I sense Michelle Donelan is the most sensitive to the reality of what confronts us. We are told it will now be one-to-one meetings with the PM rather than the delegation as originally planned. Nadhim is first to see the PM just after he honours his slot in front of the Liaison Committee, a performance later described by Canzini as 'as bad as it is possible to be'.

There is much pacing, tea-drinking, phoning of colleagues,

advisers, spouses and, of course, journalists. Speculation is rife as to what has become of Nadhim, who hasn't been seen for several hours. He only went for a few minutes. He is now either held hostage or has fled.

I am second last to see him [Johnson], as Brandon is still heading back from Northern Ireland. It's 8 p.m. and as I am summoned into the Cabinet Room, the band rehearsing for the Beating the Retreat in Horseguards starts playing 'Myfanwy', the famous Welsh anthem about unrequited love. It's me, Boris and CH-H, alone for the first time since my appointment in the very same room nearly three years earlier. Boris was positive, polite, amusing.

We spoke in sadness, not in anger. I explained how I liked his anarchic approach to politics, but we had run out of road. If he didn't go, I explained, then the '22 would get him; and if they didn't get him then the Standards Committee would have a damn good go. Akin to Michael Caine in the closing scene of *The Italian Job* as the bus balanced precariously on the cliff edge, it was a case of 'Hang on, lads, I've got an idea.' Except in this case, he said, 'Just give me till Tuesday.'

'Why?' I asked, 'What's happening on Tuesday?'

'I don't know,' said Boris, 'but something is bound to crop up.'

And then we hugged. We never hug, but it seemed like the right moment to give it a go.

I left my letter, explained that I wouldn't go public about resigning until tomorrow, and headed for Victoria Street to meet Jack.

I had just arrived when TC called. 'Have you been sacked?'

Not yet, I told him.

'No. 10 has called and offered me your job. I told them to fuck off.'

'You don't have to do that,' I replied. 'I'm basically toast so you might as well seize the moment.'

'Fuck that. It's dirty money.' What a hero.

Robert Buckland later accepts the role from which only yesterday he demanded I resign. Not such a hero. No. 10 then leak like a sieve, so I call CH-H, activate my departure and order a gin.

Thursday, 7 July

Return very early to Pembrokeshire for the Prince of Wales's visit to Narberth. No car, no box, no plans. There is a strange feeling to being so instantly irrelevant. As Malcolm Rifkind once said, you know when your ministerial career is over when you get in the back of the car and it doesn't go anywhere. Robin Cook was much the same, but he also added how much he would miss the handy little diary card that the Private Office gives you first thing every morning which tells you what you are doing all day.

And so, less than 12 hours after resigning, I am in a line-up in Narberth High Street and shaking hands with the Prince of Wales. 'Weren't you once Secretary of State for Wales?' he asks.

Then the PM finally confirms he will go (Brandon and Michelle had also gone overnight).

So much arguing could have been avoided. Boris is Boris, but Guto Harri and the inner team had the chance to manage the pain. Easier said than done that's for sure, especially with someone like Boris. TC and Jack will be remembered as loyal soldiers.

I speak to Rishi several times and agree to back his bid early. We need a grown-up, but above all else we need someone kind. And there aren't too many of them left . . .

Friday, 8 July

I film a lengthy segment for Laura Kuenssberg's *Panorama* (at home). It's not the time to stick the knife in any deeper but given

the nonsense observations from people who played no part in all this, a little segment of truth may not go amiss.

Tuesday, 12 July

My diary is empty, and London is sweltering in a heatwave.

The 'Ready for Rishi' team is well organised and resourced and meets every day at 9.30 a.m. under the direction of the excellent Mel Stride [Chair of the Treasury Select Committee]. It deserves to win, yet the 'right of centre' candidates – Braverman, Truss, Mordaunt – are getting quite a bit of traction. Rather too much traction this early on.

The 1922 rules set out the timetable of two ballots this week and the rest next week, accompanied by various hustings.

I have no facilities as such, so most meetings take place in the oppressive heat of the cafe on the corner of St James's Park, just opposite the Treasury. In fact, every cafe in SW1 is populated by huddles of anxious MPs and staffers. No matter who wins, their CVs will stress – disingenuously in most cases – they 'worked with xxx on their successful leadership campaign'.

Briefings are frequent and I do a couple of media rounds on behalf of the centre. Disingenuous attacks on RS vary between him being too closely aligned with BJ, to him having single-handedly brought BJ down.

Wednesday, 13 July

Lunch with Dan Hodges [newspaper columnist] at the Union Club, Greek St. Nice place, full of 'media types'. I like Dan. He feels our man will make it to the last two. The first ballot is announced at 5 p.m. by Brady (who has clocked up a bit of experience of this kind of thing by now). Graham is a commanding figure for the '22. Big in every sense, he has an air of unflappability about him.

Round 1: Sunak 88; Mordaunt 67. The rest of the votes are spread about, but Zahawi is out. A 'solid start' is how we describe it and move to Round 2 tomorrow.

Thursday, 14 July

I cancel England vs India at Lords for the second ballot (that hurt, but we can't risk being off-site). We need about 100 to keep up the momentum. We get 101 and Mordaunt gets 83. Again, the rest are evenly spread but Braverman drops out this time. We go again on Monday, so we are now at the stage where the real poker game begins in earnest. Deals will have to be done . . .

Friday, 15 July

First of the (rather pointless) TV debates on C4. A resounding victory for Sunak, especially on the vital gravitas-related points. Good timing too for the undecided and wobbling MPs.

Temperatures up to 40 degrees in the UK are adding to the tension . . .

Sunday, 17 July

Second TV debate – scrappy and acrimonious, so unappealing to pretty much everyone.

RS did okay and 'wins', as far as public support indicates.

The heat is blistering and the tempers all round match it. Everyone hates everyone else (at best).

Tuesday, 19 July

I'm appointed Honorary Colonel of the Royal Wessex Yeomanry, to the general amusement of the small number of people who

noticed. I inform Ben Wallace that I expect him to salute me in future. He sensibly and predictably told me to fuck off.

Another ballot. We move to 118 – 1 vote short – which is better than a thumping win as it will remind people we are a long way off being safe.

Tom T drops out, and Truss is now better placed than Mordaunt – super odd if Truss gets anywhere. Are people blind or delusional? Another (the last?) ballot tomorrow.

Wednesday, 20 July

BoJo's last PMQs, with lots of references to 'I'll be back', etc. Very Trumpian. I was not there, but plenty of Cabinet colleagues who wanted him out were cheering him to the rafters – mega hypocrisy. Do they not realise we can see through it all?

The final ballot puts us at 137, followed closely by Truss. Mordaunt, surprisingly, drops out.

We have done well: not too vulgarly large but not too close either. It will be hard from here on in, as the members can be insane and totally ignorant of what skills are needed in a crisis. I dread to think what a Truss Government would look like, or if it will even last. One of my most astute friends, Justin MacLaren, says it wouldn't last till Christmas, but it never works like that. Once they are in, it's bloody hard to get them out again. 2024 looks like an increasingly attractive exit point from politics for me.

Monday, 25 July

BBC TV debate – Sunak vs Truss. By all accounts it was ghastly; I am so glad I didn't watch. It was acrimonious and portrayed both candidates in a poor light. Why do we do it? Everyone I speak to says they will vote Rishi, but the polls lean towards Truss.

Summer recess

Dominated by Truss vs Sunak. TV debates, hustings, Zooms, media, visits etc. To be honest the Rishi team effort is slick and polished, but the question is whether it is targeted enough at members? We are on holiday in Austria, but I carry out a canvass of Carmarthen West and South Pembrokeshire Constituency Association members and guess what – it's 17 RS, 25 LT and about 40 undecideds. So, all to play for.

Yet there remains the risk the members will be obtuse and deploy spite. In addition, they now seem to want BoJo back!

In polling terms, the dividing line is Truss borrowing to fund tax cuts and RS relying on growth . . .

Saturday, 20 August

The polls still put Truss in No. 10. The whole thing is mystifying, and if true then a total disaster. MPs made it very clear LT poses a real danger, yet the members are on the cusp of knowing better. We need to unite the country, the Party, restore the economy and win an election. Liz can't do any one of these things, let alone all of them.

Monday, 22 August

RS ploughs on. Turnout is stuck at 50%, and Truss is convinced she has won. Rupert Yorke [Deputy Chief of Staff at the Treasury] tells Jack that if RS wins I'm in for a 'good job' – oh the irony; so close, yet so far – or is it?

Friday, 2 September

Final day of polling, and we are told there is a surge in turnout. I'm assuming/hoping that means all the cautious undecideds

will align with RS. He has been brilliant recently and the London hustings revealed an embarrassing gulf between him and LT. If the Party members decide to override the views of the MPs, then they deserve what they get. The odds are 9–1 at the bookies for Rishi.

Saturday, 3 September

We sit and wait and pray. Maybe a miracle will occur? Maybe the Truss vote was noisy and visible, but RS quiet and determined?

Monday, 5 September

On the early train with Fay Jones [Brecon and Radnorshire] in time for the 12.30 announcement. The mood is febrile, and I appear to be the only person left who thinks a shock is even possible. Most people intend to watch live at the QE2 Centre, but I would rather see it all unfold at the Blue Boar with James W [former Chair of the Boris election campaign, now Lord Wharton]. At 12.30 we go live to the result where the current (and likeable) Party Chairman Andrew Stephenson has to deliver the standard (and lengthy) Party speech, before handing over to Sir Graham for the numbers. Brady makes the most of yet another coronation on his watch. There is only one thing we need to know.

I was wrong. RS at 60k and LT at 80k. We have lost – a swing of 7% would have done it, but it seems our members know best and have rejected the views of those who know and work with these people. It's hard to see this as a triumph for anyone. Truss fails to embrace or shake Rishi's hand, fails to give her husband even a token gesture of intimacy, and then makes a very moderate and wooden speech, promising whatever it was we promised in 2010/15/17/19, which for some reason we haven't yet done.

We are joined by other members of the Sunak friendship group, Fay, Ruth [Edwards, Rushcliffe], Clare [Coutinho, East Surrey] and Craig [Williams] and then adjourn to another pub as Team Truss arrive at ours. There we see Darren Mott [chief executive of the Conservative Party], Ben Elliot, and various other RS supporters and think (and drink) about what could (and should) have been. We have quite simply 'picked the wrong Miliband'.

Liam Booth-Smith [RS's Chief of Staff] appears, magnanimous in defeat, but also with some recollections about the means by which BoJo (or his people) deployed everything to destroy RS early in the campaign.

He is discreet enough to resist revealing all, and there were journalists lurking, but the only conclusion that I could reach was that Boris has run an uncharacteristically effective 'anybody but Rishi' operation which had undoubtedly contributed to this outcome.

What hope we had of hanging on in 2024 has gone.

Tuesday, 6 September

Boris goes to Balmoral to resign, after having made a slightly unusual speech at No. 10 at 7.30 a.m. He is quickly followed by Truss appearing with HMQ for the kissing of hands. She returns to No. 10 at 5 p.m. to make another rather dull deputy head girl-style speech in Downing Street.

Then the reshuffle begins: Kwasi Kwarteng to CX; Braverman to HO; Cleverly to FCDO; Wallace to MoD; Coffey to Health, but also Deputy PM; Lewis to Justice.

Then there were multiple sackings, many of which were carried out by Thérèse Coffey in extremely short phone calls. Shapps, Hands, Spencer – about eleven in total from Cabinet. She appoints Buckland to the WO [Wales Office], thus affirming my belief neither has any intention of 'doing the right thing'.

By the end there are no Sunak supporters left in Cabinet at all, a terrible mistake and one which may well haunt her.

In No. 10 she makes the brave announcements of Mark Fullbrook as her Chief of Staff and to even greater surprise Wendy Morton as Chief Whip. Mark is a former Crosby Textor apparatchik with good contacts and a dollop of wit and charm, but no real experience for this kind of role. Wendy will have an uphill struggle marshalling support from a Party deeply fractured by the outcome and the deliberate policy of casting out anybody who failed to publicly support her leader.

I spend the day in Portcullis House with various bemused journalists, Jack and others. We try to make sense of it all. Justin rings again to say 'it won't last to Christmas' but I tease him for not really understanding the way it works here.

What is beyond dispute is I am out, unlikely to return, and with increasingly little desire to. We have failed to even slow down the Party's drift to the right and she has constructed a Cabinet with a mix of the clever and devious or simply the compliant. The backbenches are also replenished with a new influx of the dispossessed.

The first meeting of the Privy Council is postponed as HMQ is not up to it – I can't say I blame her!

Wednesday, 7 September

PMQs. I couldn't face it so stayed in PCH. By all accounts, it was 'okay', but then Starmer is quite bland still. However, I made it over to the Cinnamon Club for Rishi's thank-you drinks. Nice people, with a decent and humble speech from RS. What have we done?

Thursday, 8 September

PM Truss makes a huge announcement about the introduction of a two-year energy price cap at £2,500. The largest peacetime

intervention ever and twice the scale of furlough. It is a massive gamble on her part.

I wander over to the Commons to see TC who is already plotting the downfall of his new SoS Buckland. Apparently, he has already been frozen out of WO matters, which is bizarre given there are only two ministers in the department, of which he is one.

As I get there, I notice Nadhim Zahawi (now CDL) arriving in the Chamber and passing messages to the PM, Starmer and the Speaker. The Chamber is quite empty, so all of this is very visible and extremely unusual. Something is afoot. The journalists sense it also and start appearing in Members' Lobby. The rumour is HMQ has been taken ill at Balmoral. The Speaker makes a brief statement. This doesn't feel at all good.

News then breaks the Prince of Wales and other Royals are making their way to Balmoral as soon as possible and the BBC cancels all programming for the rest of the day. As if the world is not uncertain enough it seems the inevitable is unfolding in front our eyes. HMQ's long reign (over seventy years) is coming to an end. I race home to west Wales in time for a 6.30 formal announcement that she has 'died peacefully at Balmoral'. Operation London Bridge, the code words in Whitehall for the death of the monarch, is under way, and years of planning deployed. Hushed crowds gather at the Palace.

This is probably the biggest moment of change the country will witness for a very long time and will define our politics for a while too. When everything else seems so unpredictable, the presence of the Queen, even to those sceptical about the monarchy, provided a sense of security.

The PM makes a rather wooden statement – there is no other word, I'm afraid. BoJo issues a very much better one and we await further orders. 'The Queen is dead, long live King Charles the Third' is the order of Parliament.

Friday, 9 September

The death of HMQ is having a tangible effect on the nation, the media and especially politics. It also triggers an overdose of sanctimony from some quarters. Pretty well every MP makes a speech paying tribute. I'm not sure why because most are hardly public figures and some of the Left have been pretty critical of the Royal Household and the Civil List for years. Many colleagues adorn themselves in full medals and mourning dress. The BBC has been dubbed 'Mournhub'.

Monday, 12 September

The King comes to Westminster Hall to receive addresses from the Speakers of both Houses. Thank God Bercow wasn't one of them. It's quite a ceremonial occasion with trumpeters and music and is quite upbeat. The King's Speech was excellent, very formal. But it ended quite abruptly, as if they left out the last page. I doubt we will ever know.

We then returned to PCH to resume discussions about how bad Liz Truss is coming across. Steve Double [St Austell and Newquay] was one of those sacked by Thérèse Coffey; he was told they needed 'fresh blood' in Defra. He'd only been there seven weeks! George Eustice ended up having to sack himself as Truss couldn't actually get the words out and the meeting was significantly over-running. Then to lunch at the pub with Craig, Steve Barclay and Clare C where we bemoan the fact this is the new order of things.

Wednesday, 14 September

Privy Councillors who are not going to the funeral are summoned to Westminster Hall to receive the coffin of HMQ to lie in state. I thought it would be a rather low-key event – how wrong

I was. There was a full ceremonial turnout with massed bands and horses of the Household Division, as well as members of the Royal Family. All the way from Buckingham Palace there were huge silent crowds with just the occasional clap. The only sound we could hear was of an approaching muffled bell. New Palace Yard was covered in sand for the horses pulling the carriage and a consignment of the Grenadier Guards carried the (obviously very heavy) coffin with the heralds, Beefeaters and Household Division in close attendance.

The Archbishop of Canterbury conducted the service, and the choir of Westminster Abbey sang. The most moving part was the silence. Not a cough, shuffle or murmur, other than the distant commands of the military and the crunch of the guardsmen's boots on the floor of a building that has seen more than its fair share of history. We filed past the coffin and out through the north door to a beautiful September afternoon and a quiet reflective London.

A queue four miles long was already in place, snaking its way through Victoria Gardens, over Lambeth Bridge and down the South Bank reaching as far as Tower Bridge.

It was an historic moment.

5
LIBERATION

October 2022–March 2023

As I languished on a riverbank in Scotland during the September recess, watching the Conservative Party eat itself alive, I never anticipated it would all crash down quite so soon or quite so spectacularly, or that Team Sunak would be back in business before the year end.

Most of the polling companies had by now put us between 20 and 25 points behind Labour, a margin that would stay largely unchanged until the 2024 election.

Like many, I did not predict at the time how the Truss-inflicted wounds would still be festering two years on. What the Boris years had done for our reputation for integrity, Liz had now repeated in terms of economic competence. In electoral terms we were never to recover.

I believed that was it, my time as an MP would be drawn to an unremarkable conclusion. It was beyond the realms of possibility that within weeks Liz Truss would be gone, or that I would be the Government Chief Whip.

When I first thought about publishing these diaries, I was a bit worried the inner workings of the Whips' Office might be a bit dry, but re-reading my notes made me change my mind. Nothing else in politics is quite like the Whips' Office. It is the field hospital, into which damaged colleagues are delivered, patched up and returned to front-line duties. It is the funnel through which absolutely everything is channelled.

So this part sees the election of Sunak and my chance to be a central part of the Herculean task of rebuilding the Party's reputation, against a ticking clock.

I had mentioned to Rishi's friend and confidant Oliver Dowden that if there were to be a vacancy, then I wouldn't mind being considered for the role of Chief Whip. I have been around a bit, have good contacts across the Party (and the opposition) and am reasonably calm under fire – although this would soon become tested to the absolute limit.

Recorded here is what I learnt about the mysteries of this office. No matter what's going on in the life of a government or PM, absolutely nothing happens unless the whips provide confidence that colleagues will support it. From the most serious legislation, to who gets an office overlooking the Thames, it is the whips who decide. (There is widespread agreement the 'accommodation whip' – the person who decides who gets which office in the Palace of Westminster – is the hardest job in government.)

I record what really happened at the various reshuffles we conducted and in the process saw the very best, and I am sorry to say, the worst, of many colleagues.

I discovered the Whips' Office is also expected to be a trauma counselling service, an HR department, a hub of legislative expertise, to offer legal and financial services, and have the power of foresight to boot.

There is an expectation that we have to deploy dark arts to achieve our aims, but this is the 2020s and we are bound by the same workplace standards as everyone else. Our job is to cajole and persuade, but to always retain our ultimate weapon: the removal of the whip. We deal with MPs of many decades' standing, and some who have been here just a few months. Some have specialist knowledge, or hobby horses, and some have none. We have to get them all in the same lobby, voting the same way, every single day, often on multiple occasions. Our fundamental purpose is, and always will be, to 'get the government's business done'.

And we 'did the honours'. I nearly called this book 'About my Knighthood . . .' due to the large number of colleagues who either started or ended their conversations with me with those words. Some made compelling cases, some were brazenly entitled. With each passing day I came increasingly to realise that our system of candidate identification, selection, training and mentoring was flawed and is at the root of almost every challenge the Party and the Government was facing. We were getting some of the best onto the books, but also some who were not ideally equipped to deal with what lay ahead of them. Maintaining a democratic system of appointments, whilst ensuring only the best get through has become a recurring dilemma.

——— • ———

Sunday, 2 October 2022

Well, I've been away, cut off the outside world in Scotland with Adam. Has anything happened? Judging by my inbox and WhatsApp feed the world might as well have ended.

It seems the CX's 'fiscal event' last Friday set off a bomb that was anticipated by Rishi during the leadership bid but dismissed by others as 'project fear mark two'.

The CX cuts corporation tax, income tax, the 45p top rate, lifts the bankers' bonus cap and even brings down the axe on National Insurance. But it's all on borrowed money, which triggers a market meltdown and the pound going into freefall, nearly reaching parity with the dollar for the first time ever. The Bank of England steps in to shore up the gilt markets, the IMF issues warnings and Tory MPs explode in numerous different directions.

Four opinion polls give Labour a lead of 20–30% – total annihilation territory. Truss and Kwasi say very little, but she appears on the traditional pre Conference local radio media round and gets a proper kicking eight times on the trot.

Labour's Conference must be overjoyed and as we enter

our own Conference, experienced hacks and commentators (including Laura K, Ben Riley-Smith [*Telegraph*], Hodges, [Ollie] Wright, Young, Wells and numerous others I've spoken to) think she has done irreparable harm to the Party, the Government and her own brand.

All of this burns brightly at the same time as there are hints of cuts to public services. So we MPs will be forced to vote down pay rises for nurses at the same time as lifting bonuses for bankers. It is absurd and cack-handed but, worst of all, widely predicted.

Her speech will no doubt try and reprise Thatcher (and will fail as she isn't really a platform orator) and will most likely end up annoying members and spooking the markets even further. 40% of the mortgage market has now been suspended.

Gove goes on TV to torpedo her budget whilst Jake Berry – the new Party Chairman – is threatening withdrawal of the whip from those who refuse to support it.

Monday, 3 October

Impossible though it might sound, the situation goes from bad to worse. There is a late-night meeting between Truss and the CX where they agree to junk the 45p tax rate policy. So, after a huge build-up, lots of brave talk and ministers roaming the airwaves in support, there comes the inevitable capitulation, thanks to the realisation they couldn't win a vote. Politics is about what is numerically possible, not the stuff of dreams.

The same will now most likely happen with bankers' bonuses and benefit reductions. Now that backbenchers know the Government is on the run, there will be no stopping them.

It's fair to say this is all going very badly indeed. Instead of feeling smug, I just feel angry. This was not unforeseen. Even more polls (six in total) now giving Labour a 20-point lead. Whether we believe it or not, Boris crashed our reputation for

integrity, and now Liz has managed to do the same with our reputation for competence.

The CX (who is not a bad person) gives a flat-sounding speech in which he talks about years of 'managed decline', failing to mention it is our Party that has been in office for the entire period he refers to. Truss talks about reaching out for the 'hearts and minds' of colleagues which seems a bit late given her dismissive approach of anyone who didn't support her.

Wednesday, 5 October

I watch from behind the sofa Truss's main Conference speech. She speaks for 25 minutes (including a welcome interruption by Greenpeace). It was thankfully dull with lots of platitudes and some weird hand and eye movements which I imagine she has been encouraged to use by some media trainer but has failed to totally master. The whole thing is reminiscent of a runner-up in the sixth-form public-speaking performance. I fear little has changed.

Saturday, 8 October to Sunday, 9 October

The fallout continues, as does the very poor publicity. Ministers are out on the airwaves demanding unity whilst simultaneously briefing against Truss and the CX. Journalists et al are busily speculating as to how long it can all last. It feels to me like it could drag on longer than we all think.

Tuesday, 11 October

We return from recess to a cauldron of anger and frustration. I have lunch with Katy Balls at which we discuss only one thing – how long can the PM last? Extraordinary given we are barely thirty days

in. The No. 10 message is they are standing by one another, as well as the mini budget, yet literally everyone else says they are mad.

Dinner in Mel Stride's office with like-minded, pro-Sunak MPs, including my idea of solid colleagues like Halfon, Cartlidge, Hollinrake and Chalk. They all want her gone.

Wednesday, 12 October

PMQs is dull, the main observation being Starmer still can't land a painful blow despite the PM already being covered in bruises from her self-inflicted injuries. The CX is in the US, which is probably a mistake.

The '22 is a disaster for her. Her demeanour is of being completely oblivious to, or unaware of, the gathering storm. Her response to a series of horrible attacks is a stubborn 'not my fault'. Rumours about the CX's future also begin to circulate.

Thursday, 13 October

The tea-room talk is of another major U-turn coming from No. 10. Lobby hacks smell blood in the water. I speak to Hodges, Groves [*Daily Mail*], LK, Watt [BBC] and deduce they feel she cannot continue but a 'consortium' of sorts might just enable her to cling on without consulting our members.

I am as close to calling it a day in 2024 as I've ever been. We are eating ourselves alive.

Friday, 14 October

Here we go! The CX arrives back from DC to read on Twitter he has been sacked. By midday he is gone, for the crime of implementing plans that she and he had mutually agreed. Jeremy Hunt is wisely installed as CX, being calm, and above all, sane. The PM holds a press conference at 2.30. Even by the standards

we have become used to, it is dreadful. Cold and dull and it concluded with her taking only three or four questions before walking out. (I am told she burst into tears the minute she left the room which, at a human level, is concerning.) She is now terminally damaged. Her entire economic pitch is destroyed along with our credibility in the one area where we still had some.

But what do we do? I call Rishi and others, and we agree to speak over the weekend.

Sunday, 16 October

Hunt's appointment seems to have calmed nerves. His tone is emollient, but it is now clear Truss is even less 'relevant' than ever. She literally has no authority any more. For the first time ever, I actively consider sending a letter to Brady tomorrow. I never thought I would do such a thing, but what other options are there?

I have a long chat with Rishi as he's walking the dog. He will step in if the Party wants him, but he is nervous about 'unity' in the current situation. Now we are implementing the Sunak plans, we need to prove they could win a general or Party member election. If we can manage that, then we have a chance, but we have our doubts about whether a 'unity' candidate is even a realistic prospect these days.

The papers report I am supporting Wallace, which is a total myth. Have they muddled me up with Simon Clarke [SoS Housing]. I am not even sure Ben will run.

Monday, 17 October

Meet with Chief Whip Wendy at the third time of asking and am surprised that her tone is one of, 'it's all fine and we just need to get behind the PM'. I explain why it's the other way around

and she thaws a little but is clearly stressed by the whole edifice collapsing around her. Moments later I have a similar chat with Jake Berry, who teases me with a potential deal over parliamentary boundaries, due to be announced tomorrow. Little does he know I don't think I want to stay on anyway.

Tuesday, 18 October

The new boundaries are published and turn out to be much as expected. CCHQ boundary guru Roger Pratt estimates we can retain 11 seats in Wales, but he has based this assessment on the artificially high 2019 GE result, which seems unlikely to be repeated. The view of Welsh MPs is that we will be lucky to hold 4.

Wednesday, 19 October

PMQs is odd in so far as the PM reprised the Mandelson 'I'm a fighter not a quitter' quote, which didn't work that well when it was last used twenty years ago. The Government benches were glum despite a few noble attempts to pretend she was still in charge. The truth is, she is political toast whichever way you look at it.

We are whipped heavily to reject a Labour motion to, 'take over the order paper' and force an anti-fracking vote. It's a bizarre turn of events given it's highly unlikely there will ever be any UK-based fracking anyway. Dozens of Conservative members are publicly pledged against fracking (as was our own manifesto) so this has triggered a rebellion. Now there is a threat of whip removal because No. 10 has decreed it a 'confidence motion'. Oh dear . . .

This looked kind of manageable until [Energy Security Minister] Graham Stuart announced in his speech, moments before the 7 p.m. division was due, that it wasn't a confidence

motion after all. Chaos and disorder ensue as those who were minded to rebel felt able to do so, resulting in both the Chief and Deputy Chief Whip resigning whilst in the lobby, the PM forgetting to vote at all, and Labour claiming Conservative members were being physically bullied by the whips. Where I was (up by the tellers' boxes in the Noe Lobby) there just seemed to be a long delay, although a colleague who asked Wendy what was going on was told, 'I don't know, I am not Chief Whip any more.' It really is the icing on the cake.

It looks and sounds like 'the end' and I would be amazed if more letters don't pile in to Brady.

Thursday, 20 October

One of our doctor MPs describes the situation as the 'moment you get the family in to say goodbye'. Brady is in No. 10 – his arrival is akin to that of the undertaker – followed by Berry and Coffey.

News breaks the PM will make a statement at 1.30 and so, after just a few weeks, Truss resigns with a short, perfunctory and emotionless speech, an appropriate reflection of her time in office.

The 1922 meets and agrees a short sharp process of election and transition, running from Monday to Friday. A threshold of 100 nominations is required, there will be only one ballot, and members will be able to vote online. We have one last chance.

Mordaunt and Sunak will run, but people 'close to Boris' hint he may have a roll of the dice too – insane though that seems.

Friday, 21 October

Rishi surges to 100+, Mordaunt to 30 and Johnson to 70ish. If he gets to the membership, we could have another Truss moment.

Sunday, 23 October

The temperature approaches boiling. Boris claims he is close to 100 (now, there's a surprise . . .), as does Penny – but we know RS is already north of that point.

Monday, 24 October

We are told BJ is at 102 and Penny at 90, so it's all down to Brady now. At 3 p.m., I head to a packed Committee Room 14 to be told only Rishi has the magic number. At the second attempt, and out of nowhere, we have won. An extraordinary turnaround, in the most bizarre of political circumstances. But now for the hard part . . .

7.10 p.m. I am in Central Lobby when I get a call. 'Rishi Sunak' it says on the screen. He sounds somewhere between overwhelmed, motivated, excited and grateful. After a few niceties he said, simply and slightly awkwardly, 'Will you be my Chief Whip?'

Slightly awkwardly, I agree. I feel pride, but a sense of terror too. There is no hiding place now, no one else to blame, so yes, it's terrifying. The risk of failure, the hate, the inevitable wall of pressure that comes with this role . . . There is a reason there have been eleven 'Chiefs' in twelve years.

I am told to report to the Old Admiralty Building at the top of Whitehall in 15 minutes, in order to 'assemble a government'. Our task is to build a team that includes supporters of Liz, of Boris, of Penny, and others; a list that will pivot to being Rishi loyalists, along with all the other criteria we should seek to include anyway – a decent geographical spread, old timers as well as young thrusters, gender, diversity and the dreaded 'left' or 'right' wings of the Party. And not forgetting competence of course . . .

This was to be a government of unity, all to be nailed down by Thursday.

A few moments, and a few calls, later I found an innocuous door off the street, behind which it was all happening. Civil servants led by Cabinet Secretary Simon Case dealt with the essential matters of machinery. As yet, we were unable to move into No. 10.

Liam Booth-Smith, Rupert Yorke, Oliver Dowden [Deputy Prime Minister] and Rishi himself and others made up the rest. I passed the *Spectator*'s James Forsyth leaving as I arrived. As the PM's oldest friend, I guess a friendly face was just what he needed, but we both pretended not to notice the other.

And so, to the 'whiteboard', that thing of many scurrilous rumours. We are still relying on a manual version at this stage of proceedings as we are some way off the formal appointments process getting underway. In other words we are sketching out options 'in pencil'.

One of SW1's oldest jokes is of the final version of a reshuffle – crafted over many days and signed off at the very top – being shrouded by a blanket overnight pending the big reveal. But, in the middle of the night, a Downing Street cleaner knocks it over, causing all the Post-it notes to fall in random batches across the carpet of the White Drawing Room. Recognising the unfolding disaster, the cleaner sets about replacing the notes as fast as they can, but paying no attention to which department the names might now be assigned to . . . which, as the joke goes, explains the more baffling appointments . . .

The process is complicated. We need to keep a tally of appointments we have made, so we don't accidentally exceed our statutory limit of 96 paid government positions. As the hours drag on, we add and discard the hopefuls more disdainfully than ever. And then we had to move the whole thing back into No. 10, setting up behind the heavily locked double doors of Margaret Thatcher's old study on the first floor. We blocked

out the windows too, just in case interested observers across in No. 11 could get a clear camera shot, just as they had when Boris was pictured with a glass of wine in the garden during lockdown.

Some work had already been completed. Braverman to the Home Office ('That'll be trouble,' I said, but was told 'a deal had been done'). Mercer to Veterans Minister made sense, as did putting Cleverly in the FCDO.

Tuesday, 25 October to Thursday, 27 October

We start with the Cabinet. Hunt is first on the board, continuing as CX. A continuity message is crucial as far as the economy is concerned.

For three uninterrupted days we put this impossible jigsaw puzzle together. Two steps forward, one step back. Names go on the board, then come off again. Some people, Ministers of State especially, frequently go from one department to another. One was pencilled into nine different slots before we found the one that fitted. The raw maths meant we had 96 paid positions to fill, but 353 qualified (and hungry . . .) colleagues.

By Tuesday we had a Cabinet, by Wednesday full departments, and by Thursday a Whips' Office, Lords ministers and some thoughts around PPSs. At each stage the PM would come upstairs, assess the board, make some changes, challenge some decisions and we would move on to the next.

And now to make it happen. The first job was sackings, or as the civil service calls them 'departure interviews'. The PM insisted, as is the tradition, of doing these himself in his own office, with me discreetly, yet visibly, present.

Rees-Mogg, Brandon Lewis, Buckland were exemplary, others less so. Some were just chippy and, as Charles Walker later said to me, 'just not officer class'.

Sackings complete, we moved to No. 10 for the hirings. Mostly warm, some ecstatic, some using the moment to leverage

or even to suggest other roles. Appointing TC to my old position as Welsh Secretary was an especially good moment, partly because he was convinced he would be sacked, but more especially as this was payback time for his classy reaction a few months ago when he refused the post from Boris as his administration fractured.

Senior roles complete, it's then down to me as well as Rupert Yorke (as the PM's eyes and ears) and other occasional contributions from Dowden, and Craig Williams as the new Parliamentary Private Secretary [PPS] to appoint Parliamentary Under Secs [PUSSs], whips and assorted odds and sods. Most of this done by phone, and the reactions were equally upbeat.

The brilliant Marcus Jones comes in as Deputy CW and we reappoint Stuart Anderson, already a legend in the hardest job in government, as pairing whip.

It doesn't all go our way. Some brilliant individuals don't make the cut, often for the flimsiest of reasons.

And before the ink is even dry, Braverman is in trouble for leaking confidential info to a backbencher, Sir John Hayes [South Holland and the Deepings]. It was discovered only down to lazy misuse of the internal email system. By unhappy coincidence for Suella, there is more than one person on the parliamentary email system of the same name as Sir John's staffer to whom she had intended to send the 'protected' information. The other happened to be a rather good friend of mine, startled to receive such sensitive material out of the blue and rightly minded to 'do the right thing' by alerting the authorities. Understandably, the PM is loath to lose her this soon, so we gloss it over, at least for now. Let's hope she remembers.

Monday, 31 October

The insanity continues. Rupert and I meet with SNP/DUP plus a range of exhausting one-to-one meetings with the displaced

and disgruntled. Some very compelling and sad, some rather entitled. I commute about ten times between House of Commons and No. 10 in the process.

We start work on appointing the PPSs' network, about sixty appointments in total and in which the PM is determined to have a say. It is obvious at this end of the Parliament they aren't quite the gateway to ministerial greatness they might be at the start of a five-year stretch.

I meet Labour's Chris Bryant as Chair of the Standards Committee. He has some sensible ideas about how to improve the current rather clunky and unjust system. I had no idea he and the Speaker are sworn enemies.

An urgent meeting request from Matt Hancock. I suggest tomorrow (Tuesday) or Wednesday, which to me met the definition of urgent.

'I really need to see you now,' came the response. My heart sinking, we created a slot and in he came, cheery and upbeat as ever. 'I need to get permission for an extended period of absence,' Matt suggested.

Naively, I asked exactly what this meant.

'A couple of months maybe.' He then explained the reason; he had accepted a chunky fee [rumoured to be £400k] to go on *I'm a Celebrity*. I explained I would need to speak to No. 10 and get back to him.

'When are you planning to leave?' I asked.

'Tonight at nine.'

'So, Matt, you aren't so much asking me as telling me,' I suggested.

'Well, yes, I suppose that's it really.'

So off he went and off I went. No. 10 said no way, so I put a short message together, sent it to Matt (who was an hour into an 18-hour flight) and briefed the media of our belief that this was serious enough to 'warrant suspension'. His local Conservative

Association Chairman was less mealy mouthed: 'I am looking forward to seeing him eat a kangaroo's penis.'

Tuesday, 1 November

A reception in No. 10 for the disaffected. The PM found it hard, but it was a good use of his time. We have another one tomorrow for ministers which should be easier.

Thursday, 3 November

Breakfast for the new Whips' Office with the PM in the Cabinet Room. A jolly gathering and I'm very pleased with the team we have, as it seems is the PM. It was a good move to pick a team of the best rather than just make best use of what was left over. He makes sure everyone around the table has the chance to speak.

We have instantly been handed ongoing troubling cases of claims made against serving MPs.

The first is a long-standing case of multiple alleged rapes and coercive control by an MP against two women on the Parliamentary estate.

In a separate case it looks like the CPS is considering charging a separate former MP with child sex offences.

PMQs reverts to being quite flat after a lively couple of opening exchanges. The PM's references to Corbyn aren't really having much of an impact any more and will need to be written out of future scripts.

We nail down most of the PPS jobs other than those the PM feels passionately about.

Sunday, 6 November

The *Mail on Sunday* does a hatchet job on Gavin [Williamson] for allegedly sending rude texts to former Chief Whip Wendy

Morton and, comically not addressing her as 'Chief', a traditional custom of the House. It's hardly worthy of a national outcry. I have been in the job for just a few days and have already been called much worse. But Gav is in trouble, and he does have a few enemies. The No. 10 view is to rescue him if we can. Gavin is 'one of us'.

Monday, 7 November

I am blessed with the use of a car to share with Commons Leader Penny Mordaunt. On its first outing, the Government Car Service send a very pleasant driver who has clearly never been outside the M25 and thus is totally unfamiliar with the rural, unlit lanes of west Wales. We crawl along, following the verge in and out of every yard and gateway until we get to a road with white lines, where normality is restored.

Tuesday, 8 November

4.30 a.m. start to get ahead of everything. The Gav situation is getting worse with other complaints, including some former MoD SpAd claiming Gavin told him to, 'slit his throat and jump out of a window'. It was obviously in jest (according to Gav) but no one will believe him except me and a few close mates who understand his turn of phrase. Former colleagues of his in the Whips' Office tell me he could be quite forthright and former DCW [Deputy Chief Whip] Ann Milton goes further with a full 'spill your guts' moment on Channel 4 news. There is now a lengthy discussion in No. 10 (a whole team effort) in which we all try to save him. I even suggest some kind of middle way, for example a suspension of some sort, but everyone except Oliver worries it will make us look weak.

Liam B-S takes the lead and agrees to call him and reach an agreed position. We all know that will probably mean stepping

down. So, Gavin is sacked three times by three separate PMs. Yet he remains one of the sharpest operators we have, and not the least bit scary.

The alleged rape case rumbles on. We desperately need to resolve this. Palace of Westminster officials and I talk to the Met, who aren't a lot of use, they just keep repeating (I suppose with good reason) that they cannot launch an inquiry without a complaint.

We ask Colonel Bob Stewart [Beckenham] to step down from the NATO Parliamentary Assembly. It was not easy and Bob is quite upset, but we need the space, and it's emerged Bob's humour doesn't work as well in the 2022 parliamentary environment as it did when he first joined the army. He is what the *Telegraph* would call a 'character', and he is clearly very hurt.

Back-to-back meetings with MPs which reveal our unity position is already only skin deep.

Wednesday, 9 November

Maria Miller [Basingstoke] harangues me and Emma [Whips' Office Special Adviser] about the lack of female representation in the Government. I assume the sub-text is she is annoyed to have missed out on the recent appointments. We have tried to maintain representation in Cabinet as well as the wider ministerial ranks, but it isn't always as easy as it seems. A number of our female colleagues have already been ministers and have no desire to return to Ministerial Office, and some are very junior but will make great appointments one day. The big question is why only 25% of our MPs are women, not why only 34% of the Cabinet is. Maria tries to make a valid point, but her manner puts everyone's back up, including most of the women on our team.

Helen Whateley, on the other hand, made the same case without winding everyone up.

PM was fine at PMQs. He's not flashy like BoJo but he is

sound and decent, even if uncomfortable when quizzed about Gavin. Aren't we all?

Monday, 14 November

The PM is in Bali with the G20, providing welcome peace in No. 10. There is time to regroup and plan for 2023.

Tuesday, 15 November

Old lag Sir Bill Wiggin [North Herefordshire] drops in. He was Shadow Welsh Sec many years ago when I first got involved and is the son of Tory stalwart Jerry Wiggin. He is also sound on most key issues. What he really wants is to trade his rock-solid Herefordshire seat closer to the GE, in return for a place in the Lords. He makes his pitch with charm and conviction. Dehenna Davison [Bishop Auckland] also alerts me to her wish to stand down in 2024 too. Dehenna has created quite a brand for herself but has openly struggled with some aspects of the job.

Wednesday, 16 November

There are now two official complaints in about Raab for bullying at FCDO and MoJ [Ministry of Justice]. It's hard to verify, as others have told me that whilst he is demanding, he is not a bully. Under current terms the definition of bullying is whether a victim considers he or she is being bullied. (That is clearly the case in this instance.) Setting the threshold this low could catch out a lot of people. It seems Secretaries of State are held to account for the performance of their department but largely forbidden from insisting on the highest possible standards or drawing failures to anyone's attention. He agrees with the PM to launch a pre-emptive inquiry, which hopefully will take ages.

In the absence of the PM, he does PMQs with Rayner and puts up a decent performance.

Thursday, 17 November

PM back from Bali at 6 a.m. Team meeting at 8.30* – Cabinet at 9.00, statement at 10.30, followed by a budget statement from the CX. A tough timetable for anyone.

The budget statement was delivered in a deadpan style by Hunt (which was just what was needed) and it all seemed to land rather well. To some it was too socialist, with tax hikes by way of threshold adjustments, but there were also spending freezes and money available for public services.

The main thing is it steadies markets and restores our credibility, and for most colleagues it managed that, with widespread support, if through gritted teeth. It's remarkable how quickly they have forgotten the Truss explosion.

Tuesday, 22 November

Two days' debate on the Finance Bill followed by a vote on 'resolutions' on Tuesday evening. The PM's orders are not just to win, but to win well. To that end we need to neutralise dissenters, Redwood, Drax [South Dorset] and even IDS [Iain Duncan Smith, former Conservative leader].

The PM wants the 'scalps' of any rebels but if we do we will have to be consistent, and that would mean de-whipping Kwasi,

---

* Every morning at 8.30 (when the PM was in London) his whole Private Office, along with other advisers including me, would gather for a 15-minute gallop through the immediate challenges we faced. Chaired by Liam B-S, it was preceded by his own smaller group and then followed by a less formal 'coffee-and-biscuits'-style gathering of an even smaller group charged with implementation.

Liz Truss, Philip Davies [Shipley] and others. So, he eases off a little and allows us to fix some last-minute absences, the result being we get a majority of 96 and no rebels. PM is chuffed to bits, and I even get a round of applause in the 8.30 morning meeting. The PM and I agree though, a time will come when we must shed some blood.

In the meantime, the list of those lobbying to be Lords or Knights gets longer, and sillier.

Wednesday, 23 November

'22 Executive, led by Sir Graham Brady, comes to my office for what I am told is a traditional weekly Chatham House chat, with champagne. Sounds pretty good to me. We quickly establish the fact that we can share vital Party info without the risk of leaks.

We now have about a dozen colleagues saying they will step down in '24, mostly women. Colleagues are feeling the strain and pace, especially those with family responsibilities. At some stage this will become a much bigger problem for politics.

Thursday, 24 November

The phone rings at 2.45 a.m. from a 2019'er, clearly pissed but just about coherent:

'Hi Chief, hope I haven't woken you.' (It's 2.45 a.m. FFS . . .)

Me: 'What's up?'

Him: 'I'm stuck in a brothel in Bayswater and I've run out of money.'

Me: 'Go on . . .'

Him: 'I met a woman as I left the Carlton Club who offered me a drink, but I now think she is a KGB agent. She wants £500 and has left me in a room with twelve naked women and a CCTV.'

Me: 'Give me a few moments and I will call you back.'

Bloody hell, this is a mess. I ring SpAd Emma. Emma being Emma, she answers the phone with all the cheeriness of someone who has already been at work for an hour, and for whom nothing is ever a surprise. I explain our dilemma. She offers to leave her house and go personally to Bayswater on an extraction mission. I suggest not (she sounded rather disappointed).

Instead, we devise a plan to send a taxi, extract our man, return him to the safety of his own hotel. I go back to sleep. Emma assumes control.

4.10 a.m. Phone rings again.

Me: 'Are you back safely?'

Him: 'Yes, but you will never guess what happened next.' (The truest thing he said all evening.)

Me: 'Go on . . .'

Him: 'Well, I slipped out of the room and saw the taxi Emma ordered across the road, so I legged it over and jumped in. However, it turned out it was a different taxi being driven by an Afghan agent called Ahmed.'

Me: 'So . . .'

Him: 'Well he demanded £3,000 for a blow job.'

Me: 'And . . .?'

Him: 'I legged it back to the hotel and locked the door.'

Conclusions: 1) Either he is incredibly unlucky or an utter fantasist, 2) Emma is really a very, very good SpAd, and 3) I am now knackered.

Tuesday, 29 November

Neil Parish comes to the office to sound out the chances of being able to stand again in Honiton. He has had a tough time, that's true, but given he resigned as an MP he has no automatic rights to the new seat. CCHQ won't alter the rules, I'm sure. He may well stand as an independent but history is littered with the bodies who have tried that and failed.

Wednesday, 30 November

The Cabinet agenda today is on Science and Tech and the economic value of these industries to the UK, in both the long and short term. It's a much more serious, organised and less comedic affair these days.

We continue to win Finance Bill votes with ease. The office team is doing well.

Thursday, 1 December

The *Sun* also runs a story of a '50-year-old former Tory government minister' being arrested for child sex offences. We all know who it is and it has been suggested others may also have been involved.

In the meantime, Matt Hancock requests the return of the whip (declined!), Conor Burns is reinstated after CCHQ eventually concludes there is no case to answer in his Party Conference sex allegations case (there were allegations made by a third party that he had put his hand on someone's leg in an unwelcome manner at a party conference event), and Sajid Javid decides to stand down. We also try to quell two planning rebellions on the Levelling Up Bill.

Sunday, 4 December

The *Sunday Times* names Charlie Elphicke [former Dover MP] in relation to the arrests for child sex offences which prompts a threat by him to engage in legal action against them, a big mistake, I would suggest.

Monday, 5 December

The 'overnight' commute is knackering but unavoidable if I'm to be in No. 10 by 8.30 on Mondays. I will end up having to

leave home earlier on Sundays. The GCS [Government Car Service] surpassed itself on the trip home late Thursday night – having missed the turning off the A40, he stopped and reversed 50 metres down the main road into oncoming traffic.

I meet later with Bill Cash [Chair of the European Scrutiny Committee] about EU matters. Old Bill has no other cares in the world. He has been in Parliament for decades and is a living example of someone who is both obsessed and institutionalised, as well as being pleasant and well mannered. Given his vast experience he is surprisingly wrong about many things, the most obvious being the realities of Parliamentary maths.

We win the Online Safety vote by 66 despite Labour fielding 242 votes, their highest ever number in this Parliament.

Tuesday, 6 December

Meet with John Redwood, who is like Bill Cash but twenty years younger and somewhat less humorous. His interests also include the EU but extend into the finer detail of economics too, about which I have no doubt he is an expert. He has no doubt either but until he gets appointed into the Treasury he is going to have to put up with the existing team. Then it's another old hand, John Hayes, about onshore wind. John is threatening to trigger 'the biggest rebellion we have ever seen' unless we drop any plans that facilitate onshore turbines. He is pompous but also passably funny and melodramatic. He won't muster that many, but we have to assume, for management purposes, he could.

One colleague of my 2010 intake has let it be known the 'gong' (about which she has received official notification) is not the damehood she is convinced was promised. I am put out, as some effort went into landing the lesser (but nonetheless much sought after) alternative.

The situation with the alleged rape case is heating up to the extent that we have taken extensive legal advice.

Wednesday, 7 December

Meet with head of Commons Security Alison Giles to discuss the the most appropriate way to tackle cases of serious misconduct.

We agree that the 'sequence' is vital. Firstly we must make sure that any allegation is treated seriously and that complainants are signposted to the help they need, including the police. Then they need an open point of contact in our office, for which Emma is designated. Then we need to make sure that the Speaker's Office is looped in, the Party Chair where appropriate, and in the most serious cases No. 10. We remind ourselves that we are dealing with situations where people's entire lives, hopes and dreams are shattered. It has to be right, for everyone's sake.

Thursday, 8 December

Emma picks up further info about other possible cases of concern, but of different levels of severity.

Monday, 12 December

Meeting with Priti Patel. She really has got it in for Suella, and a few others too. I am not sure why we have met, but we touch on tonight's vote on the Online Safety Bill. Labour pulls all our pairs, but we still win comfortably.

Tuesday, 13 December

Cabinet, and we discuss a small boats announcement, which remarkably hasn't leaked in advance. The PM makes a balanced and compassionate pitch, to which Starmer's response seemed strangely unprepared. Why? All he needed to do was ask searching questions. However, we need to get on with it as

people will want to see planes full of Albanians taking off before they believe anything.

Late night 'catch-up' pizza with Rupert, Liam, Craig, Claire C and Julian upstairs in No. 10. Joined by the PM a bit later (who was going round turning off the lights) and who wanted above all to make sure we tidied the room afterwards. He also wanted to know my most interesting whipping experience so far so I told him the brothel story – poor Rishi, he doesn't believe such things happen! He is refreshingly straight-laced and tends to see the good in most people. He should work in the Whips' Office for a day and that would soon change.

Wednesday, 14 December

The King comes to unveil his new lamp posts in New Palace Yard – the latest present I believe us MPs have given him. Michael Ellis is beside himself with excitement, this having been his idea from the start. I have received weird texts from the MP in the rape case, which I assume do not come with his lawyer's blessing.

To Rules in Covent Garden for a catch-up with Nigel Adams. We chatted about BoJo's resignation Honours List, the Privileges Committee (which Nigel thinks Boris will 'sail through') and various other issues.

Monday, 19 December

Lunch in Strangers with the 'Soho House Four' [friends from very different political backgrounds]; a lunch so good they all ended up in my office for the afternoon.

Chat with Conor Burns. He's been through a bit and whilst his life is never simple, on this occasion the Party has fucked up. He would like his job back (I don't blame him) but is wise

enough to realise it won't happen any time soon. Politics can be very unfair and unforgiving at times.

I also grabbed a drink with Michael Fabricant who I've never really got to know. He and Boris will be remembered for their hair as much as anything. He was polite and amusing and reminded me he has done thirty years as an MP and was once a pirate radio DJ.

Tuesday, 20 December

A suitably straight-faced and standard ministerial security brief reminds us that on no account should we engage in a chat with any unusually beautiful Chinese women (or men, I guess), to which Alister Jack added, 'If you think you are punching above your weight, ask yourself why.' My phone would be a fascinating mine of information.

Then to the FCDO drinks at Lancaster House before No. 10 and a late-night chat with the PM. He arrived with a very nice bottle of red, partially drunk by William and Ffion Hague on an earlier occasion and now wrapped in cling film. The PM is teetotal, but he said, 'William seemed to like it so I hope you do too.' We had a good time telling each other how brilliant we both were.

Wednesday, 21 December

It's recess.

Wednesday, 4 January 2023

Back to reality with a drama about the timing of the PM's 'Big Speech' which was originally due next Monday. We have heard Starmer is making one tomorrow and Harry and Meghan are planning to self-destruct on TV so the decision (against my

instincts) is to go tomorrow, although as yet we have no venue and for that matter no speech either.

Activity ensues, at pace, which at least produces some usable words.

Thursday, 5 January

A venue is identified in Stratford, East London and the speech is crafted, drafted, re-drafted and delivered as if it had been planned this way for months. If only they knew. Overall Party (and press) reaction is pretty good although the cliché count is always a little high for my taste. As with everything with RS though, he had given it great thought, so it was a decent and professional effort.

So, that little drama over, we are all set for our return next week.

Sunday, 8 January

Everything seems unusually aligned and ready to go although Boris is agitating in the background. Then Sky News cooked up some puerile version of an expenses scandal, which they have amusingly managed to cock up on take-off. They have paired up with some left-leaning PR outfit called Tortoise Media to produce an interactive website where, if you are sufficiently outraged by the very existence of politicians, you can search to find what heinous sums they have claimed. As ever, they make no attempt to separate 'expenses' from 'costs', meaning the sums look large as most of it relates to staff salaries and rent and the money never goes anywhere near the MPs themselves. It is all rather overly gleefully reported by one of my favourite people Sam Coates. And they wonder why we don't get decent people into politics.

Drinks over at No. 11 with CX and others makes me marginally less irritable.

Tuesday, 10 January

Plans afoot for the REUL [Retained EU Law] Bill, Online
Safety and strike legislation all next week. There will be
blood. In a publicity stunt, Grant Shapps manages to strangely
airbrush Boris out of a photo which gets noticed by everyone,
following which BoJo attends the Carlton Club to unveil a
portrait of himself. We send some Whips spies over who report
there are almost no MPs there and that Boris looks like he has
got dressed and shaved in the dark. Not sure his comeback is
nailed down yet.

I find a mobile phone left in the men's loo in No. 10 which
turns out to be the PM's. Lucky I was the next in. I don't think
he even knew it was missing, as we slipped it back on his desk
when he wasn't looking.

Wednesday, 11 January

The PM wants to alter an aspect of the 'Machinery of
Government' to split BEIS into two halves – Energy, and Science
and Tech. This won't change the world, or even be noticed but
it's the sort of thing the PM will have been agonising about
because he is frustrated by the illogical nature of the structure
as it is. However, from my perspective it means only one thing,
the triggering of a mini-reshuffle. We are required to operate in
secrecy.

Then, just before PMQs we get a call to say one of our MPs,
Andrew Bridgen, has made a Twitter connection between the
vaccine rollout and the Holocaust. No. 10 is initially inclined to
'demand an apology' but due to Bridgen being an utter knob,
we agree the more decisive and meaningful course of action is
to suspend the whip with 'immediate effect'. The anti-vaxxers
go spare, to them our move confirms the Deep State is at work.
The reality is he is a malevolent creep whom nobody likes, and

we really don't need him in our Party. A massive cheer goes up in the Whips' Office when I tell them.

Sunday, 15 January

It's another big week with strikes legislation, Online Safety and the dreaded REUL. All have a raft of amendments we need to deal with and in the case of Online Harms Bill [OHB], one has the support of nearly fifty MPs. At that level, a rebellion has the chance to be successful, so we deploy the excellent SoS Michelle Donelan to work her magic. By late Monday, the rebels have been broken up or talked down to the point we win quite comfortably.

Jamie Wallis [Bridgend] is in a bad place about Conversion Therapy. He is one of our few colleagues in the process of transitioning, so he acts as a vital test of opinion when it comes to our plans and of course, when the more strident of our colleagues say silly things. At the moment we don't have a plan, but we do have a stack of colleagues saying mind-numbingly insensitive things.

Dinner at the 'Chief Whip's Table' with Simon Clarke. Simon is always so polite and engaging I assume he is deploying exaggerated good manners as a means of averting my attention from what he is really up to, which is chipping away at our authority or panicking about our popularity. I won't quickly forget the way he torpedoed Boris on the issue of lockdown when he aligned with Gove et al to try to bring in another lockdown.

Monday, 16 January

We devote the entire day to negotiating soft landings for all the amendments, with success, as we defeat/agree every single one.

Wednesday, 18 January

The early decisions on the Levelling Up Funds [the distribution of large sums of money to the most deserving and needy community projects in the UK] have come out and it's quickly clear DLUC has rather screwed up on the comms. There are up to twenty colleagues who had been given every assurance their bids were going to be successful, but who now discover this is not the case. Worse for them is the fact they were given a hint they could 'own' the projects in anticipation of them coming good, only now to find they are being slammed locally for having failed. The spread also looks a bit too southern and Labour-leaning too. That said, there are winners aplenty, including me.

One of the early complainants was Philip Davies, normally full of bluster but not this time. He was very dispirited, but the good thing about Philip is he never bears a grudge, or at least I hope not.

Thursday, 19 January

There is a gathering army of MPs agitated about asylum seeker accommodation being set up in their local towns, Wiggin and Leigh [Gainsborough] to name but two. They all blame Jenrick who looks and sounds increasingly beleaguered. Jenrick thinks the Home Office [HO] doesn't give a shit whether the scheme works or if our people are offended. In fact, it looks like the HO has deliberately chosen hotels in Tory-leaning areas. However he is the minister in charge.

The *Mail* runs a story that Rishi was seen without a seatbelt whilst on a visit to Lancashire. He was recording a Twitter clip in the back of the Range Rover when this terrible crime was perpetrated. It really cannot be a big deal, but some are determined to make it a 'thing'. It really is absurd.

Saturday, 21 January

The seatbelt story gathers pace. It seems to me No. 10 is missing a trick. The PM's vehicle and convoy are provided by the Met, not the Government Car Service. As such, they are police cars and exempt from a range of traffic regulations, including the use of seatbelts. I have no doubt that every day the convoy exceeds the speed limits, jumps lights and fails to buckle up, all for good security reasons. Lancashire Police should have been told to fuck off and stop trying to jump on a populist bandwagon. I wonder how many FPNs [fixed penalty notices] they have issued for seatbelt violations this year? I suspect none.

Nadhim Zahawi's tax matters are also beginning to cause a headache.* It's just that the numbers (well over £4 million) are so huge.

Sunday, 22 January

Meeting with PM set up on Nadhim's tax position. It seems No. 10 is split on what to do – sack or save? The PM will want a full and detailed explainer.

Monday, 23 January

Both Emma and I are now getting multiple messages from a victim in one of our many cases of misconduct, often late at night. They are getting quite desperate, which is very upsetting, for Emma especially. We are only trying to help, but it is clear she is very troubled and in need of a level of help that the Whips' Office is not really equipped to provide.

---

* A story emerged that Nadhim Zahawi's complicated business tax affairs resulted in a dispute about a sum of £4.6 million still being due. Zahawi is a co-founder of the global polling company YouGov.

Tuesday, 24 January

News reaches us that the Zahawi tax inquiry doesn't look at all good. We should know by the weekend, so in preparation for the worst I sketch out a few changes which might be possible at the same time . . .

HO – Barclay for Badenoch or Cleverly

MoJ – Atkins or Prentis? Chalk to Attorney General?

Party Chair – all sorts of options.

DIT – Braverman

And for the new Department of Science – Huddleston

Andy Stephenson has the best ground operation in play, judging by the number of colleagues suggesting him for a bigger role.

Thursday, 26 January

To Chequers for the Cabinet awayday. These things always fill me with a sense of gloom and end up exceeding my worst expectations. It must be odd for PMs having this rather stately second home. I wonder if it ever feels like a private place or just a smart hotel in the middle of Buckinghamshire. Isaac made an upbeat polling presentation suggesting there is a path back into public favour, so long as we don't fuck up. That's a big ask these days. To round things off there is 'the Dinner' to which people like Kemi [Badenoch, Women and Equalities Minister] declined to stay, and to which the PM had asked William Hague to provide some morale-boosting contribution. Being William he did so with some skill. He has a remarkable knack of hitting the right notes in the right order. He started by explaining why someone with his questionable track-record of electoral success should be opining on our election chances at all, going on to remind us that during his career we had lost 37 consecutive by-elections, only to win a GE in the midst of it all. It was

clever and funny and above all, timely. If only the whole Party could have been treated to it.

Friday, 27 January to Saturday, 28 January

It's all about Nadhim. The noose is slowly tightening, and it looks like we will have to make our inevitable move on Saturday or Sunday. What a shame.

Sunday, 29 January

It's Sunday morning, when I get the early call from the PM. Just the two of us to start with, mapping out the options and agreeing the form of words he will have to use. He wants me to join the call with Nadhim which is set up straight away by Switch. He made some brief opening remarks and then the business is done. It's always sad to see a good man dropped but the Independent Ethics Adviser had made it clear to the PM the Ministerial Code had been broken so we really had no choice. Nadhim was pragmatic, raised a couple of legitimate questions about process, but accepted his sentence with as good a grace as feasible at moments like this. For most people, a tax discrepancy may not be career-ending, but most people cannot easily relate to a £4.6 million version because we haven't created a multi-million-pound enterprise (in his case YouGov). He will bounce back.

It looks like we will now launch into a slightly bigger round of changes.

Monday, 30 January

There is limited fallout from the Nadhim sacking. The news is mainly 'we did the right thing'.

The process of finding the right replacement starts in earnest.

The list of hopefuls is extensive, the list of good people, less so. We can't have anyone with a question mark over dubious behaviour, and it seems we are looking for a combination of a gritty northerner and a southern schmoozer, a marginal-seat champion who has a safe seat, someone who can mix with the high-net-worth community and our grass-root members, all at the same time. Our female colleagues are lobbying for an experienced woman, our gay colleagues want a gay person, Brexiteers want a Leaver, Remainers want a one-nation centrist.

I suggest we should consider someone competent, triggering much laughter.

I get a call from Simon Case, the Cabinet Secretary. He is concerned certain MPs are being overtly rude about civil servants (at least our people are doing it on the record) and asks: 'Could you find a way of getting people to dial back a bit?'

He asserts if there's 'open season' in which MPs and ministers blame all of our problems on the civil service then we could trigger a go-slow on areas of controversial legislation. In other words, if you are rude to the waiters don't be surprised if they eventually spit in your food.

He is right to raise this as politicians are being a bit cavalier about this relationship, it's important it works. The worst offenders are people who have never worked in a proper workplace or managed a team. But there is also an irony in his comments given the propensity of civil servants to leak shitty stories to the media. We are in a vicious circle but there are more of them than us, and they have the protection of anonymity.

I grab a drink in the House of Lords with Jonathan Evans [former Head of MI5 and Chair of the Committee for Standards in Public Life] at which we bemoan the fact the current model of politics makes correcting these scenarios nearly impossible.

And then to the Whips' dinner down in the City. We chip in £50 a month so Mike Wood [entertainment whip] can lay on a decent dinner at which we can be indiscreet about our

colleagues and friends in the optimistic hope it won't appear in Guido.

Wednesday, 1 February

Yet more 'Witherspoon' meetings and discussions about the new Chair. Witherspoon is the code name given to this mini-reshuffle.

Julian, Olive, James F, Rupert, Craig and I in attendance. We go round in many circles but it's worth it to get the right outcome, assuming we ever reach a conclusion. We cover dozens of names, but our problem is not really who we want, but that we can't really agree what we want.

And then the 1922 dinner at the Hurlingham Club, possibly one of the least accessible venues in London, and definitely the least conducive to the poor sod who has to conduct the auction. 550 people present including all the 'great and good' you could muster. Not too many speeches, luckily, and the ones we did have were sound, in particular Brady and the PM. My table was a bit flat, probably due to my barely concealed indifference to these events, so I engineered an early escape, but not before the newish Home Office PPS Colonel James Sunderland shared some barbed critique of his department with James Forsyth, not realising he was no longer the *Spectator* political editor but the PM's Political Secretary. We won't forget. Whips' intel (our permanently live feed of questionable behaviour across London) also learnt a senior married MP got a bit fruity with a journalist, suggesting her 'lovely dress would look better discarded on my bedroom floor'. Groan . . .

Thursday, 2 February

Meetings with the PM re Operation Witherspoon. It looks like the shortlist for Chairman is now down to Greg Hands, Andrew Stephenson and even possibly Gillian Keegan [Chichester], with

Lucy Fraser [South East Cambridgeshire] to DLUC if Gove takes the new Science and Tech role. Final decisions to be taken this weekend.

Over to Horseguards [the Treasury] for the Honours Committee, a rather arcane but hilarious three hours of discussion (light lunch included) about deserving and less-deserving political nominations for either the King's Birthday Honours or the New Year's Honours. During this short space of time, Alan Campbell [Labour Chief Whip] and I wield more power than at any other moment in our lives. We can dish out joy and disappointment, and nobody much is any the wiser. The committee is chaired by the wily old cross-bench peer Stephen Sherborne, with lay members and former politicians making up the numbers, plus the two Chief Whips, opposition and Government. Cabinet Office Clerks oversee the process. The list in front of us is the product of many months' work. Our allocation is roughly four knighthoods, four CBEs, four OBEs and a few MBEs for good measure to share between us. The Chair also guides us in the direction of diversity and gender targets. We all speak to our own Party nominations, but generally support those put forward by our opponents.

One thing for sure is the civil service knows how to write a citation. They love this stuff and their own nominations have been crafted with the greatest of care. None of them is rejected and as far as Alan and I can tell, never have been.

Sunday, 5 February

Witherspoon is on! We gather in secret in No. 10 at 5 p.m. The PM, James, Liam, Rupert and me. It's all casual kit, RS in his Adidas tracksuit and trainers, sharing cookies his daughter made upstairs. We go through the lists yet again, trying to reach a situation where there is minimal wider disruption, bearing in mind we are already at our statutory maximum number of

ministers, so we have to do all of this from within existing numbers. Eventually we settle on Greg Hands as Chairman and most other departmental roles, like the new ones, are internal. Greg is the nearest thing we have to a doughty campaigner who has been around the Party and Government for many years. The final proposal is therefore: Gove to Science and Tech; Fraser to DLUC; Shapps to Energy; Badenoch to Biz and Trade.

I am sent to the Chelsea Arts Club in Greg's Fulham constituency to sound him out and 'agree terms' whilst James Forsyth is tasked with the more uncertain job of landing Gove. The scene is set.

Monday, 6 February

Overnight the PM wants us to give a final thought to Ranil [Jayawardena, North East Hampshire] for a mid-ranking ministerial post. He declines as he wants something more senior, so that's scuppered. Gove also now changes his mind, we think due to the influence of Henry Newman, and wants to return to DLUC. The PM agrees as he doesn't want this whole exercise to be 'all about Michael' as usual so we revert to Lucy at DCMS and Michelle at Science and Tech (or STI as it is now known). So much for this being all agreed.

We now have nine changes, no sackings and only one 'new entrant' – the popular Ruth Edwards to the Whips' Office.

The PM and I hit the phones. Grant Shapps is slightly less than ecstatic, but he knows more than most how this all works, whereas others are delighted. At MoJ level, Nigel Huddleston is incredibly grateful but Andrew Stephenson, whom I backed to the hilt, declines the housing job as he can't stand working with Gove. He then resigns as a whip and it requires deft work and some promises of future senior roles by LB-S to get him back on board. Andrew is one of our best operators, but I can't get to the bottom of the rift with Gove. MG is affable but perhaps

a bit disdainful of his ministerial team. Whatever the root cause Andrew is adamant. He is also close to Boris and we want to avoid creating a new victim at times like this. We give him a coded guarantee that next time around we will check in advance that the position works for him.

One lucky Cabinet appointee is less grateful than her promotion deserves and more entitled than professionals should be when selected by the PM for high office. 'Let's all agree about one thing,' says the PM, 'she is fucking useless but we can't get rid of her.' (Every time we appoint for reasons other than merit it goes totally wrong.)

By 3 p.m. we have a new team and for the first time for a long time there are no old Etonians in the Cabinet.

Tuesday, 7 February

BoJo comes to the office to pester me about his resignation Honours List. (The list former PMs are entitled to submit when they leave office. It is always the source of much media tittle-tattle as they invariably include the PM's hairdresser, school mates, shooting companions and the like.) His people are claiming that he is making substantial changes, accepting that the current version is too optimistic, even for Boris. To add to this, Rishi has decreed that he will play no part in expressing views or editing Boris's list. It must be his and his alone.

Boris has suggested his landlady, Carol Bamford, and his father Stanley Johnson would fit better on any future list we have in mind, rather than on his. To be fair to Boris, both Lady B and Stanley are legitimate nominees, but as he doesn't really explain what's in it for us, there is no way I can make any meaningful contribution. Also, we are just not in the business of horse trading for honours. In fact, it might even be a breach of regulations.

In a separate secret plan President Zelensky is in town, coming to No. 10 and then addressing both Houses in Westminster Hall.

BoJo's team is rumbled trying to cook up a plan whereby he greets Zelensky at the airport. No. 10 has spiked it, so instead we all line the hall in No. 10 to clap him in. He is the same (tiny) size as the PM, with a big smile and plenty of charm and charisma. His close protection team, on the other hand, is the most menacing outfit I've ever seen. His speech in Westminster Hall is remarkable for its good humour and thoughtfulness and is delivered in English. If we weren't already standing, we would have been at the end of his 30 minutes. All he really wants are planes and my guess is that at some stage we will oblige. Being the slick politician that he is, he presents us with the Ghost Pilot's flying helmet (so named as the Russians couldn't catch him) as an opening bid for us to provide the jets to go with it. He caressed his audience with plentiful references to Churchill and landed an absolute bullseye when he said that 'in England the King is an air force pilot; in Ukraine every air force pilot is a King.'

Then he was off to in Dorset to see some of his soldiers being trained on our tanks. What an existence he is living. It is claimed he will wear army fatigues every day until the Russian Army is defeated.

Wednesday, 8 February

The Government Car Service is now becoming a fixation of mine. This time it is the issue of the latest driver's endless yawning after we had been on the road a few hours which culminated in the car going so slowly I thought we had actually broken down.

I am told not to worry as it was probably the 'same guy who couldn't find the duty free on the Woolwich Ferry'. And that's not all, I also hear of a driver whose car was booked by a traffic warden outside a church, fully 'ribboned up' as he was moonlighting as a wedding driver with one of the government Jags.

I have no business being so entitled so instruct myself to get back in my box.

Thursday, 16 February to Friday, 17 February

It's all kicking off with the NIP [Northern Ireland Protocol]. The PM goes to Belfast so we are all 'stood to' in order to prepare for an inevitable vote next week. The expectation is this will be hostile as it will be a trigger for the smouldering remains of the ERG. Any excuse to exhume the bodies of the past will be too tempting for them to miss. No. 10 is keen for yet another scoping exercise around NIP. We aren't quite ready, and the PM rightly wants all the pieces in place first.

Monday, 20 February

A drink in the Pugin Room, my favourite hospitality spot, with the ever-affable Robert Buckland. Robert has considerable charm, but simultaneously triggers my less sympathetic side. He is pretty certain he is going to lose his seat and is hence making an early pitch for the Lords. I make all the usual noises about the election being a long way off, the PM concentrating on other things, but stop short of reminding him that the centre will not easily forget his very public defection from Camp Sunak to Camp Truss in the middle of summer 2022. I know by the time the election comes round the list of hopefuls will be very long and I fear he won't be very near the top.

Tuesday, 21 February

Cabinet. Wallace and Mercer are sparring about veterans. The issue is Ben believes the Defence Secretary is the ultimate authority and the plight of veterans should be under his jurisdiction. He resents Johnny for manufacturing this job by

strong-arming Boris and for having a glamorous and substantial social media presence. They are both credible figures in the veterans' world so this needs early and mature resolution.

My weekly meeting with Sammy Wilson [DUP] is dominated by him explaining they will never agree to a deal. Never. Sammy is what is commonly known as 'unreconstructed', but polite with it.

Dinner in House of Lords with Michael Dobbs and Jesse Norman [Decarbonisation and Technology Minister]. Dobbs is still writing political novels well into his seventies and is one of the funniest story tellers I know. We parked ourselves at the corner table in the Lords dining room, which is so much nicer than ours, and spent two happy hours laughing about the almost invisible line between his imaginary vision of the Whips' Office and my real one.

He also revealed the significance of 'FU', the initials of his two main characters, Francis Urquhart and Frank Underwood. He was on a cheap sunshine holiday back when he was Chief of Staff to Margaret Thatcher and getting increasingly frustrated with the trashy political novel he was reading. As he cursed each page, his wife got more and more irritable and eventually snapped, telling Michael, 'If it's that bloody awful, write your own bloody book,' to which he replied, 'Fuck you, I will'.

Wednesday, 22 February

Another timely lesson about cyber security. As ever it produces a short period of panic and observance followed by a return to our usual sloppy habits.

Sir Jeffrey Donaldson [DUP leader] tells me progress is being made on NIP and to ignore Sammy.

Thursday, 23 February

Coffee with Rob Shrimsley and George Parker of the *FT*. They are old-school hacks. In the glory days this would have been a four-hour lunch, and more rewarding for all of us, whereas now it's all much more guarded. I trotted out the Government line word for word, and we all left none the wiser.

Back to No. 10 at 10 p.m. (having left home at 6 a.m.). A NIP deal seems very close. The plan we agree is to spend all day on engagement, following which the PM will meet EU leaders at Windsor (in a golf hotel not the Castle) followed by a statement to the House and then to Belfast for more ceremonial celebrations.

The hastily assembled engagement team is Dominic Raab, Michael Tomlinson [Solicitor General for England and Wales], the PM, Steve Baker (now emotionally fully on board) and NI SoS Chris Heaton-Harris. Each has a list prepared by us of colleagues rated red, amber or green. Their task, to start with reds, work through each section and submit to us to enter in the main spreadsheet. They do sterling work all day and it seems we not only have a deal that goes further than anything BoJo got, but we have colleague support too. We agree a process with the Speaker and will announce tomorrow at 3 p.m.

Friday, 24 February

We are off! The media has hardly seen any of this coming, especially the 'Stormont Brake'.* This is a tribute to John Bew (the NI expert in No. 10) and the discretionary ability of the rest of the team. This could have been destroyed before it even got as far as Parliament if we had leaked. The overall reaction is

---

* The Stormont Brake is the mechanism by which the Northern Ireland Assembly can object to changes to EU laws that apply in Northern Ireland.

therefore better than we could have dreamed of. The Agreement is universally and internationally well received and colleagues even line up behind it.

We go to the statement at 7 p.m. and there are nearly three hours of intense questions. The PM was on top of the detail and determined to deliver this first big test of his international status. If we go to a vote, then we should get widespread support. He's then off to Belfast at 10 p.m.

Saturday, 25 February

Good media fall out. The ERG has split, again. Sarah Dines [Derbyshire Dales] is the only payroll problem and the 1922 were (in the main) fine when we met later. There is no sign of BoJo who, like a submarine, seems only too happy to sink beneath the surface when things like this go badly. (One of our new female whips described him as 'like a foreskin, he always disappears when things get hard'.) There is a rump of MPs, around 25–35, who simply cannot take yes for an answer.

Wednesday, 1 March

Coffee with Steve Swinford and Olly Wright of *The Times*. They are incredibly well informed. Everything they tell me is word perfect, but they need me to stand it up. I try to maintain a poker expression, but I would love to know who is leaking to them. Whoever it is must be very well placed. Wright is more charming, Swinford sharper. It's like facing Anderson from one end and Warne the other.

Harriet Harman drops in to say the Privileges Committee (which she chairs) will produce evidence on Friday to which BoJo will be required to respond. Her main point was we should be ready to protect the Tory members of the committee (Jenkin, Walker, Costa and Carter) which makes me think it could be

spiky. Harriet discloses nothing more but is keen to heap praise on our people for 'the professional way they have conducted themselves'. Oh dear.

And then the St David's Day reception at No. 10.

Last up to see me are John Hayes, Fiona Bruce [Congleton] and a few others from the Christian wing to lobby me to lay a Government amendment to the Public Order Bill to allow 'silent protest' outside abortion clinics. At present the proposal is we should forbid people hanging around outside clinics to express their anti-abortion beliefs, as we feel women using the clinic are probably experiencing enough trauma as it is without having dear old John Hayes staring them down.

They say it's an issue of freedom of speech but the harder they explain this the less convincing they become. What could be worse than groups of people gathering creepily outside your clinic in eerie silence? To my mind this is an attempt to use the so-called 'right of protest' to intimidate. No. 10 won't go near it, sensibly.

Thursday, 2 March

We all decamp to a smart golfing resort in Windsor for the Parliamentary awayday, normally a thing of dread. To my surprise at least 240 colleagues made the effort, and the event was something of a triumph.

First, there was a compelling polling prediction from Isaac Levido; then a brilliant speech from Michael Howard on the perils of disunity and opposition and finally a good after-dinner leadership lecture from Andrew Strauss, former England cricket captain. Strauss got everyone in the best place I've seen for a very long time, but how long they will remain this unified is another question. It reminded everyone we get along quite well when we want to. The PM even stayed in the bar until 3 a.m., not bad for a teetotaller.

Remarkable news has emerged. Sue Gray is to become Keir Starmer's Chief of Staff. Colleagues united in their amazement that a Permanent Secretary could do that without at least a year off in line with ACOBA [Advisory Committee on Business Appointments] rules. Colleagues are livid and of course it's allowed Boris to say he was tried by a dodgy and partisan judge (a disingenuous claim, but still it is Boris). I suspect much of the anger is a means of venting frustration that Sir Keir has taken us all by surprise with a rather eye-catching move.

Friday, 3 March

The Privileges Committee publishes its 'charge list' which is pretty devastating, whichever way you read it. It focuses on the key question of whether Boris misled Parliament – the ultimate charge – and gives every indication the vultures are already circling.

Saturday, 4 March

Boris comes out fighting, making the claim the report vindicates him. I am all for the fight but that really is nonsense and erring towards Trumpian. By lashing out at the Committee, the media, Sue Gray and worst of all, advisers and officials (whom he cheerfully throws under the nearest bus) he has alienated just about anyone who might have been able to save him.

6

CORONATION

March–July 2023

One of my older Parliamentary friends Andrew Percy was one of our MPs elected in 2010. He won the seat from Labour and by the time it was dismantled by the Boundary Commission in time for the 2024 election he was nurturing a majority of 24,000. He is therefore an original 'red waller'. He was one of the few Conservatives from a deprived northern background, brought up on free school meals. A former comprehensive teacher, he now volunteers for the NHS. Why is this relevant to this part? Because Andrew never really mentioned small boats or Rwanda to his constituents. As he put it, in the eyes of the residents of Brigg and Goole the policy is either far too strong, or far too weak, for him to glean any great advantage. And this is partly why we became so deeply entangled in this complicated web.

So, as I recall the agony the Party experienced getting the Rwanda Bill through Parliament, it is with the realisation that it won't make much electoral difference, even if the subject itself is of enormous importance.

Talking of controversies, we deal with the ban on imports of hunting trophies, which like all animal welfare law, always generates more heat than light. Dominic Raab is found 'guilty' of bullying and resigns on the flimsiest of evidence – putting at risk any secretary of state who demands high standards and isn't afraid to say so.

It's a period when the house of the once untouchable Nicola

Sturgeon is raided by Police Scotland following theft allegations involving her husband, the SNP Chief Executive. It's also when we get in a terrible tangle with Boris Johnson's complicated resignation Honours List. As ever with Boris, nothing is ever simple.

Being awarded an honour is an important incentive to many people, and hence is a crucial weapon in the Whip's armoury.

Whilst I have been careful in reporting private conversations about honours, I cannot hide my indignation at the level of entitlement I witnessed. Rishi's take on the honours system remains that it should, where possible, be open only to those who have gone beyond what their role as an MP or Minister requires. Honours shouldn't just 'come round with the rations'.

Inevitably some deserving names slip through the net, some whose names are put forward in good faith I then feel guilty about as they are unlikely to make the final cut, and some nominations are so absurd I will lose little sleep when they don't appear in the *London Gazette*.

And it was, of course, the time of the biggest constitutional and ceremonial event for seventy or more years, the Coronation. Once again, we were at the centre of the world's attention at an event designed to have 'something for everybody'. Even the Whips' Office had a role, facilitating the ballot for the hottest tickets in town, causing an occasionally undignified clamour among MPs. And Leader of the House Penny Mordaunt stole the show with an epic display of flawless sword carrying.

——— • ———

Monday, 6 March 2023

A meeting of Ministers to work out the details of the legislation on small boats. It all sounds okay although there is an element that leaves me queasy. The Home Sec [Braverman] is far too gleeful about aspects of it, especially the modern-day slavery

elements. She really does give the impression of disliking asylum seekers, who are in the main the innocent victims in all of this.

Our tone should be more in sadness than anger, yet we seem to have been cornered by the Braverman group of right-wingers who claim the whole nation is longing to be far more radical.

All that said, the Home Secretary's statement to the House is just about okay even accounting for the fact some of our colleagues don't think we have gone far enough. Some would be more than happy to abolish the legal system, including the ECHR, if that's what it takes, without understanding that the more swivel-eyed we become, the less likely it is we can win votes in Parliament.

Tuesday, 7 March

For some reason the issue of Politically Exposed Persons [PEP] came up in Cabinet, prompting Jeremy Hunt to admit he had been refused a Monzo account.* I have also been caught out by this and found it impossible to open a new account as well. This can't have been the intention yet no one wants to fight it.

Sir Jeffrey Donaldson calls to implore us not to opt for an early vote on NI. Everyone in No. 10 agrees with him, except for the PM. We will need to steer carefully.

The PM is off to France to bond with Macron and then the US to do likewise with Mr President, whilst I have the unenviable task of arranging a system by which a very limited group of MPs get tickets to the coronation.

In the meantime, Gary Lineker tweets provocative comments about small boats (comparing Tories with Nazis) and creates a

---

* Since the creation of PEPs under Gordon Brown, the regulation has been widely overinterpreted, meaning that simple things like opening a bank account have become almost impossible for many people in public office.

huge storm. Instead of leaving the BBC to sort it out amongst themselves, some of our people, including the increasingly voluble Sir John Hayes, weigh in making it look like it's 'Tories vs Football'. There will be only one winner, and it won't be us.

Monday, 13 March

In a packed Pugin Room for a drink with Thérèse Coffey [now SoS Environment, Food and Rural Affairs] about hunting trophies. It's by far the best drinking hole in Parliament. The staff have become friends, Keith in particular, and we are treated like long-standing guardians of a decent private members' club, which I suppose we are. It's a whip's dream too. There is much to be seen; the regular 7 p.m. champagne twosome of Shami Chakrabarti and Diane Abbott to *Line of Duty* actor Vicky McClure supping wine with Vernon Coaker. All human life passes through here daily. It's the place of scandals, illicit liaisons and deals. More business gets done in here than in any other part of the estate.

Thérèse is a frequently misunderstood person. We did our Parliamentary Assessment Board together and I remember coasting along until she did her bit, whereupon I knew I had to raise my game. Then we met again in the final of my selection for the Carmarthen West and South Pembrokeshire seat. On that occasion, I had filled the room with my own supporters, so she was less of a threat. On the import of hunting trophies, she is also very sensible. We have inherited a nonsense proposal from the previous team, which we assume is a relic of Zac [Goldsmith] and Carrie's appetite to legislate on as many animal welfare issues as possible, irrespective of whether they make any difference. I had done my best to explain to the No. 10 team that animal welfare stuff always goes too far for some and not far enough for others. We will end up pleasing no one, and my message to the PM that 'nothing good will come of this' attracted sympathy. But their

conclusion was that junking it would look callous and it was in part in our manifesto anyway. As it is, the number of trophies imported to the UK from other countries caught by this will be so small as to make zero difference anyway. Thérèse's point is exactly that, let this go through or else Labour might introduce a much more draconian version if they win a GE.

In other news, the head of the China Research Group, a body set up to expose the deviousness of the Chinese regime, is arrested by the Met for spying, for the Chinese! Got to hand it to the Chinese, they don't piss about when it comes to a bit of spying.

Tuesday, 14 March

The '4 BMs' (the House Business Managers: me, Penny, Nick True and Susan Williams) meet with HO officials to discuss the Internal Markets Bill [IMB]. What could be more exciting? As ever the officials are proceeding at the slowest possible pace and seemingly determined to aim for the long grass. We tell them we want two days in committee before the Easter recess – needless to say they describe it as impossible. The PM will be livid, and it will be down to me to tell him.

Then a delegation to see me of the Northern Research Group led by John Stephenson [Carlisle], who want to moan about their concern no one loves them. Not true of course, but we can't love everyone equally all the time. Or maybe we can. My mood is restored by the ever-helpful Will Quince [Colchester] who never really complains and always wants to help. Maybe that's why he isn't in the Cabinet.

Wednesday, 15 March

It's Budget Day. As I arrive at the office just off Members' Lobby there is already an occupied row of chairs lined up outside the

Chamber as the keenest members assemble to get their Prayer Cards* in first. I used to be that person once, but I now realise I have become too grand . . . Hunt briefs the Cabinet and then comes to the Whips' Office to repeat the process, as it will be our team who bear the brunt of colleague reaction, good or bad.

Hunt is a cool operator. He never raises his voice, never gets needled and always treats each inquiry with respect. Then he gave a solid one-hour speech in the Chamber. He is quiet and diffident. He is an effective Chancellor, and he needs to be serious. We have plenty of jokers elsewhere. It is competent sensible stuff on tax, borrowing and childcare, and shoots Labour's pension fox also. My fears of a substantial rebellion are allayed. The tea room is a bustle of noise and activity. Whips have carefully fanned out across the estate and are reporting calm, but the bars aren't open yet.

I see Bill Wiggin to find out if we can resolve a gathering storm over trophy hunting. Bill chairs the Committee of Selection, a little-known procedural committee which has the power to ambush stuff we don't like. With Thérèse's words echoing in my mind, I suggest he thinks carefully about the committee's next move. Cash has a 40-minute meeting with me and Emma in which he fails to listen to a single word I say about NIP. He really can be the most awful old bore when he wants to. I know I am not allowed to speak ill of such a revered figure, but I just don't buy his 'I'm only trying to help' refrain.

Thursday, 16 March

To a pleasant lunch at Langan's with Nigel Adams. It's one of those occasions where we both try to politely extract information

---

* Prayer Cards are a small green or pink credit-card-sized slip that members insert into a slot on the green benches to reserve their seat for the day. However, they have to then be present at 'prayers' at the start of business for this reservation to be validated.

from each other without being vulgar enough to admit it. I am not sure who did best. I have always got on okay with him and intend to continue to do so. He has a dry turn of phrase and loves cricket and shooting. In fact, he holds the record for the highest score of an MP in the Lords and Commons vs the MCC at Lords where he smacked 134 not out, an achievement that warranted a letter from the great Geoffrey Boycott. We talked about BoJo, whose demise still clearly agitates him, as does the length of time his honours nominations are taking. I am not sure how much I can help, if at all.

Lo and behold Boris then calls me to remonstrate about the injustices of the Privileges Committee. He swings between threatening a by-election to promising to cooperate fully with all they suggest. I think he was a little taken aback by: a) my refusal to commit to whipping colleagues to support him (which would be a fatal repeat of the Paterson fiasco) and b) my not trying to restrain him when he threatened to resign.

It was all vintage Boris, but for the first time ever I was left with the impression he felt outraged by anyone questioning him. Herein lies the problem. Bluster is fine up to a point, and has been fine in every other role he has occupied, but it's not fine when you are PM or former PM. I'm afraid colleagues have sensed it and for the moment feel we are better off in a Boris-free world.

Friday, 17 March

The Import of Hunting Trophies Bill goes through, so it's a Lords problem now. The SNP is having an ironic moment of internal meltdown as Nicola Sturgeon, her husband and some comms bloke all seem to be on the way out due to financial scandal. Alister is loving it and feeding it. He is good at this kind of thing. The big mistake Nicola made is to have been relentlessly sanctimonious about everybody else's behaviour for years, so when the light shines on her we are all especially smug about it.

Monday, 20 March

Another meeting with John Redwood about Northern Ireland, about which he knows much more than me. Our meetings are always polite, but completely devoid of humour. Like Cash, he purports to be on the Government's side but sincerely believes he knows better than everyone else on every topic. Politics just doesn't work like that. It is a collective endeavour, involving compromise and agreement. It leaves me reflecting, more and more, about how these people get through the process of candidate identification and selection. By chance my next meeting in my sweaty, airless Commons office is with Bernard Jenkin [Harwich and North Essex], another one with the rather unfair reputation for being contrary. The big difference is he argues his position with charm, humour and manners. It is said that in every Richard Curtis film (which includes *Four Weddings*, *Love Actually*, etc.) there is always a sad loser of a character called Bernard, an act of revenge by Curtis after the real Bernard (Jenkin) stole his girlfriend when they were at university together. I have no idea how true the claim is.

Tuesday, 21 March

Whips' breakfast with the PM over in the Cabinet Room at No. 10. Despite the early hour, 7.30, these are good uplifting occasions and recharge the depleted energy levels with some real appreciation from Rishi for the substantial office efforts.

Today's task: to nail every possible dissenter on the question of Northern Ireland. Promises will be made which we have no intention of honouring. People are absurd. Can certain colleagues not remember the night we rescued them from a brothel; or realise their peerage might depend on their 'cooperation' with the PM? They are idealogues, oblivious to the fact that if we lose crucial votes on these flagship issues we will be swept away.

Jonathan Gullis [Stoke-on-Trent North] decides to vote against us after changing his mind three times and giving me a personal assurance he will support us. I find Jonathan harder to dislike than some in the Whips' Office do, despite his best efforts to piss me off. It's like owning a Labrador that can't stop stealing from the table. He knows he will get in trouble but does it anyway.

Next, Andrea Jenkyns [Morley and Outwood]. What can I say? It was she who was photographed giving the finger to reporters outside No. 10 during her forty-four-day ministerial career under Truss and who has been bad-mouthing the rest of us on Twitter ever since. Yet she has always had the help and support of the Party and its donors and was elected under our brand, not hers. She spends 20 minutes telling me how crap Rishi is. I remonstrate to no effect. We should remove the whip of course, but I know the reaction from the centre will be, 'she is an attention seeker, ignore her.'

In the meantime, the ERG is talking up the numbers they think will rebel on NI but Stuart Anderson is rock-solidly confident there will only be around 23 rebels. We check, recheck and recheck again.

Wednesday, 22 March

At the daily 8.30 meeting in No. 10, I make the mistake of giving the PM a range of voting outcomes on NI, ignoring Liam's grimace from across the Cabinet table. I ventured that the range of potential rebels was 19 best-case to 28 worst-case. The PM instantly snapped back at me, '28 is unacceptable.' The lesson, keep off the actual numbers when briefing the PM, he is fixated by spreadsheets and their accuracy.

BoJo is to appear before the Privileges Committee at 2 p.m. and the big NI vote is at 2.21 precisely. To no one's surprise both Boris and Truss announce they will vote against the Government.

Nakedly opportunistic, but we must hold our ground yet again. This is now a test of whether Rishi commands the Party. We work through, yet again, the red and amber risk register. The instruction to the whips is not only to check attendance, voting intention, but also to double-source our information. Whips Stuart Anderson and Marcus Jones, along with SpAd Emma Pryor and I remain certain it will be 23 against, a long way from the 35 claimed by the ERG and nowhere near the 100 the *Daily Telegraph* is spouting.

So, both these SW1 melodramas kick off at roughly the same time. The 'trial' of Boris Johnson is interrupted at 2.20 by the division bell. Will Boris bother to vote? After all, he is in mid-flow over in PCH, but as always, he gives in to bad advice. Labour vote with us, as expected, so the final score is 515–29. An absolute slam-dunk of a result. Twenty-two rebel (a triumph for Stuart Anderson's data and nerve), seven DUP and the rest with us. This is a huge result for the PM as it asserts his authority, convincingly, over Boris, Truss, the DUP and the ERG in one move. RS and No. 10 are chuffed to bits. A lot more rode on this than anybody realised, including my survival as Chief, for that matter. The feeling of relief and pride is tangible. I go over to No. 10, grab Rupert, Liam B-S and Craig and head for the Two Chairmen pub. The team fizzes. A substantial rebellion, one that enabled Labour to say they had saved us, would have been a terrible look. Perhaps the press too, might listen to our version of 'the numbers' a little more carefully.

Back in PCH, BoJo is getting a hoofing, courtesy of the Privileges Committee. As ever he adopts an 'attack is the best form of defence' approach. Mainly, he denies it all, then he prevaricates, and then just blames everyone else for letting him down. All this playing out in the cold light of day is a horrible reminder of what a chaotic regime had taken root in No. 10 and how right we were to move on. I guess the committee will find him guilty but won't suspend for more than 10 days. One thing

is for sure, he is poorly advised, and the certainty with which he expresses his innocence is really now at Trumpian levels.

Dinner with one of my oldest friends, the very civilised John Gardiner (Lord) and a late-night call to the PM – still massively on fire about the vote – made this the most intense day to date.

Thursday, 23 March

Stephen Hammond [Wimbledon] pops in. He is very decent, old school, honest, conservative. He is one of a handful of MPs who have been stitched up by a dubious web-based campaign group known as 'Led by Donkeys'. It's a typical gobby and permanently angry group of ex-Greenpeace activists. The scam? To pretend they represent a bunch of South Koreans who want to bring MPs onto their board. As it turns out, none of the MPs signed up, so it came across as all somewhat confected outrage. There will be those who are a bit sniffy, but why shouldn't MPs explore offers as they get closer to the end of their Parliamentary careers?

Monday, 27 March

Yet another 'big day' as we deal with day one of the committee stage of the Rwanda Bill. Home Office is crap as usual in dealing with amendments from both left and right. For numerical reasons the so-called centre or centre-left amendments are the only ones with any chance of success because they will attract Labour support. As things are we only have a majority of 4, but good whipping gets us to 17 and we don't think we will divide anyway. In truth, all we have done is buy time by pushing it all back to report stage on the 26th. It remains intense and evidence these ERG battles are not over yet.

Tuesday, 28 March

Cabinet, and an excellent energy presentation by Grant Shapps. He's highly competent in a polished, slick sort of way. We get a Whips team pic with the PM – for most of us it will be a historic (one-off?) political memento.

We conclude committee day two with a decent majority and then I go to dinner with Nadhim in Oswald's, Albemarle Street. We have Dover sole, and our evening is regularly interrupted by visits to the table of those who wish to be around Nadhim. (They have no idea who I am.) He grips their hands with both of his, a touch on the shoulder maybe or for some a full-blown hug. These are London's richest and Nadhim is very comfortable in the centre of it all. He's thinking of some kind of comeback and why not?

Wednesday, 29 March

Coffee with Chris Hope before he heads to GB News and then a rather raucous lunch at Boisdale's with Craig, Rupert, Julian and James. We were interrupted by veteran MP Mark Pritchard [The Wrekin] sitting down at the next table – he tactfully retreated to another one when he saw who his new neighbours were.

The Met tell us that they are not proceeding with one of the misconduct cases they are currently looking into, a decision that will no doubt be analyzed in detail. Unfortunately they had not warned any of the complainants (or my office for that matter) in advance, meaning we had no time to help people prepare. You would think they might be slightly more sensitive of their current reputation.

Emma calls in to report another four cases of concern that we didn't know about, taking the total to eight (we know of).

I take a long-standing friend Michelle Hakim, her husband

Richard and their young family to see the PM. A couple of weeks ago, their son Rudy came home from school with a headache which just a few days later was diagnosed as an aggressive brain cancer. It's too tragic for words. He had already had one serious operation, so he was self-conscious about how his head was half shaved. Lisa [Lovering, Rishi's PA] had put aside a little time as a huge favour to me so I showed them around No. 10 and then into Rishi's office for what I hoped might be a few moments and a pic. Instead, Rishi gives them more time and love than I dared to ask for. We sat in the office for nearly 40 minutes as the children played and he gave them as much support as he could. It was a lovely act of kindness, way beyond the call of duty. I hope it helped.*

Thursday, 30 March

As the misconduct stories worsen, I go to see the Speaker about access to the estate by MPs under investigation. There isn't much he can do apparently. We are powerless to do any more than withdraw the whip.

One of our new, younger whips arrives at the office with a broken rib, apparently the result of an energetic night with his new girlfriend. Oh, to be young again! He is mercilessly teased, but then he shouldn't have been so honest as to the cause of his discomfort.

Wednesday, 5 April

Drama in Scotland as the police raid Nicola Sturgeon's home and start digging up the garden. This is getting really interesting.

They arrest her husband Peter Murrell, who also happens to

---

* Rudy died a few weeks later.

be CEO of the SNP, but no one really knows what the police are looking for. It looks serious though.

Blackpool MP Scott Benton is 'stung' by *The Times*, offering to ask questions and provide information for money. Unlike some of our cases this one doesn't seem to have an innocent explanation, unless rank stupidity is included. Offering to provide access to sensitive information before Parliament is an offence in anyone's language. As it is so clearly outside the rules, we all confer (including the PM) and agree to withdraw the whip. He thinks he will get it back, but I have my doubts, especially as he has been in the *Express* recently, slagging off the Standards Committee he is going to be up in front of.

'I'll sleep for the first time in two weeks,' he tells me now the story is out. Will we have to do the same for the fastidiously honourable Steve Brine [Winchester] as he was even more unfairly tangled up in the 'Donkeys' scam. His position does seem to be a genuine error.

It's Easter recess still, so peace for the time being. The PM is in Belfast with President Biden for the twenty-fifth anniversary of the Good Friday Agreement so the mood in No. 10 is a bit more relaxed than usual. CCHQ recommends Bridgen is expelled from the Party and someone hacks into the Whips' Office Admin Unit and sends spoof texts to certain MPs telling them I have issued instructions for them to be suspended. This is total fiction, so House Security is roped in and an inquiry launched. We think it is most likely a media hack but will have to keep quiet until the spooks have had a little look around.

Suella Braverman is head-to-head tonight with Flick Drummond [Meon Valley] for selection in the new seat of Fareham. Flick should win on merit, but the whole Home Sec persona (including armed bodyguards and convoy of blacked-out cars) may just dazzle the members into endorsing SB.

Saturday, 15 April to Sunday, 16 April

Fab weekend in London for Nell's 21st but inevitably interrupted by the need to pre-plan what we need to do, a) if Raab has to go, and b) for some maternity leave cover for Michelle Donelan and Julia Lopez [DCMS Minister]. We have a few thoughts for each scenario, but it will be for RS to decide.

As it is, the PM is pretty pissed off that the Standards Commission is looking into why he didn't refer Akshata's care home interest when he appeared before the Liaison Committee. The media is making this a thing, which is totally unreasonable given the interest is already a matter of public record and has been declared in the proper manner. He (or any other MP for that matter) cannot be expected to recall every detail about everything, all the time.

Monday, 17 April

Early meeting in No. 10 to resolve all the above. We have a clear shortlist for Raab replacements in the form of Chalk [MoD Procurement Minister], Atkins [Financial Secretary to the Treasury] or Prentis. Prentis is much valued as Attorney General so he [RS] won't want that. Atkins is great but she has a knack of annoying colleagues and Chalk is the best lawyer, as well as being a great mate of RS's.

On the question of maternity leave the PM wants to appoint people who are not current ministers, so not to put pressure on Michelle or Julia to come back earlier than they need. So, we look at Wright, Norman, Warman, Damian Collins, Whitto [John Whittingdale], Crouch, Double and others, including Rupert's suggestion of Chloe Smith.

I meet separately with Atkins who is not shy in setting out her ambitions and therefore ruling herself out on this occasion (in

my book) but probably in at a proper reshuffle down the line. She wants a cabinet role, and will definitely get there.

Separate discussions with Marcus and others in the Whips' Office about Rob Roberts (suspended since July 2020 on sexual abuse allegations, he was rebuked by the Party, served a six-week suspension and had the whip withdrawn back in 2021). He wants the whip back, which is probably justified at one level, and he makes a compelling written case. However, our whip colleagues are far from happy. By restoring the whip, they believe (not unreasonably) that young men and women on the estate will be given the impression we don't take their well-being as seriously as we do securing the Government's business.

Hence the current position is unfair on everyone involved as it involves one punishment irrespective of the offence, the length of which is determined solely by the Chief Whip, and dependent on political circumstances at the time. At the very least we should have a 'tariff system' which explains to MPs roughly how long their suspensions may be for certain offences, and even some independent system of appeal.

Tuesday, 18 April

Political cabinet on local elections and main Cabinet on AI. The PM opens the general discussion with 'please keep your questions short'. First question, Rob Jenrick: 'I've got four points.' Read the room, Rob.

Looks like the Tolley report (into Raab) will be out on Thursday.

Wednesday, 19 April

Coffee with the BBC's Ben Wright and Vicki Young. They both agree that if Raab goes down for being 'demanding' we have a much wider problem. Everyone in No. 10 wants to keep him,

but he has unwisely (but decently) said he will go if found 'guilty of bullying'.

I meet with Nusrat Ghani (at my request) to talk through the inquiry into allegations she made claiming Mark Spencer told her she was sacked for 'being too Muslim' whilst he was Chief. The whole thing is extremely awkward and made worse by both individuals having an entirely different recollection of events. What I hoped would be a friendly meeting at which I would try to help her 'move on' ended up being anything but. She wants Spencer convicted, but the inquiry concluded that as neither of them had taken an official record of the meeting it was unable to reach any sort of safe judgement. Other sources make the outlandish and unproven suggestion the Muslim comment was made by Boris at Chequers and Spencer had been offered a knighthood to cover it up. I am glad I had Emma in the room as a witness.

The Speaker is fretting (again) about a *New Statesman* claim that a senior Conservative MP, and friend of the Speaker, has been inappropriate with someone within the Parliamentary eco-system. I told the Speaker I thought the claim was unusual as the man in question had made no complaint, whereas his unnamed 'friend' had. I would be amazed if the *New Statesman* get this one to stand up.

One of our female colleagues has had her damehood rejected for tax reasons which she accepts with surprisingly good grace.

The Raab report has been received in No. 10 and by Raab himself.

Thursday, 20 April

My diary cleared for the day as we cram into No. 10 to digest the Raab situation. The team and I read the numbered report in stony silence around the table in Room G39. Forty-five pages of legal-speak in which there is just one paragraph that poses a big

problem. A single meeting with a foreign ambassador, three years ago, is cited as intimidating and demeaning. If it wasn't for his own commitment to resign, he could survive. What was said at the meeting is unclear, but it seems to be around the time the ambassador in question was summoned back from his post to a 'meeting without coffee' for saying some unhelpful comments in public.

In one of many subsequent meetings in the PM's office with Rupert Yorke, Julian, Craig the PPS, Amber [de Botton, Director of Comms in No. 10] and James Forsyth, I stress he is guilty of being abrasive but not for a sustained pattern of behaviour which could constitute bullying. If he goes for this, I said, then God help us manage the situation with other ministers, such as Wallace, Coffey and Spencer who are known to speak their minds and demand high standards.

SoSs will no longer be able to run their own departments, and civil servants and stakeholders can dangle any threat they have, however historic, over us. Ministers will however be responsible for anything that goes wrong, and seemingly unable to do much about it. The PM agreed but we are trapped. LB-S does the direct liaison with Raab, and the PM rightly wants to consider it overnight and then move quickly tomorrow.

It is hard to describe the intensity, drama and pace of days like this one. The entire machine kicks into a new gear. The PM also stress-tested Tolley personally, grilling him for over two hours to make sure he wasn't taking the course of least resistance. RS knows, like we do, this is probably the wrong outcome, but we have no choice.

Friday, 21 April

We gather back in No. 10 at 8 a.m. The PM speaks to Raab who has already decided he will go. Yesterday's planning takes immediate effect as we exchange the pre-drafted letters and line

up Chalk for MoJ, Chloe Smith for DSIT [Science, Innovation and Technology] and Whitto for DCMS.

We get Cartlidge [Treasury Exchequer Secretary] lined up for the MoD procurement role and Gareth Davies to replace Cartlidge. All 'blokes', some will say, but the PM is still disappointed with Braverman and a few others, who seem remarkably silent in their public support for him given the confidence he placed in them on several occasions. He wants loyal and competent people and is increasingly less afraid to say so.

And then, as is so often the case, the storm has blown through. A few gusts here and there, but for now it's back to the ever-present headache that is the Home Sec.

Monday, 24 April

We have a problem. The opposition day tomorrow (which has been sanctioned by me) on the question of river pollution has, with the help of Mr Speaker, morphed into a Humble Address, the ancient process by which a vote can be binding on the Government and therefore embarrassing. Sewage in UK rivers is currently one of the most divisive and misleading policy areas there is. This is much more serious than a run-of-the-mill opposition day debate (on which we would normally abstain) and will require us to reject the motion.

We will now have dozens of colleagues at risk from hostile Lib Dem propaganda in our key rural marginals. The truth is we have done good work on sewage discharge by introducing monitoring, setting targets and putting the water companies on notice. However, the Lib Dems are happy to lie about it, and Labour now see a bandwagon they can leap on (even though in Wales – where they do have control of this problem – incidents of pollution are twice as bad as in England).

Asking colleagues to vote down pollution control measures is

a nightmare especially as it wasn't long ago we got a beasting for doing exactly that.

RY [Rupert Yorke] and I agree we need to conjure up an amendment allowing our people to vote 'for' a reasonable-sounding alternative rather than just close our eyes and vote it down. Cue a rather brilliant suggestion from a junior civil servant. Why don't we, he suggests, simply remove 95% of the opposition day text (the bit that takes over the order paper, etc.) and leave in the first three lines which we all agree with about making rivers nice and clean. If we do this, some ancient custom allows for our vote to come first, and then the vote for the Labour proposal 'as amended'. It's genius.* We can kill the proposal but remain on the side of the angels. It's too good to be true so we get written agreement from the Clerks and then keep quiet as surely someone in the Labour Whips' Office will rumble us . . .? Surely . . .?

To maximise our chance, we table the Government amendment at the very last moment, making it impossible for them to counter-amend. The trap is sprung. They have not rumbled the ploy.

Tuesday, 25 April

Cabinet was fine, so we now anxiously await the debate. The Defra team is ready to go, so we launch into the opposition day with a rare confidence. With only ten minutes to go Labour realises what is happening.

We vote first, kill the oppo proposal stone dead and then put the main question, forcing both Labour and Lib Dems to abstain on their own proposal.

---

* These processes are arcane in the extreme but have a basis in logic. To be 'permissible' and thus voted on first, the Government can only remove text, not alter or add to it.

As their minister angrily said, 'They have made us look like twats.' Indeed, we have. It's a very 'village' event but one that adds further credibility to the Whips' Office reputation and our relationship with No. 10. These little victories (and defeats) happen on multiple occasions most days. In some ways, the sweeter the victory the less noticeable it is to the outside. Each day and on every subject, we spar, jabbing away, landing the odd punch and ducking a few too. 'Getting one over' like this may seem a bit childish on the outside but it's a bit more important than that. It reassures our side we aren't idiots; reduces friction in our own ranks. And it frustrates the opposition thereby creating tension in theirs.

Wednesday, 26 April

Report and third reading of the IMB. Last-minute agreements result in four straightforward votes which we win with majorities of 60 or so. We still have some headaches ahead, but it's a good outcome for now.

I really need to see the PM to explain why Suella is not his friend. The problem we have is that the Whips' Office is seeing the real Suella but No. 10 sees the more house-trained version. We see the leaks, the tea-room briefings and the general lack of solidarity. Troublesome MPs think we don't know but fail to understand that almost everyone is talkative. They all tell a friend, who tells a friend who tells a journalist, or even a whip.

Dehenna Davison tells me she is to stand down from the Government at the next reshuffle. She does so with decency.

Thursday, 27 April to Friday, 28 April

Local Authority election campaigning in a very wet Swindon with the excellent Justin Tomlinson [North Swindon] followed by Welsh Conference and a meeting with Sir Mark Rowley of

the Met. I feel obliged to apologise for the grubby way he was treated by Lee Anderson [Ashfield] at the Home Affairs Select Committee yesterday.

The Coronation is getting closer.

Tuesday, 2 May

A reception in Westminster Hall for the King and Queen. Either I am not an especially dedicated monarchist or colleagues are somewhat overexcited. MPs and Peers were arranged in small manageable groups around the packed Hall to which both Royals would be taken for a quick handshake and a few moments of instantly forgettable banter – or at least that was the plan.

Instead, it became a scrum with some MPs manoeuvring themselves so they could have a second or even third attempt at a selfie or, in examples of very poor form, monopolising HM King which included, in one notable instance, producing an envelope of poetry to read! Poor show, everyone knows you don't hand him things, and even if you do, he is well trained in ensuring it gets passed to one of the multitude of hangers-on hovering nearby for just such an occasion.

I was one of the introduction party for HM Queen. She seemed somewhat bemused by the whole thing. She asked what I did, so I just said I was the 'whipper-in' – a joke that I thought she might appreciate given her many years in the saddle with the Beaufort Hunt. It was an 'occasion', I suppose, so I mustn't get too sceptical about the whole thing, as they don't come round often.

Wednesday, 3 May

Met Henry (Lord) Bellingham [former MP] in New Palace Yard who is currently, due to some Lords whipping cock-up, sponsoring the hunting trophies Bill. He doesn't seem interested and

is ready to hand the whole thing over to Janet Fookes [Deputy Speaker of the House of Lords] unless I can think of something sufficiently valuable to trade with him. I can't, or won't to be more precise, as this thing is going to founder this time round anyway and I don't want to waste my depleting supply of goodies on a doomed endeavour. Nice try though.

Thursday, 4 May

Local elections – Nick Watt [BBC] thinks we will all do badly – or at least underperform. I would settle for that, and he does make more effort than most to understand the numbers.

Friday, 5 May

London has become a sea of red, white and blue as thousands of excited visitors prepare for tomorrow. It's a happy atmosphere, contagious even for those who take a more republican view. Tents appear on The Mall, aged couples adorn themselves in Union Jack clothing and people talk to each other on the street in a way that never happens normally.

Overnight election results are a mixed bag. We probably do slightly worse than the anticipated loss of 1,000-plus councillors, but it is not Armageddon, and everyone is thinking about the Coronation anyway. We lose some vital councils like Medway but gain others like Torbay and Wyre Forest. We do brilliantly in N Lincs, prompting Percy to remind me where councillors work bloody hard, the result is people will still vote for us. No one can blame RS either so we should be able to get them back, especially those who are 'protesting' by supporting Liberal Democrats, Independents or Greens.

And critically, a 7% swing from Conservatives to Labour is not enough for them to win the next GE . . . Is it game on?

It all fades quite quickly as the news moves swiftly to the

Palace reception for foreign dignitaries and of course, to the 'main event'. As I return home around 9 p.m., my passage is blocked by rank upon rank of uniformed services, starting by County Hall and snaking all the way back to the main entrance at Waterloo Station. It is the final dress rehearsal and is quite a spectacle. Senior NCOs, boots and buttons like mirrors, line up the ranks, snapping out orders to cold-looking bandsmen and nervous-looking officers. I doubt it was much different in 1952.

Saturday, 6 May

Coronation Day. I've opted for the civilian not military dress as the latter leaves me feeling far too self-conscious and in danger of suffocation. I leave the flat early to assemble with the rest of the Cabinet in Westminster Hall. It's lucky I do as the bridges have closed, making progress through the crowds and police a nightmare. Never have I been happier to see Robert Jenrick or even Nadine Dorries. Charles Walker was there too, so excited, he explained to me, that he had put his pants on backwards that morning.

So, at the appointed hour (9 a.m. for an 11 o'clock kick-off) we head over to the Abbey. Lines of immaculately dressed people queue patiently at every door. Ushers know exactly who is going where and have clearly worked every hour to create a seamless procession. Joanna Lumley waited her turn, as did Stephen Fry and Ant and Dec. For some strange reason I greeted Ant and Dec like old friends. Maybe I thought I knew them. Anyway, they handled it better than I did. I'm in a fantastic seat in the choir which is as close to the action as it's possible to be without being either Royal or Clerical. Opposite me were Karl Jenkins, Bryn Terfel and Andrew Lloyd Webber. Slowly it dawned on me what a historic British and global occasion this is, and I was there. Every leader, former PM, minor and major Royal swept passed us. Trudeau was cool, Prince Harry cut a lonely figure, Boris

was, well, just as expected, Carrie striking, Drakeford likewise and Humza [Yousaf, Scotland FM] looked like he was hosting a barn dance. But none of it mattered.

The procession of all the officials and their obscure titles was something only Britain could do. Charles looked serious, Camilla mesmerised, and Penny Mordaunt stole the show as the bearer of the sword, in a magnificent dress she designed herself. She is terrific. Rishi's lesson was faultless and the music – from the Byzantine Greek chants to the gospel choir – was the best in the world. Bryn Terfel sang in Welsh and as the choir left (they put in a heck of a shift) the whole congregation applauded them.

The Archbishop declared 'Long live the King' and it felt for a moment all was well in the world. What an extraordinary thing to be able to say, 'I was there.'

Once out, Hoare, Quin, Tugendhat, Spencer, James, Williams and I went to lunch in St James's, struggling to make any progress at all across the park as crowds milled about and demanded pictures with us.

Tuesday, 9 May to Thursday, 11 May

It's all about REUL and the apparent unwillingness of Kemi's team to properly engage or take people seriously. There are grumblings 'on the right' (aren't there always?) so we agree to meet Kruger [East Wiltshire] and his gang in the lower Whips' Office to see if we can find common ground. Marcus Jones and Michael Tomlinson appear for moral support as well as expertise, so the line-up consists of Bill Cash, Mark Francois, JR-M, Simon Clarke, Priti Patel, Nick Fletcher [Don Valley], Miriam Cates [Penistone and Stocksbridge], Craig Mackinlay [South Thanet], David Jones [Clwyd West] and inevitably John Redwood. It was turbulent, each one outdoing the demands of the one before. At the start I said I would listen rather than

speak, which was just as well, as I've seldom heard such a long list of clearly undeliverable demands. These are experienced politicians of many years' service, but they seemed oblivious to the numerical realities of what they were demanding. They think they represent a mainstream view, but they cannot command a majority, which is the only thing that really matters. Afterwards, I took Kruger back to my office and explained in words of one syllable why I thought he was dicing with death. Our Party will die if we don't face these people down. Of course, none of this was helped by Kemi winding them all up but that does not alter the fundamentals. I go and have dinner with David Davis who talks much more sense on the issue. To think he used to be the one people thought was the 'far right' of the Party. I've seldom seen a starker example of why we need to alter our candidate selection programme.

Monday, 15 May

A large group of Ministers meet to puzzle out Gove's Renters Reform Bill, a proposal that stands the unique chance of irritating the remaining segments of the Party who are so far un-irritated. There is a feel of anti-Conservatism about it, and of course, many of our colleagues are landlords. However, we can't ignore the fact that renters also need protection. As we've already voted to delay until the next session (called 'carry over') it may well wither on the vine.

Michael has mastered the art of appearing thoroughly engaged whilst completely ignoring the argument. But he does it with charm and humour, so we forgive him. A mistake.

There is a Conservative Democratic Organisation meeting in Westminster at which various Conservatives speak – including the Home Secretary – I'm assuming without anyone's consent. Basically, it's another group of right-wing fundamentalists who are dragging the Party into unelectability. I think we are in

last-chance saloon with her and a few others. They are not the future, added to which they are not even that good.

There is a UK 'Farm to Fork' summit at No. 10 just after Cabinet. The PM has insisted on it as he is increasingly baffled that we seem to be annoying farmers, usually amongst our most loyal friends. It's a rather good event and the NFU seems a little warmer to us, even if they still don't really 'get' Thérèse Coffey. Kaleb Cooper and 'Cheerful Charlie' from *Clarkson's Farm* were there and did a decent job making the case. They are superb advocates, and now the show is such a success absolutely everyone wants a bit of them.

Have a meeting with Mark Francois in which we try to find some common ground. He is not malevolent in any way. In fact, we have fun, as we both have a Reservist background. However he is defeatist, which is a contagious disease if allowed to go untreated.

Oliver Dowden is the chosen one for PMQs as the PM is in Japan. Olive, who has been focusing on little else for days, was understandably nervous but did well. He landed an absolute zinger on Starmer's stand-in, Angela Rayner, early on. 'When they told me I was up against the deputy leader of the Labour Party I assumed it would be a Liberal Democrat,' he joked, a reference to recent news reports about a Lib/Lab pact. Much guffawing ensued and poor old Angela (to whom humour seems to be a dirty word) never really recovered.

The storm over the Conservative Democratic Organisation intensifies. There are now numerous messages of dismay heading my way about Suella, and from the sensible wing too. Unless we

move, this will all rub off on the PM and frame him as weak. If we do move, we will trigger a wave of confected outrage from the Right, who will describe it as some kind of Remainer conspiracy (forgetting of course that RS voted to leave).

If we are going to take action, we need to move before she does as next week's migration figures look rough, and we don't want her using that as a platform to walk.

Thursday, 18 May

Liam Booth-Smith convenes me, Rupert, Forsyth, Julian Smith and Craig [Williams] to discuss the 'Suella problem'. As ever LB-S is on the money by stating we need to move from 'damage limitation' mode to much more daring politics and with some new faces around the table. We float the notion of dropping a weekend media story about a 'performance review' of the whole Cabinet, giving us cover to 're-assign' the Home Secretary and trigger a far-reaching reshuffle, probably around the week ending 21 July. I produce the one I've been toying with as a starter and we kick around a few names. Michael Tomlinson is a popular option, respected by the Right and the Left, and doing a great job in some challenging areas. Is it too soon to bring back Raab? He's a solid performer, as are both Liam Fox [former SoS] and even David Davis.

When we are done, LB-S whispers in my ear that this meeting 'must never have taken place . . .' making me worry the PM may be about to be blindsided, which we know he hates. But we have to start somewhere, and one thing is for sure, when we do meet, the PM will have expected some prep to have been done.

It transpires that lawyers acting for Boris in the Covid inquiry have unearthed sixteen examples of breaches of Covid regulations, over and above Partygate. They include hosting family lunches, on one occasion the same day as telling the nation they could not leave their homes. Given this possibly constitutes an

offence that meets the threshold, the lawyers have no option but to share this with the cops. As is also correct, the civil service has no option but to pass this to the Privileges Committee.

I later discover the committee was at this stage split on the 'sentence' but agreed on the verdict (guilty) for their inquiry; this is now likely to lead to a recall vote and therefore a by-election.

If this happens, do we allow him to stand as a Conservative? What are the risks? What if he wins or loses? Every possible scenario is damaging and divisive.

This has come up now because Sue Gray was asked to only look at parties, not other breaches. Boris resolutely maintains 'no rules were broken' but once again this is getting very, very messy.

Saturday, 20 May to Sunday, 21 May

A story appears in *The Times* that Suella Braverman attempted to use the civil service to get a one-to-one speed awareness course rather than join in with a bunch of other reckless drivers. Quite rightly the service has refused. It's now blowing into a 'thing'. Colleagues who don't care for her much are livid she has again shown scant regard for the Ministerial Code, and her apology was that the Home Secretary 'regrets' what she did rather than being actually apologetic.

The PM is on the way back from Japan but the very least we should do is refer her to the Independent Ethics adviser as we have an opposition debate heading our way and HO Orals this week. Labour and the Lib Dems are sharpening their knives.

Monday, 22 May

Meeting with Bill Cash on the crushingly dull subject of REUL. He had spent the entire weekend ringing people to pester them, so I wheeled in Tomlinson to help manage my blood pressure, something he is fast becoming adept at doing. At eighty-three

years old Bill is a mix of benign elder statesman and mischievous
time waster. I will be patient for a little longer.

Off to the Chelsea Flower Show (thank you Lloyds), where
I discover most of the Party with a glass in their hand. Hague,
May, Rudd, Mordaunt and others plus a few better-known types
like Clarkson, Fogle and of course the King and Camilla. On
every avenue of the show lurks a waiter armed with a large bottle
for top-ups which was a dangerous precursor to sitting next to
Jon Sopel [journalist] at dinner. I have no idea what I may have
told him, but it can't have been interesting, or maybe he is very
discreet.

Tuesday, 23 May

An average Cabinet followed by meetings with Robin Millar
[Aberconwy] and Tom Hunt [Ipswich] on immigration and
REUL. Robin and Tom are both earnest, and especially exer-
cised about immigration issues, both legal and illegal. They are
also sensible, and I think understand there is no silver bullet and
whatever we propose has to get through both Houses.

Wednesday, 24 May

It's the 'Big Day' for REUL which concludes with at least six votes,
all of which are complicated. Tomlinson does well at the dispatch
box and our vote is carried with a majority of 60–80 with NO
rebels at all. This is not a stroke of luck, I immodestly explain to
everyone. We have spent months speaking to colleagues collec-
tively and one to one. We have persuaded, forced, bribed, cajoled
and pleaded with colleagues not to fall into the trap of gifting a
victory to Labour and opening old EU wounds in our own Party.
The media did its best to talk up the scale of a rebellion, with a
little help from Francois inevitably, but sense prevailed, which
was extraordinary given the noise everyone has been making.

It's another great whipping success, but this one down to quiet diplomacy and painstaking engagement by Tomlinson.

Jubilant, it was off to the rooftop garden of Carmelite House for [former SpAd] Cleo Watson's book launch for *Whips*, a political Jilly Cooper for MPs, most of whom had turned up to drink someone else's champagne. Cleo was in her most mischievous mood, largely refusing to confirm on whom the raunchiest characters in the book were based. Tim Shipman was chuckling about how she had managed to get onto unlubricated sex on page one. Gripping stuff.

Thursday, 25 May

We had to pull the Margaret Ferrier [Ind., Rutherglen and Hamilton West] suspension motion as MPs were lining up to save her skin. Our colleagues do behave strangely at times. Ferrier had been found guilty of a major Covid breach when it was discovered she had travelled to Scotland on a train after testing positive. The SNP withdrew the whip, meaning she continued to sit as an independent, despite being encouraged to resign by Nicola Sturgeon. She was then arrested in 2021 and charged with 'culpable and reckless conduct'. Fast forward and she found herself suspended by Parliament for thirty days and at the wrong end of a recall petition.

I had to tell the GCS driver to stick to the speed limit on the M4 as he was doing 112 mph. I fear I am becoming very irritating, or certainly irritable.

Tuesday, 30 May

An 'all dayer' at No. 10 with James, Rupert, Craig and Julian mapping out what could be the July reshuffle. Basically, it's an exercise in 'ruling in' and 'ruling out' certain people before we get anywhere near the PM. Whatever we do will be the visible

face of the Government for the next (and maybe even the last) period up to the GE. It was, as ever, irreverent, hilarious, risqué and I hope effective, if it ever actually happens. I had a draft we started with, and which got rid of Suella Braverman, Wallace (who wants to depart of his own accord), Thérèse Coffey and Barclay (this was No. 10's scalp not mine).

We planned moves for the whole HO team and butchered the MoS and PUSS ranks, getting rid of the deadwood, and bringing in new ones to more visible roles. Coutinho to CST, Jacob Young to DLUC. We floated whether to move Mitchell in favour of Leadsom to rebalance the gender numbers but he is considered a safe pair of hands on FCDO issues so I know that will make little further progress. We question putting Mordaunt in a more prominent and demanding role such as Health or even back to Defence, but anticipate the PM is happy with her current role.

It was a mammoth job but better to do the basics now, so we are ready when the PM presses the button. By 7 p.m. we retired to the pub, for too long.

Monday, 5 June

Meeting with an inconspicuous red waller; defeatist, negative and uninspiring. Some of these people are no Thatchers, that's for sure, yet they often cite her as their inspiration. Then a meeting with Jerome Mayhew [Broadland and Fakenham], son of former Attorney General Sir Anthony Mayhew. What a contrast.

The PM is off to Washington so the machine has time to cool down a little.

Sarah Atherton [Wrexham] drops in to tell me she has pulled out of 'New Conservatives' (a right-wing evangelist splinter group led by Danny Kruger) because of her concerns about their funding sources as well as their fundamentalist zeal. At their recent meeting in Kruger's house Suella spent all evening in a bedroom with John Hayes – and an anonymous funder. Nothing

untoward implied, just odd they never joined the other guests. Sarah has made a wise choice.

Wednesday, 7 June

Harriet Harman calls by to tell me her committee will publish the Privileges report into Boris on 29 June and hand it to him on Friday at noon. It will recommend a 20-day suspension, which will almost certainly result in a recall motion and by-election. Brace for impact.

Thursday, 8 June

BJ is in Lagos but starts phoning everyone to find out whether they know what he is going to get. CCHQ is on by-election alert too. Jo Churchill [Whip] is also hearing of further complaints coming in about an unnamed MP.

As Boris's resignation Honours List is imminent this is relevant. It looks like the original list has now been revisited by his team and a final version is doing the rounds and is the subject of plenty of media speculation.

No. 10 (and the PM in particular) make it crystal clear to me that they will not interfere. In other words, this will be Boris's list, not Boris's list 'as edited by Rishi Sunak'. This is made similarly clear to BJ. I also remind the relevant hopefuls of the rule that stipulates that peerages cannot be assured more than six months out from an election and, as none of the four MPs currently lined up for peerages are stepping down, this option is not currently available.

BJ now rings me repeatedly from Lagos demanding information I simply don't have.

Back in a world of things that matter, the DC trip is going well for RS and he – we – are being taken seriously again.

Friday, 9 June

I speak to BoJo again who is questioning whether there is any procedural route by which we can kill-off the Privileges Committee report or at least vote it down. In any normal circumstances a former PM asking for special treatment would be a big deal but this being Boris, it doesn't surprise me at all. Worryingly, it doesn't even annoy me that much either.

So, I remind him, as nicely as I can, that it was he that set this process up, he who approved its terms of reference and he that accepted Harriet Harman as its Chair.

'But I was in India and I wasn't concentrating,' comes the reply. 'I left it all to the whips.' Not sure that will wash, even if it was true. After all, we all know he thinks this whole saga is irrelevant in the general scheme of things.

As ever, he has convinced himself he is the victim; we were all wrong and that we should all acknowledge we 'owe him one' for our 2019 election victory.

The Honours List saga is slowly progressing. Most people understand the complexities, although others are less sanguine about their last-minute disappointment.

Then Nadine Dorries calls – several times. She clearly does not grasp the very simple convention in relation to the six-month limitation period however many times I tell her. And she is not short of threats either, including a promise to 'reveal all she knows about RS' and to 'oust Simon Case', both of which can be averted, she assures me, if she is reinstated.

She repeated the 'Why have I been taken off the list by No. 10,' question numerous times, despite my insistence, with evidence, that this is not what has happened. As far as she was concerned this is all one big establishment conspiracy, the origins of which lie in a deep-seated misogynist mind-set that also preju-dices against people like her who have 'come up through the ranks'.

She asked if she would remain automatically entitled until the next GE (no) or if she were to resign totally whether she would get it (again no). So, she resigns her seat in a massive tantrum, and we have a by-election in Mid Beds, all because she considers she was promised (or owed) a seat in the House of Lords. The expression 'unfit for public office' comes to mind if for no other reason than she is now putting colleagues, volunteers, the Government and others, including voters, into an incredibly toxic position without a care in the world. Her constituency officials get in touch expressing, amongst other things, significant relief.

And then by 8 p.m. and in a 1,000-word essay BJ goes too. It's an extraordinary bit of prose, every sentence dripping with exasperation, disbelief and only loosely based on the facts. In one way I'm quite relieved. He has many attributes, is immensely likeable and amusing company. I know one day we will realise that whilst we have parted company with someone who had unique leadership skills, he also lacked a few of the essential ones to succeed in today's politics.

The weekend will be lively!

(I also get a polite note from Dame Andrea Jenkyns saying that she has been diagnosed with ADHD, a relief, she added, as this 'explains my tendency to say what I think every five minutes'. 'And I thought it was because I was a northerner . . .')

Saturday, 10 June

Nigel Adams and I speak as he has decided to resign his seat also, but with great decency. So, we have three by-elections heading our way.

Sunday, 11 June

To London (again) for a meeting with the PM and team. We know we have three by-elections but a fourth is also possible.

Our preference is Thursday 13 July, so that means moving the writs on Wednesday. Greg Hands is charged with making the plans with the Local Authorities and I will see to the House requirements with the Speaker.

Nadine Dorries in the meantime is digging an even deeper hole. She seems to think she can now shoehorn her way onto Liz Truss's resignation list (without Liz apparently knowing anything about this). To achieve this, she submits a written threat to agitate, coerce and persuade civil servants, poor Simon Case in particular, to adopt her plan. She does not seem to realise the considerable risks attached to the use of such pressure in order to leverage an honour. She seems too obsessed to realise her other threat 'to hold out until the election if needs be' is exactly what we all would prefer.

However, the PM is in good form and greeted me with a large hug. The general view of colleagues is that BJ is buggering up his response to the Privileges Committee yet again, probably on the back of poor advice.

Tuesday, 13 June

Drinks with an affable Simon Clarke who whilst very pro BJ is minded to abstain on the Privileges Committee vote. This is the effect on colleagues that these acts of self-indulgence are having.

Wednesday, 14 June

PMQs was preceded by me moving the writs for BJ and Nigel Adams's seats. I managed to get the 'de Pfeffel' out without a hitch and there were just a few sarcastic murmurs from Labour. That was the easy bit as it seems CCHQ may have fucked up the dates, with the Local Authorities squeezing us into the 20 July date rather than our preferred option. This is the last day before the recess and messes up the reshuffle plans.

Embarrassment over in No. 10 as the PM goes on a 'dawn raid' with Border Force with a view to getting some 'man of action' photos of the PM arresting some illegal immigrants. Everyone lines up as planned and hammers down the doors only to find the bleary-eyed occupants had all the correct permissions and paperwork. Whoever in the Home Office signed that off needs a quiet word. They never miss a chance to fuck up.

However, a party in the No. 10 flat for Cabinet partners was a great success and Akshata was a great host. Abi reports it was like going through the looking glass as you enter via the work lift and pass open-plan offices with printers in the corridors. Then through an unremarkable door and into what feels like a luxury hotel suite with thick carpets, Diptyque candles and smoky mirrored walls. There were a few personal photos dotted about and Akshata made a heartfelt speech about how 'cruel' politics can be, especially for the partners.

Friday, 16 June

Michael Naughton, our candidate in Selby, has had an unforeseen family emergency. The poor bloke has to withdraw so we are searching again.

(P.S. However, given he once worked for Abramovich and a Polish fascist, it may be just as well. According to the new normal, parliamentary candidates can at no stage of their lives have ever done anything remotely interesting or risqué, or made any kind of error.)

Saturday, 17 June

We hear David Warburton [Somerton and Frome] will resign on Monday ahead of the ICGS finding him guilty of various sex and drugs charges.

Sunday, 18 June

If we are quick, we can move the writ on Monday and have the by-election on the same day as the others. At least we might as well condense the inevitable agony all of this will cause.

Monday, 19 June

The only story in town is the vote on the Privileges Committee report. A lot say they will abstain, and it turns out that's what happens. 360-odd vote in favour (including 120 Conservatives), 7 against, who now all look rather stupid. As the PM was unable to vote both Craig and I voted in favour.

There were some sensible speeches but also some curiously tone-deaf ones, Lia Nici [Great Grimsby] being the most obvious. It's not their opinion that is the problem, but we all voted in favour of dealing with the matter via this committee working to these terms of reference. However, BJ keeps his dogs at bay so it becomes a relatively calm occasion.

Tuesday, 20 June

Political cabinet was okay (but flat) so today's drama is seeing off Priti Patel's amendment to the Finance Bill. To be fair to her she is proving to be a model colleague, and we quickly strike a deal which averts any need for a divisive vote.

Lunch with Alok Sharma. I like him but he wants the peerage promised to him by BJ guaranteed and a golden ticket! Golden tickets are granted to the PM, Home Sec and occasionally Foreign Sec, allowing them to skip votes in all but emergencies. It's a bold ask by Alok but we agree to reaching a discreet and flexible arrangement.

Wednesday, 21 June

Opposition day on Kept Animals. I was expecting trouble, but we didn't get it. Maybe that's why.

We defeated the Labour motion and our amendment was passed with no vote against. So off to Michael Ellis's birthday party at the Goring Hotel which was very typically Michael. Various flunkies from the Royal Household, former PM Theresa May, current PM Rishi and the Cabinet Secretary for good measure. Michael has spent months working on the guest list and is a generous host.

Thursday, 22 June

News Corp party at Spencer House. I looked over the balcony to spot Nadine Dorries holding forth about her peerage, so after bemoaning the state of the nation with the thoroughly decent Tristram Hunt [former Labour MP], I made it a brief stay.

Monday, 26 June

Gove briefs us in the Whips' Office on Renters Reform. Everyone still hates it and we are therefore nowhere near a good place. Michael is compelling, and most likely right, but that's no good if our people have stopped listening.

Meetings with various colleagues such as Natalie Elphicke [Dover], Jo Gideon [Stoke-on-Trent Central] and Joy Morrissey [Beaconsfield and a Government Whip] confirm this lack of enthusiasm.

Dinner with Alun Cairns, one of life's most energetic, cheeky and thoughtful colleagues. Alun has done a long time in elected politics and was SoS Wales for three years. He is also an astonishingly good marathon runner. Everyone loves Alun, except it seems No. 10, who are not forgiving his moment of madness

when he deserted Camp Rishi in favour of Camp Truss. He seeks forgiveness and rehabilitation, and is genuine, but I am not optimistic.

Tuesday, 27 June

Dinner with James Wharton in the Lords. Splendid as ever. The requests for peerages from Commons colleagues are now coming thick and fast. I reckon we are getting two a day. Some attempt to be subtle, from the old favourite of 'so many of my friends have mentioned it, I feel I would be letting them down if I didn't put my name forward' to the more wheedling, 'But Boris promised me'.

Adam Holloway [Gravesham] puts the boot into Tugendhat too. Nothing like former servicemen for a bit of aggro.

Thursday, 29 June

Train from King's Cross to Selby for the by-election. We have demanded maximum presence. It feels like voters are pissed off with us but unlikely to vote Labour quite yet. More are likely to stay at home or grudgingly support us. Hence why the polls are 50:50 at the moment. I am far from convinced that flogging round empty streets knocking on doors makes any difference. Most people are out, for a start, and those who are in are rarely in the mood for a chat that might change their voting intention. I reckon the lifespan of any literature we leave is the time it takes to pick it off the floor and chuck it in the bin. There must be a better way, I am just not sure quite what it is.

Pressure builds around the Foreign Divestments Bill too, resulting in us having multiple battlegrounds, very much not what we want at the moment. The Bill seeks to stop Local Authorities having their own foreign policy in relation to places like Israel. The best example is in Wales where Welsh

Government has banned LAs from using JCB owing to evidence that some of their kit gets used to demolish property in Gaza. Added to this, the Privileges Committee has named several members in their contempt report for using language that suggested the committee was either a kangaroo court or in some other way invalid. This will mean another vote and even more tension.

The quicker we can move to a reshuffle and a new session the better.

Monday, 3 July

Issues with the Foreign Divestments Bill continue, mainly because Israel is named in the Bill, and is dividing the Party, quite passionately. Oddly, the most controversial bits have gone unnoticed, but since it became public I have had yet more delegations of colleagues. Gove has done some limited engagement, but it may be enough to play the 'it's only a second reading debate' card and get away with it for now. This we do and beat the Labour amendment by 60 and pass the Bill 198–2.

Tuesday, 4 July

Cabinet on NATO but not without a speech from Jenrick, the content of which was fair enough, even if its length was a bit unnecessary. Meeting with Brendan O'Hara, the sanest and most amusing SNP member and also their Chief Whip. Like many of the SNP he is invariably clad in a thick tweed and the sort of brogues you could go stalking in, but he is keen on the whisky, so we retire to the Pugin Room to start a rumour just by being there. He was incensed to have been physically manhandled by his gobby SNP colleague Angus Brendan MacNeil and intends to settle the score.

Then off to see John Benger and Eve Sampson [senior Clerks

of the House] about amendments to the Privileges Motion. They gave the impression (in their very particular civil service-style) that Mr Speaker will be advised to 'reject all amendments', meaning backbencher attempts to be mischievous will be thwarted.

Wednesday, 5 July

To the *Spectator* summer party in Old Queen Street where the great and the good were gathered – PM, Nigel Havers, Grayson Perry and every MP and lobby hack you could mention. Unlike previous occasions there were no fights.

Thursday, 6 July

The Standards Committee publishes its report on Chris Pincher, concluding with a 40-day suspension. He is finished. On the face of it, the sentence seems unbelievably harsh given he has lost his job, all his money and most of his friends. On the other, maybe we are all discovering that 'squeezing people's arses' is not acceptable, however fleetingly, or however drunken the circumstances. For some generations, this will come harder than for others, especially in this place.

There is a worrying build-up of colleagues talking of low morale, lack of vision and hopelessness. The PM is also picking this up. He needs a break and a lucky break also.

7

CONFRONTATION

July 2023–January 2024

Nothing galvanises SW1 quite like a reshuffle rumour. All hell breaks loose. Existing ministers fear they will be sacked or moved, aspirational backbenchers agitate for a 'turn on the carousel', and former ministers argue that what we need is some grey hair back around the Cabinet table (i.e. them). For the Prime Minister and Chief Whip, reshuffles are a moment to make a small number of already happy people even happier, and a large number of slightly grumpy people even grumpier. We seldom disappoint.

By now we had quite a lot of experience of these things and knew that the faintest rumour would be seized upon, and our lives would be a misery as a result. We also knew that nearly fifteen years into a term of office our gene pool was running quite low, especially if we were to maintain our diversity and gender targets. In other words, we had reached the stage where we knew we would be making appointments on criteria other than purely talent. Added to that was the realisation amongst MPs that this would be their last opportunity. Miss out this time and there was a good chance they would never get their hands on a coveted red box or arrive grandly at a destination in the back of a black GCS Jaguar. Why not therefore agitate for a change of leader and hope the next one would look on you more favourably in return for your support?

But where reshuffles work, they work well. The return of

David Cameron was an inspired move by the PM and his Chief of Staff, Liam Booth-Smith. The whole project was spread over a matter of days not weeks, and to our total amazement nobody leaked. No. 10 kept quiet, the Cabinet Office, HOLAC (as Cameron had to be rapidly ennobled), and my office all kept schtum. Even David himself, who can be talkative, managed to keep it quiet right up until he stepped out of the car in Downing Street, taking the press by storm.

Much more confrontational was the departure of Suella Braverman. It was never going to be easy, but what happened raises questions about reshuffles more broadly and how they create an everlasting headache for whichever PM is in charge of them and our criteria for high office in particular.

We changed the leadership in the MoD, always a big deal, and started to get more strident warnings from Alex Chalk in the Ministry of Justice that we were running out of prison places fast.

And amidst all of this Dr Lisa Cameron of the SNP defected to us.

By now we were bleeding, but we were still standing.

—— • ——

Monday, 10 July 2023

Things are heating up in the Illegal Migration Bill [IMB]. It looks like we will get a raft of stuff back from the Lords and multiple votes are on the cards. Tim Loughton [East Worthing and Shoreham] is batting for the moderates and knows the clock is ticking so holds out for a deal. We just need to get this done. It's not a hill worth dying on.

Tuesday, 11 July

And so, it happens, eighteen consecutive votes starting at 5 p.m. and to conclude by 8.30. We think this could be a possible all-time

record. We face down Tim and win all of them with majorities between 42–76. The lower numbers will almost certainly be seen as worth another push by the Lords and so it will come back again. The challenge with these vote-fests is there is just enough time between votes to slip back to Strangers or the Pugin for another quick one. With each circuit the mood changes, and generally worsens, as MPs get more tired and emotional.

The Whips' Office Admin Unit (run by a very good team of civil servants) reports Suella's office has this morning applied for a slip to miss the vote in order to go to the opera. There are gasps of incredulity across the whips team. In our world this is an unbelievable request, akin to a leading actor missing the opening night to go to the pub. This is her (controversial) Bill, which comes with an expectation, and long-held custom, that the Cabinet Minister responsible is there throughout to comfort and thank colleagues for putting in a lengthy shift and for voting in some cases against their personal beliefs. Her cheeky request is soon buzzing around the office and the lobby. The slip was rejected of course, and Suella is present throughout, claiming it was all a misunderstanding caused by a junior diary secretary. Our records point to a different cause.

I'm just over Westminster Bridge and nearly home. It's about 10 p.m. when Suella calls me, initially to thank the team for delivering the votes (which is good of her, to be fair) but then to get stuck in for what she calls a high-level leak about her opera plans. She promises (threatens) an HO leak inquiry, all of which is ironic given her own department's long history of extensive leaking. I refuse to concede it was the whips behind the leak as numerous people were in the loop including her own advisers and team. I expect this won't be the last we hear of it.

Wednesday, 12 July

Craig seeks me out and worryingly suggests a meeting in secret on the balcony of No. 1 Parliament Street. I've seldom heard him so worried so make immediate arrangements. We meet in the lobby, take the lift to the top floor and go onto the very plush balcony overlooking Whitehall and Parliament Square. Being Craig, beer is on hand. It turns out he has acquired intelligence to the effect that there are 'people close to the PM' who are thinking about bringing Cummings back in from the cold. For a range of reasons, Craig argues, this is mad. It shows panic, breaches promises RS has publicly made and will trigger absolutely everyone in a negative way. The close teams are all against it and they need me to step in. The problem is, I don't officially or unofficially know and to acquire this info would reveal a breach of confidence. We agree to speak later.

BBQ (a good one) at No. 10, spirits were quite high considering the expectation we will lose all three by-elections next week.

I'm back in the flat when Rupert Yorke calls to summon me to another secret session, this time at the County Hall Hotel at 11 p.m. to consider the Cummings problem. RY, Craig, James F and me. The PM has now been alerted to the idea but wants to speak to me tomorrow.

Back to bed by 1 a.m.

Thursday, 13 July

I eventually see the PM and others at 6 p.m. to discuss the reshuffle, about which he clearly needs some persuasion. He is nowhere near where we are, that's for sure. We defer the DC chat to the phone tomorrow.

Friday, 14 July

PM (or Pam as he's now known thanks to spellcheck) and I have a 40-minute call. We spend five minutes on bringing back Cummings (he recognises the concerns) and 35 minutes on the reshuffle. Understandably, he wants to be certain we have stress-tested all the plans for a potential upside before we move. So, it could be next week, or next month . . .

Monday, 17 July

It looks like the Cummings proposal is already dead. Thank God for that. I am not sure how serious it ever was. It felt like the PM went through the motions of considering it but never felt that it was sensible or that the Party would swallow it. We move on to the second round of ping pong on IMB [Internal Markets Bill] and a mere nine votes all of which we win between 50–90. Better than last week which should head off any further noise from the Lords. It does, and they capitulate with a day to spare.

Tuesday, 18 July

PM very happy with the IMB outcome as is the whole Cabinet. Extensive reshuffle work (I think we are on edition 20) just in case he wants to go next week, but I think it's looking less and less likely. He clearly is not ready. However, he is in much better form and starting to agree with us again – a good sign.

Wednesday, 19 July

First PMQs for a bit and he was a different man – back to his best. Then a good speech at the '22 as well so somehow his mojo is restored. He wants to meet later so we reconvene at 8.45 (dodging the lobby drinks in the garden in the process) where

he effectively sinks the reshuffle idea at least until September unless Suella resigns on Friday (which she won't). At least it is a decision.

It's about 9 p.m. and we are mid-meeting in the PM's office when his phone rings. We sit in silence as he has a rather oblique conversation with someone in which he tells them to, 'take the package to the black gates halfway up Whitehall and someone will meet you'.

Faintly alarmed, Rupert asks him to explain and it turns out to be his Nando's order as he hadn't eaten all day. Rupert reminds him that as PM he can ask other people to do that kind of thing, but he seemed rather hurt by the suggestion.

Friday, 21 July

A chance one-to-one with the PM so I broach the whole issue of the future of my seat (which is a casualty of boundary changes). He seems okay with my idea of applying for other seats – we shall see. He is adamant though that all Cabinet members must be up for fighting the election. Alister is the exception, because he has announced already and there is no obvious alternative SoS Scotland ready to step in. But the rest of us are lashed to the mast.

It's recess, so we have lunch at Gordon's and collapse.

August – recess

All a bit too peaceful. PM off to Santa Barbara, California, everyone else to their own destinations, including us to South Africa for a couple of weeks. There was a time when the Whips' Office would acquire the destinations and emergency numbers for all MPs during recess, in case of the need to recall Parliament, but that is no longer done, and I have no intention of reviving it. It's so much harder to trigger a recall if we don't know where anybody is . . .

Otherwise, it's just the usual August media, football, wild-fires and the disturbing case of Lucy Letby, the children's nurse accused of mass murder. And then it's the botched 'small boats week' in which the fifteen people we manage to put on a barge had to come off due to an outbreak of Legionnaires' disease. HO useless as ever, but quite why we want to make a media spectacle of a challenge we don't seem to be able to crack, I will never know.

PM seems to have gone lukewarm on the idea of a September reshuffle – will this ever get done?

Tuesday, 22 August

A quick trip to London to advance the reshuffle – or at least the Wallace part of it. PM seemingly energetic and refreshed but settled on Oct/Nov reshuffle with a quick reset now to deal with the MoD as Ben is anxious to go. Or so we thought. The PM's preference is for Liam Fox or possibly Shapps to go to Defence but there are still question marks around Liam's last departure from Government [from the Dept of Business] when he was accused of improper use of private email addresses by Theresa May. He very reasonably maintains his innocence, but we are paranoid about this sort of thing these days. The PM hates the risk that every time an appointment is made someone rakes up some historic question mark over their propriety which then backfires on him and his judgement. At this rate we will make no progress at all.

Thursday, 24 August to Friday, 25 August

I declare the reshuffle officially chaos. Too many cooks and a dollop of indecision. Everyone is whispering in his ear and no two bits of advice are the same. I need to speak to the PM over the weekend and explain again he is in danger of looking weak

and untidy unless this is gripped. Either that or park the whole project.

Saturday, 26 August

Nadine is 'smoked out', thanks mainly to slowly building pressure locally and nationally. However, her resignation letter to RS was the very worst example of why our candidate selection process is so flawed. Bitter, chippy, delusional, paranoid, vicious and vindictive. It was the perfect example of how not to show a bit of class or depart with honour. In fact, it was a terrible example to other colleagues and the wider public who already view us with a great deal of scepticism anyway. Luckily, it was so awful no right-minded person would be swayed by it.

Wednesday, 30 August to Thursday, 31 August

And back into reshuffle mode we go. At last, we have agreement – of sorts – between us all on who is replacing Wallace at Defence. Fox is finally out of contention as are Mordaunt, Anne-Marie Trevelyan, Tugendhat and even, for a few short seconds, me as I made one of those last-minute desperate suggestions just to try to conclude the process. Quin [Horsham] has been in strong contention throughout and comes with the support of numerous colleagues. As a former Procurement Minister he knows the department and is solidly loyal to RS. The PM fancies him in another role and thinks that Grant may have a more versatile media role to play too. So, Shapps it therefore is, with Coutinho to Energy and David Johnstone [Wantage] in as PUSS to Education. The thinking is Shapps has run multiple departments. He can come across to some as almost too smooth and hence may not appeal to the military traditionalists. However, we think he will administer competently, won't

use the role to undermine the PM and might introduce some new thinking to this vast spending department. Claire is a RS loyalist, good on the media and her appointment sends a clear statement of intent, which is: 'if you are good enough, you are old enough.'

So, with the prep eventually done we do the formal stuff tomorrow. Off to the pub with the team for one last rehearsal.

Friday, 1 September

New positions are announced. Reasonable reaction internally and externally and a slight scepticism about Grant. Otherwise, colleague feedback is reassuringly muted and neutral – even from Francois and Chope [Christchurch] from whom I expected opinions, whether invited or not.

As ever in No. 10 I then get sucked into other meetings to discuss the abolition of smoking, the cancellation of HS2 and the impossible conundrum that is conversion therapy. It never stops.

Monday, 4 September

All go re the Energy Bill* with Sharma (who like me, gets angrier with age) and Clarke (polite but not 100% reliable). They are pressing all the onshore wind buttons again. They will probably get their way but it won't change much.

1922 reception on the Terrace which is better than usual. The PM gets the tone about right. We always fear some kind of mutterings among disloyal colleagues but they never quite materialise.

---

* The Energy Bill sought to deal with issues of production and security, CO_2 transport and storage as well as hydrogen production and transportation.

Tuesday, 5 September

Cabinet about India which fits into the 'dull-but-important' category. A bit of eye-rolling between Jenrick, Mercer and John Glen [Salisbury] when Grant spoke so we will need to alter the seating plan in time for next week. We can't risk a naughty corner at the moment.

Glen – a decent man – has convinced himself he was in the running for Defence Sec but was then done over by No. 10. He was never actually an option, so perhaps we should have been clearer with him at the outset instead of leaving the possibility open.

Dehenna Davison is desperate to step down and plan for her future outside Parliament. Unless we are careful, she will go anyway and it will look like a desertion.

Wednesday, 6 September

PMQs was a surprise success for the PM, in fact a great one, given we were wrestling with the RAAC concrete scandal. Anything built with this stuff all those years ago is now falling down, resulting in important public buildings like schools and hospitals having to be closed. Needless to say, it is all our fault although whilst apparently a catastrophic scandal in England (under our Government) it's barely worth a mention in Wales (under a Labour Government).

To a very entertaining *FT* party in the Strand where I had to separate Craig and veteran journalist Robert Shrimsley who were having a row about concrete.

Monday, 11 September

Another week, another writ. This time it's Pincher for whom I issue the last rites. One or two colleagues get rather sad letters of

goodbye from him which worries both Andrew Mitchell and me. Friends in the form of Simon Hoare [South Dorset] and Michael Fabricant thoughtfully volunteer to offer support.

Tuesday, 12 September

The Cabinet agenda is 'Winter Preparedness'. Given what is happening, this feels quite low down the risk register at the moment. Even a Chinese spy entering Parliament doesn't get a mention.

However, the latest three ideas, to scrap GCSEs, abandon HS2 north of Crewe and abolish smoking seem to be gathering pace. We also appear on the cusp of a reasonable deal with Tata at Port Talbot.

Thursday, 14 September

Lunch with Michael Ellis at the Goring, which was as delightful as ever. Michael is a kind man (as well as generous!) but longs to be the Attorney General again. He would be rather good of course, but I am not sure the stars will align in his favour any time soon. Michael always prides himself on being a politician and a lawyer, not the other way around. It's an important distinction.

DLUC sources apparently brief the *FT* that the Renters Reform Bill is being stalled by whips as we are all landlords and have a vested interest. It's generally deemed as being a wankerish thing to do and is extremely counterproductive should they need help getting this Bill through. We may have some landlords (me included) but we do have professional standards too.

Thursday, 28 September (and thereabouts)

Back from Scotland to a frenetic day in No. 10. LB-S needed to nail Alex Chalk down on prison numbers which he did with

some skill. However, Alex is clearly having sleepless nights as the system is just a few places away from total collapse, yet a vote on early release (the only solution . . .) will be impossible to win. We buy a little time, but that's all, and we are probably making the issue harder in the long run.

Conference planning with RY and the whips team. A rota of spying and reporting is set up. We will have eyes and ears everywhere listening for the faintest whiff of challenges, or letters to Brady, insurrection or rebellion. We will be in bars across the conference area to ensure drunken colleagues get home on time (and alone) and journalist honeytrappers identified and outed before they can ply their trade. We will meet every morning for a full debrief and then deploy a process of aftercare where necessary.

I bump into the PM and talk about the reboot of the TV show *Frasier* – of which he is also a huge fan. He likes *Friends* too and says a bit of light-hearted comedy helps him relax. He should read my whips notes if he wants a laugh at night.

Suella has screwed up again, this time making unnecessary and clumsy references to gay people in the asylum system. As ever she manages to put her foot in it and offend another group of people who look to us for understanding. Less than 2% of asylum seekers cite their sexuality as the cause for their application, so why does she do it? Answer: because she is fast becoming a glove puppet for the 1950s wing of the Party.

I get to see the early version of Rishi's 'big speech'. It's a good, well-thought-out and intellectually compelling offering, but for some it will be seen to lack real political sex appeal. It deals with HS2, smoking and education thoughtfully. It's hard to disagree, even if it is a speech that highlights three things we don't like and fixes them rather than providing the 'big vision' some of our colleagues keep banging on about.

News reaches us that Craig Mackinlay is gravely ill in hospital with sepsis. Surely not another by-election? It sounds like a

50:50 situation at best. Adam Holloway is keeping us abreast and is a godsend to the Mackinlay family.

Sunday, 1 October

Any Party Conference is my worst nightmare. I travel up to Manchester with Craig from mid Wales during which the Government driver made much of having overheard my conversations about Grant Shapps being appointed Defence Secretary the week before: 'I reckon I was one of the few people in the country who knew he was getting the job and could have made a fortune down the bookies.'

I know they can't help but listen to our calls, but it's not unreasonable to expect them to at least pretend otherwise. As Mark Garnier once said to me, 'They should behave like a long-standing butler in a decent country house.'

Then to an endless round of receptions, each with an even worse selection of wine and nibbles, in soulless conference rooms dotted around the 'secure area'. Apparently, the purpose of Conference is to make money (I am told they clear a million quid profit), although we always claim they are family occasions for the great and the good to come and get involved in the sharp end of policy-making. Nonsense from where I was sitting. Almost everyone there these days is a lobbyist, stakeholder, journalist or some other poor sod who is armed with the company credit card. The PM dutifully did the rounds – Scotland reception, Wales reception, Young Conservatives et al. Each requires a grand entrance to cheering (and mainly inebriated) supporters followed by a short, funny and identical speech, after which he is whisked away to repeat the process somewhere else. He was good in the ones I was at, and I think unexpectedly enjoyed it. Whether he will still be as upbeat in a few days' time I doubt. Emma had worked the system so I am staying in the main conference hotel where we argued the 'whips operation'

needed to be based. The PM presence is a full floor of the hotel, into which the entire CCHQ/No. 10 operation appears to have decamped.

Braverman's upsetting of the LGBT supporter base means RS is rapidly running out of patience. So bad is the situation it was almost impossible to find a venue in the city to host our LGBT reception. Wherever it is to be held, I make it clear I will be going, along with some No. 10 bods, to show solidarity.

But the main talk is of Wednesday's PM speech and what is in or out of the latest version. James Forsyth is doing great work on the words, and we have a pre-speech handling plan to head off the potentially disaffected.

First, a thorough media operation by No. 10 and a carefully selected team with a clear objective – to ensure positivity is spread far and wide. It goes well and certainly gets the mood of the building in the right place.

Then, the line-up for the speeches. It would start with Penny Mordaunt, still a Party heroine for her Coronation sword-bearing triumph, followed by Johnny Mercer, our resident veterans champion, next Akshata Murty, then RS.

Penny kicked off with a flamboyant attempt to work the crowd into a frenzy of 'stand up and fight' type theatre. She did her absolute best, but the audience was not really in the mood and whilst receptive, stopped short of euphoric. Johnny surprised us all, and himself by all accounts, with a first-class and authentic performance, after which Akshata was genuinely warm and engaging.

Foreplay complete, RS landed all three of his policy announcements with intelligence and clarity. Members were chuffed we had some real substance, and even the smoking ban landed okay, despite our fears it might provoke some audible groans from the libertarians. Rupert, James and I lurked in the wings, scanning the audience for visible signs of dissent, for facial expressions that might spell trouble or for that conference 'protester' to

make their move. We were untroubled. I noted that every one of my suggested speech amendments has been ignored!

Given that Boris is history and Truss failed to make much impact and other leadership wannabes were muted, the verdict was a 'job well done'.

It was back to the suite on floor four for much hugging and sandwiches and some very relieved choreographers.

Monday, 9 October

All hell is breaking loose in Israel and Gaza. Mass bloodshed seems inevitable and will reignite the intense passions in the House between supporters of Israel and those who still harbour pro-Palestinian tendencies. The Conservative Friends of Israel [CFI] have become a huge part of the Party family so the politics of this are far from straightforward.

Wednesday, 11 October

To a wet Tamworth to make a speedy by-election appearance, followed by London to try and progress the conversion therapy stuff to an acceptable place as well as move the next reshuffle into a manageable starting position. Neither fill me with confidence.

News reaches us that the nicest of the SNP MPs Dr Lisa Cameron wants to defect to us. I hear it's something Gavin [Williamson] has been working on for some time (he is never far from the action) along with Alister and others. It's a welcome surprise but I'm not sure it will resonate widely. Colleagues take a dim view of defections, even the rare ones that come our way. But Lisa is well liked and has been bullied by her own Party so there is a chance it could work. RS quite rightly stops short of offering any preferential treatment otherwise the whole thing will start to look a bit grubby.

Meanwhile over in the Ministry of Justice Chalky's nightmare continues with prison places getting used up so quickly that by next week we could be forced to let some villains out prematurely.

Monday, 16 October

But he did well when it came to the Chamber operation. Fluent, persuasive and effective, a strong finish to a saga that started badly. It's only a temporary success though, as the truth remains we are banging people up in greater numbers than we are releasing them. We are building new prisons but too slowly, and we are all petrified if we let out the bad guys it plays into the hands of those who think we are a bunch of liberal apologists anyway.

Coffee with Dr Lisa Cameron, fresh from her SNP defection. It's hard to see how she ever signed up to all the independence stuff in the first place. She really isn't the type and she seems to be relieved to find her natural home at last.

Tuesday, 17 October

Seventeen consecutive votes on the LURB [Levelling Up and Regeneration Bill] a sure sign, as Theresa May reminded me rather pointedly, of a poor piece of legislation.

Thursday, 19 October

By-election. The experts predict we will lose both, probably not by much but by enough to create panic. The PM will be in Israel and Saudi which is probably just as well. We will manage the heat our end.

Sunday, 22 October

The *Mail on Sunday* runs a story placed by some of our more evangelical colleagues that I'm trying to bring them down or to 'rid the party of the evangelical right' is I think what they said. In some ways I wish it was true. The longer I do this job the more I realise that 'right' and 'left' are descriptions that trigger misgivings in the minds of a voting public that is still, in the main, quite centrist. Whilst the wings of the Party might hoover up the enthusiastic support of the like-minded, there is never enough of them to win an election.

Later, veteran MP Peter Bone [Wellingborough] rang to say he is about to be suspended for six weeks (triggering yet another recall petition) for bullying a young lad in his employment over the last ten years or so. He says it's all a bit of a misunderstanding, but the allegations included the suggestion they shared a hotel room together ten years ago whilst on a trip to Madrid. Peter is sixty and the lad was not yet twenty-five so the claims he exposed himself and had a habit of making the lad sit with his hands between Peter's legs as punishment for wrong-doing will eliminate much chance of any public sympathy. He was very calm and utterly convinced of his own innocence. Anyway, as per usual, whip suspended.

Drink with Matt Hancock in the Pugin. He wants the whip back and, to be honest, there is no good reason not to give it to him.

Wednesday, 25 October

An urgent summons to the Speaker's office (which is never a good sign) especially when head of Commons Security Alison Giles is there too. The news is that Crispin Blunt [Reigate] has been arrested for rape, incitement to rape and possession of Class A drugs. Will this ever stop?

Crispin is a former Guards officer and uncle to actor Emily Blunt. The Whips' Office cannot think of a more unlikely perpetrator of this kind of crime, thus already revealing a degree of unconscious bias.

We are told to keep quiet until more is known so we will take no action until tomorrow when he will lose the whip. As the media is reporting the arrest was made by Surrey Police, grossly unfair online speculation is it could be one of the other Surrey-based MPs, so we need to close this down quickly.

PMQs was fine (all about Israel) and we saw off Kit Malthouse's Foreign Divestments rebellion* with ease. Kit has strong family reasons for adopting his position and at least has the decency to explain in advance what he is planning and why.

Dinner with PM in the upstairs dining room in No. 10, with me, Craig, RY, LB-S, James, Julian and Lisa [Lovering]. I was whacked by Covid so poor company, but it was a civilised event even if RS was as knackered as I was. I think he might even now be content with an autumn reshuffle, or not.

Tuesday, 31 October

To No. 10 for Cabinet, to agree the King's Speech, and some associated planning. (I still have lingering flu or Covid.) Amongst today's HR joys is the report from Emma that a departmental SpAd went to an orgy over the weekend and ended up taking a crap on another person's head. To make matters worse, in a separate incident a House employee went to a party dressed as Jimmy Savile and ended up having sex with a blow-up doll, for which he has been subsequently dismissed. Just another day at the office, I guess.

---

* Kit was a consistent and passionate opponent of the Bill, despite it being a manifesto commitment, and had attempted to gather opposition to it at each Parliamentary stage.

Wednesday, 1 November

Word reaches me (via Andrea Jenkyns) that John Howell [Henley] has not been seen all day and failed to make it to a pre-planned meeting with his girlfriend this afternoon. Everybody is concerned as JH is extremely steady and 'going dark' is not his style. The Met goes round to his flat at about 7 p.m. and reports no lights or noise – an unhelpful observation as this is why we asked them to go round in the first place. Later, with the help of the Speaker's Office, we deploy the House Security and the Met plus Andrea to gain entry, having first checked he had not used his pass to access the estate (which he hadn't).

By midnight we discover he was in the flat all along having had a serious stroke and been unable to call for help or move. So off to hospital he went. Full marks to Andrea and John's girlfriend in acting quickly and efficiently.

In the meantime, the Middle East blows up, Elon Musk and co make an appearance at the PM's AI summit and more reshuffle rumours are in the air . . .

Monday, 6 November

Drinks reception with the PM. Looks like the reshuffle is ON. Suella Braverman is now pushing her luck even further, but RS is a master at not letting himself be goaded.

Tuesday, 7 November

The King's Speech, the first one by a King for seventy years. The procession from Commons to Lords, via a crowded Central Lobby, is led by the two Party leaders, followed by the Chief Whips. Well, that's the theory but I was neatly elbowed out of my place by Father of the House Peter Bottomley. As for the

speech itself, it was reassuringly dull and contained nothing to spark either excitement or dismay.

Off for a drink in Gillray's in County Hall with Anna Mikhailova [*Mail on Sunday*] who is sniffing around reshuffle rumours. As it happens, we are now in advanced reshuffle mode with a view to execute on Monday 13th, or possibly Tuesday. The Gaza conflict gets uglier and uglier, and the London protests more lively and more violent.

It looks like the centre has now eventually concluded Suella has to go. The reshuffle therefore hinges around who takes over from Braverman – Cleverly, Barclay, Harper [SoS Transport], Badenoch are contenders. Or do we bring Shapps back in after only a couple of months in the MoD?

Looks like Thérèse Coffey may have run out of road also, so the question is whether we replace her with Mark Spencer or Steve Barclay or Victoria Prentis or even Victoria Atkins – we even wondered if Mel Stride would work?

They are keen to move Greg Hands from the Party Chair role to make way for Holden [North West Durham]. Greg is good but the dynamic doesn't quite work with No. 10 and they want it humming in time for the election.

Thursday, 9 November

We are nailed on for reshuffle on Monday so the weekend is cancelled.

The big bombshell is RS has approached David Cameron to make a return as Foreign Sec and he has, subject to detail, agreed. This is huge news, sends a very clear message of seriousness and gravitas around the world and the Party. The Right will be sceptical, but no one can deny DC is a big beast and the fact he is prepared to endorse RS so publicly will impress all the right people.

Secrecy is at its highest level. Dowden is therefore deployed to make sure DC doesn't accidentally let anything slip to his old

mates like [George] Osborne, and he – DC – also needs time to wind up some business and charitable work.

Braverman then decides to put out an op ed that is not approved by No. 10 and contains highly provocative statements about police bias in handling of pro-Palestinian protests. It's an open act of defiance and surely must come at a price this time. The HO claims that the speech was 'submitted' but No. 10 retaliate by confirming that it was not 'cleared'.

The PM is livid. He feels let down and offended by someone he has gone out of his way to rescue on more than one occasion. I, on the other hand, am not remotely surprised.

Friday and Saturday are spent in London planning extensive moves. Eight people will leave, five will return. Cleverly will be asked to No. 10 on Monday and offered the HO, which I think he will take, but others are not so sure. He should, few people get to be both Foreign and Home Sec. As we need to maintain our gender targets Vicky Atkins will come to DoH [Dept of Health], Barclay to Defra (at which point Spencer will go nuts).

The appointment of DC remains, surprisingly, a total secret.

Saturday, 11 November

A huge pro-Palestine demo in central London seems clumsily managed by the police. They seem incapable of arresting Hamas sympathisers who are saying the most outrageous and provocative things, therefore increasing the tension and likely violence. The PM is irritable about it all and we are all in no doubt Suella Braverman has made all this much worse than needs be. In the end there are a couple of hundred arrests.

Sunday, 12 November

Remembrance Sunday. The first challenge is to get in and out of the back door of No. 10 without being seen, on the one day

of the year Horseguards and the back of Downing Street is alive with veterans and photographers. Our plan being we would shut down our reshuffle before the 11 a.m. service, and then spend two hours with the PM from 12–2 p.m. to get the logistics in place for Monday morning.

The service was fine, none of the threatened demos or interruptions from the likes of Tommy Robinson or other right-wing headbangers – I stood behind David Cameron and Tony Blair and chatted with Sadiq [Kahn, London Mayor] and Keir beforehand. DC is clearly itching to say something (but doesn't). Starmer really is as steady in real life as his public persona suggests. His great strength is that he looks good and isn't actually mad. Tony is always delightful, despite clearly having no clue who I am. I guess he is like this with everyone, which is why he was as effective as he was as PM.

We return to No. 10 where 'operation reshuffle' is in place, including our favourite bit of kit – the whiteboard. The plan is to see Cleverly in the flat tomorrow at 7.30 a.m., move him to the Terracotta Room at 8.00, and lock him in with [Will] Tanner [Sunak's Deputy Chief of Staff], call Suella at 8.15 (we can't call her in to do it face-to-face as she will resign before we can sack her). We then need to release Suella's hard-working PPS, Tom Hunt, and lock down their access to HO IT straight away. We'll get the new appointments out, followed by DC at around 9ish. We will then decamp to the Commons.

This complex logistical planning takes until 11 p.m., and we agree (wearily) to reconvene at 6 a.m. on Monday.

Monday, 13 November

5.30 a.m. We sneak in through No. 70 Whitehall and get going. I think Rupert may have slept the night in G39. Cleverly agrees to HO (this is mission critical). We park him with Will T and LB-S in the Terracotta Room, and then RS rings Suella. Initially there

is no answer, but then she rings back, and after some token pleas-
antries all hell breaks loose. He puts her on speakerphone in the
White Drawing Room upstairs (Mrs Thatcher's study when she
was here) and everybody is listening in around the large circular
wooden table, laden with discarded notes, open packets of
No. 10 biscuits and half-drunk cups of coffee. RS in the chair,
LB-S, Dowden, me, RY and various SpAds and essential civil
servants.

The first minute or two goes okay and then, once RS had
made clear his intentions, came this ghastly 10-minute diatribe
of vindictive and personal bile. It's hard to know how to react at
moments like this, or where to look. Part of me feels that this is a
private call and that we are all eavesdropping, but the other part
realises that for the protection of the PM and the Government
there needs to be a note taken and a record saved. Suella knows
this too. So, we sit in astonished silence, doing our best not to
grimace, smile or give any indication of what we feel. The PM's
script is polite but firm. The theme is that they have done their
best to make the relationship work, but that it is proving harder
for both of them and that's why, alas, it's time to recalibrate and
for her to move on.

If ever there was an example of her unsuitability for the
office of Home Sec – for *any* office – it was her response. RS
was far more polite than most of us would have been, but he
was clearly exasperated that someone whom he had saved from
the political abyss – at least twice – could be quite so vindictive.
We move on.

Her sacking announced, Cleverly was then appointed. And then
for the big moment: into Downing Street comes an innocuous-
looking people carrier. The media pack had absolutely no clue
what was coming until the door opened and out DC strolled, as
confident a swagger as ever. It was an absolutely golden moment,
made all the sweeter by Sky's Beth Rigby's stumbling response

to this unseen bombshell. A comment about his weight was as much as she could muster.

As the PM and I watched the 'return of David', on the office monitor inside, we both comment, almost ruefully, on the way he so naturally rises to such an occasion and how his star still shines quite brightly.

To the Commons, then, where we sacked Thérèse Coffey (who was excellent), Jeremy Quin (gets a knighthood to sweeten the deal), Rachel Maclean [MoS Housing] (awkward). We moved Hands (a tough conversation given his very long period in some difficult roles) and Barclay (fine). I felt sorry for Quin. A few weeks ago, he was in line for Defence Sec. Today he is out of Government. Then back to No. 10 where all the newbies were appointed, and the old stagers moved or sacked.

The operation went well, but with eight sackings and five retirements we will get some pushback. There were necessary jitters in No. 10 about it being a bit too left wing, but they will settle, I hope.

One minister, always emotional but bright too, saw his (really good) offer as a demotion but took it anyway. Craig and I had to listen with a straight face as he explained why he thought we needed to keep Rishi in place as otherwise: 'I will have to lead the Party and be PM and I don't want to do that.'

Other MPs – about a dozen – were also totally unrealistic about their chances, and a few – Dr James Davies [Vale of Clwyd] for example – are rightly a bit sore. It's a crap system . . .

Tuesday, 14 November

Cabinet – lots of happy faces but it was DC who commanded the room without saying much or in any way wrong footing RS. 'I'd forgotten how good he was . . .' Shapps says to me.

Braverman publishes a letter dripping with poison and hatred. I think she has gone way too far this time. We are seeing the real Suella.

To cap it all we have votes on the King's Speech, including an SNP amendment on a Gaza ceasefire which results in six Labour front benchers resigning. However, we hold on without losing anyone to that lobby . . . unquestionably the most challenging week so far.

Wednesday, 15 November

We vote on the King's Speech which as expected, and is the custom, went without a hitch, despite the SNP pulling a stunt with a vote on Gaza (an amendment to the KS and therefore a 'confidence' matter).

Persuaded or slipped anybody with significant concerns although Paul Bristow [Peterborough] was in a pickle, mainly because he had made some very public pro-ceasefire commitments a couple of weeks back. He is very troubled by it all, but we just about found a landing point, which enabled him to abstain.

Monday, 20 November

A week's work of stress counselling has been carried out by the whole office for those who missed out on the reshuffle but were convinced they were in for something. To be fair, most were okay, notwithstanding different levels of disappointment. Some were more decent than others, Quin and Higginbotham [Burnley] in particular. It doesn't matter how much 'pitch-rolling' we do, human nature is such that there is always hope, and therefore always disappointment. Others were less decent, and as I've come to learn surprisingly entitled and opinionated.

Sarah Dines disappointed me the most. Nobody is owed a job in this world, especially those who have not exactly gone out of their way to embrace the Sunak cause.

Went to collect DC from New Palace Yard as he doesn't have

a pass yet and he needed to get to the 1922 Committee weekly
meeting. He has lost none of his slickness and was brave in
the way he shot down both Kruger and Gullis on immigration
points in front of a full House. It was done decently though, and
whilst he treated their questions with respect, he dismissed their
arguments clinically.

Dinner with Tom Tugendhat, who worries we are being
dragged into an unelectable position out on the right.

The AG [Attorney General] and Justice Secretary have
become very wobbly about where the Rwanda legislation may
end up. Neither is convinced it will enable us to deliver our
commitment on time. I agree the road ahead is perilous and we
therefore set up a Small Ministerial Group [SMG] for Saturday
afternoon.

Off to the Wyre Forest patrons' dinner as a favour to Mark
Garnier where it seems his supporters are like members everywhere else, mightily pissed off by the infighting and pleading for
unity. They are not the least troubled by policy.

Saturday, 25 November

The SMG on Rwanda with a cast list that includes the PM, me,
AG, Justice, DC, Cleverly, Jenrick et al.

We sort of end up in the right place – namely a workable Bill
but will the old ERG faction agree? They never normally do, as
their desire to discomfort Rishi always exceeds their desire to
deal with the problem in hand.

Monday, 27 November

Dr Caroline Johnson [Sleaford and North Hykeham] comes
to berate me, in a semi-decent style. She's a strange combination of very disappointed yet highly intelligent. Her purpose, to
raise the two key questions of 'felching' and solar panels, two

topics that rarely feature in the same sentence, and which after checking Google left me more bemused than usual. Apparently, she explains, the rather unusual practice of felching is being taught to kids who are too young to be subjected to that kind of thing. The good doctor is on the warpath so I promise to raise felching (and solar farms) at the highest level.

Dinner with Quin and Alister Jack in Boodles. JQ is recovering his mojo.

Tuesday, 28 November

Lunch with Penny Mordaunt in Members. She is worried about the long-term future of the Party, as am I, if we keep capitulating to the lunatics.

The reality of the division Rwanda could cause the Party is gathering pace. No. 10 is being increasingly spooked by the noise, mistaking it for numbers.

Wednesday, 29 November

The mood is pretty poor at the moment. The polls won't budge, and the reality is dawning that other incentives, honours, jobs and baubles are running out too.

So, we set up the Wednesday Club WhatsApp group. It's formed of Cairns, Quince, Goodwill and Jupp – sensible backbenchers all – whose job is to seek out, identify, and report on pockets of resistance or panic. To be fair, this happens anyway, and the whips team is always on the receiving end of high volumes of intel, in which nuggets of gold are concealed. So, they are not snitches, but rather experienced hands who can spot a problem.

PMQs was grim. Rishi was unusually disengaged. He seemed more tired than ever and struggled to muster the energy the session thrives upon. Equally unusually, Starmer was rather

sharp and goaded Rishi about the Elgin Marbles – Rishi having cold shouldered the Greek PM on Monday. It was probably his worst session, but his bar is high. Every PM has one off day, but colleagues can be brutally intolerant.

To the *Spectator* Parliamentarian of the Year award at the Rosewood. Always a jolly affair, but the speeches were poor – Shapps is normally pretty good, but even he couldn't get the crowd going. Suella decided to double down on her 'hate march' rhetoric to a room full of left-of-centre political commentators triggering a predictably muted reaction. But, of course, it was the video montage of David Cameron that stole the show.

Thursday, 30 November

Liam, Oliver, Craig and James meet to discuss the PM's morale and Rwanda. Not a good sign . . . Our job is to help, but we all feel we could do more to help bolster the PM.

Never has a week felt more like the end of time. Everything we try to do is met with one group of colleagues or another rising in opposition; the media amplifies every mistake into a drama; the only reaction that is allowed any more is one of outrage. The polls give Labour a comfortable lead, irrespective of their lack of alternative ideas and even the reaction of voters locally is one of pity, along with the implied suggestion that it's 'someone else's turn'.

Monday, 4 December

From left-field comes the issue of infected blood, a terrible scandal in which – during the AIDS crisis – innocent people received transfusions of infected blood. Now, many years later, they have rightly won compensation.

But the Government is pissing about with the minutiae which is being seen as a delaying tactic, so Labour's Diana Johnson

puts down an amendment which gets loads of Tory and cross-Party support. All day we wrestle both with colleagues and James Nation [deputy head of the policy unit in No.10]. Our numbers for the vote are not great and heading the wrong way.

Stuart Anderson [pairing whip] predicts we will be 'in the red' by mid-afternoon unless we can do a deal. The logic is crazy. We have to do this, we should do it, and we will do it, so why is the department buggering about, asking MPs to vote against something we will end up doing anyway? James Nation is a fantastically clever operator, but even he cannot get the agreement we need. The clock is ticking.

It also transpires no one has spoken to Diana herself, a first-rule failure for any handling plan. At around 7 p.m. I seek her out and offer a deal which she rejects (and I don't blame her) as it is now far too late in the day.

We are going backwards with colleagues, and Stuart thinks it is now far too close to call. Ed Argar [Prisons Minister] will be winding up for HMG, and he needs to know what the hell he is going to say.

We make little progress with colleagues, and eventually reach an agreement with the department at 8.30 p.m. – which we should have reached at lunchtime. I rush over to the Chamber to inform Ed A, who handles the new policy position with great skill.

We lose the division, to mighty cheers from the opposition, by 4 votes. My unbeaten record is destroyed, and this is a humiliation we could so easily have avoided. More seriously, it makes us look ungovernable. This was not complicated, and we were right in assessing the impending outcome several hours earlier, but wrong in prolonging the negotiations.

Rishi is displeased, as am I.

Tuesday, 5 December

Cabinet, including a sarcastic comment about whipping from Esther McVey. Just what we need.

Wednesday, 6 December

PM much better in PMQs – there is still fight in the dog. Jenrick resigns, citing disagreements over immigration policy, which is pretty rich given he has been largely responsible for working it up and implementing it. There have been endless calls and meetings between him and the PM, most of which have involved him [Jenrick] layering on the charm. However, the truth is now out. Rather than help the PM see this through and delivered in the strongest form that Parliament will allow, he has run for the hills, presumably to put some distance between him and the fire.

Saturday, 9 December

To Liverpool for the weekend, just as Rwanda starts to heat up. We are told it will be the likely trigger of a huge right-wing rebellion. I'd never been to Liverpool and was in two minds whether to go. Despite my appallingly bad company at times like this I desperately needed to step outside the bubble and where better than the Dee Estuary in a gale?

Sunday, 10 December

To No. 10 to crunch the numbers for the Rwanda vote on Tuesday. Hoodies and trainers are the order of the day for RS and others. Stuart and Emma came as the numbers whizzkids, and I just knew the PM would feel confident that they knew

what they were doing. In fact, a Stuart and PM 'nerd-off' on voting trends is a great spectator sport.

It becomes clear that for Rishi this is a confidence motion, even if we are not saying as much publicly. Lose this, and both he and HM Government are on the way out.

Monday, 11 December

The stakes could not be higher. All day we speak to MPs, triage them, discuss concessions, and count numbers again and again, and then again. Stuart is as calm as a cucumber.

Our position improves a little as a few peel off to abstain, but the combined efforts of the ERG, New Conservatives, the NRG [Northern Research Group], etc. can topple us, especially as all the opposition are against, and, most crucially, present.

Alister keeps us abreast of Kemi Badenoch's attempts to sow seeds of doubt. Luckily, she's no match at all for his cunning so we can see her a mile off. Whips' operations are as intense as I've ever known. Francois is in Central Lobby claiming to 'have the numbers', but has he? We are dead certain ours are reliable.

Tomlinson does great work, and Ranil Jayawardena also enters the market for a deal. Francois storms into the office and starts bellowing, especially at our female staff as I'm not there. He comes across as an intemperate, angry little man. And to think that he was once a minister and a whip and was helped through challenging times by Julian Smith in the then Whips' Office. Why behave like that?

The PM thinks we should do whatever we have to to secure the vote, short of removing the whip.

Tuesday, 12 December

R-Day – our position improves, helped by an unfounded rumour (started by Alister I surmise) that the whip will be withdrawn

from those who vote against. It's not true, but it's a good story to have in the wind.

The PM warns Cabinet 'there will be consequences' for any payroll [ministers] who fail to support the Bill. (At one stage Sky wrongly reports I'm currently at an 'emergency meeting with the PM' in No. 10. Incensed, I stroll into Central Lobby and accost Jon Craig, the source of this myth. He didn't seem remotely concerned that my presence destroyed the entire basis of his story.)

However, Stuart A and I go back to see the PM at 5 p.m. to give him the good news that we think we will win by 20, even though the DUP is not supportive.

We then hear the rebel armies are capitulating and abstaining. We are there, I think. They have blinked first.

At seven the division bell goes, and amongst intense interest we win by 44, with NO Tory rebels. It is our best result to date. It's not the policy that matters (half the Party hates it) but the fact that we have no doubt saved the Government, and will live on to 2024. Rishi hugs me in the Chamber. We saw off all attackers, with little or no bloodshed.

So, despite all the noise, the threats, the lies, the anti-Rwanda activists have once again reminded us they just don't have the numbers, even if they shout the loudest. Although the Party remains badly split and the future is rocky, we have won a crucial battle.

Rishi comes to visit a rapturous Whips' Office (they have worked like dogs) and makes a heartfelt speech. In some ways this could keep Rishi safe, and it was us that did it.

Wednesday, 13 December

PMQs and the PM's drinks party in No. 10, a very different occasion to what might have been. We are all very, very tired.

Thursday, 14 December

My BUPA medical. Not quite the week for a blood pressure check.

Monday, 18 December

A very different atmosphere – no votes, no pressure, but a chance to decompress with a tired whips team. They have done well. They make a good team. Possibly the only real team in Parliament. But as the House prepares to rise for Christmas, there is no doubt the atmosphere remains unpredictable and brittle. If we can make it to February/March we might just be okay.

Friday, 29 December

Word comes I am required at a COBR meeting, so secret I have to be present either in person, or from a secure line in a government office 'somewhere in Wales'. So off we go to a drab building in the middle of nowhere, with spasmodic Wi-Fi and not much for me to add.

All that secrecy . . . but not sure it was necessary to miss a day shooting woodcock for that.

Sunday, 31 December

In an unsurprising development Dominic Cummings claims (in his preferred journal, the *Sunday Times*) that the PM offered him a job. Our recollection of events reads a little differently. There were discussions about options, the challenges we face and stopped well short of the 'sign here' moment hinted at in the story. For all his self-proclaimed genius, Dominic proves yet again it is all totally worthless if you cannot behave decently and carry people with you.

Monday, 8 January 2024

Back after Christmas recess to what seems to be a marginally better mood among the Party. We shall see.

I host a 'Monday night drinks' do in the PM's office for more than a hundred people. They are becoming more popular and provide just a nano-second of shared goodwill and good humour. There is an ancientness about this room. All oak panels and green leather. You can imagine Churchill or Thatcher sitting at the big oak table; so, as a drinks venue it takes some beating. Overall morale seems jovial, so I keep my speech light-hearted. It's noticeable how well our people respond to group therapy. We should do more of it.

Tuesday, 9 January

Cabinet photo op followed by a rather dreary 'catch-up'. Some one-to-one sessions on the Boycotts, Divestment and Sanctions Bill which continues to set colleagues against one another. It will pass but it's been a painful and divisive experience so far and I am not sure how much the public really care (actually I am, and it's sod-all in electoral terms).

I'm told Reform offered Scott Benton £10,000 to defect should he be kicked out by us following his Standards issue. Given that Blackpool is a key battleground for them it seems a rather paltry offer (which he sensibly declined) and which reveals quite how little money they really have.

To a wine-free catch-up with the PM at 7.15 for a general chat about his plans for the year and what we can junk and what he wants to keep. He seems quite bullish and practical and has, as always, thought through every detail. We agree that the test of every decision we make, legislative or otherwise, ought to be set against the question, 'How does this help us win the election?'

Wednesday, 10 January

Jonathan Edwards [formerly Plaid, now Ind.] popped in to talk about his trials and tribulations with his original Party. He has had a bad time of it and paid a heavy price, but it doesn't mean he isn't thoughtful, political and effective. This all started with a serious domestic altercation which resulted in a police caution.

Then a meeting with PM and others to decide on the Rwanda handling plan for next week. We have three options – full fat, semi skimmed and skimmed. We need some decent data before we can decide. To the Carlton Club for dinner with Justice Minister Ed Argar and his wife Tish. Ed is carrying the heavy weight of the prisons' crisis which gets more perilous by the day.

Thursday, 11 January

I move the writs for both Wellingborough and Kingswood (how many is that now?). The custom is you can't just resign your seat as an MP, you have to die, be disqualified or expelled. To be disqualified, so the Resolution of March 1624 says, you must apply for the 'Crown Steward and Bailiff of the Chiltern Hundreds and of the Manor of Northstead'. That short ceremony falls to me to play out with the Speaker just before main business of the day commences.

And then SpAd school in No. 10 where I was the 'entertainment'. This tradition dates back to Dominic Cummings, who deliberately held them at 6.30 on a Friday night to cause the greatest inconvenience. LB-S was a bit worried I might be too revealing. It was tempting, given the first question was: 'What's the most interesting thing you have had to deal with since being Chief?' I restrained myself, within reason.

Sunday, 14 January

It's all kicking off – the Rwanda third reading rebels are determined to sink the ship. They are being more unreasonable than usual. The once middle-of-the-road and boringly sensible Robert Jenrick even suggesting we bring back a new Bill. Is he serious? We can't even get this one through! For some reason he has been persuaded he could be a future leader, so his persona, values, hair and waistline have all been adjusted with this in mind.

Monday, 15 January

The whole week is now assigned to engagement on Rwanda. In other words, the whole of HM Government is being brought to a standstill by the usual group of about twelve people. Some are reasonable (David Jones), some evasive (Cash) and some downright awkward (Francois).

Tomorrow is likely to be sort of okay but thereafter it's anyone's guess. Most MPs I meet are cagey about their intentions, but I doubt will want to kill us completely. Tom Hunt even offers a semi-peace deal so maybe they are softer than they seem. He realises that endless niggling is pointless and damaging so if I find him a decent trade envoy role I think he will do his best to play nicely with us.

Tuesday, 16 January

Recent security news in the media makes mention of the vulnerability of politicians and especially ministers. It reminds me of a previous occasion which, as always, involved the 'experts' sitting at the opposite end of the table from the likes of me, the Attorney General, the then Cabinet Office Minister Jeremy Quin and Security Minister Tugendhat.

Me to Jeremy: 'Who's the young bloke sitting at the far end?'
Jeremy (deadpan): 'That's the director of MI5.'

What is it they say about police officers looking younger these days? Now it's the head of our security services.

From a Whips' Office perspective the most critical risk seems to be the Carlton Club bar.

David Cameron has also managed to have a spat with Gavin about Somaliland, but they have already patched it up a bit. Somaliland's recognition is Gavin's new mission in life and I guess he hoped for more from his old boss. In theory Somaliland is part of Somalia still but seeks recognition as an independent state.

Wall-to-wall Rwanda after that including a rather absurd meeting with Lee Anderson. He spells out all the things he wants in the Bill and why he must therefore vote for Jenrick's amendment – even though it doesn't actually do the things he wants either. He will have to resign of course, but I don't think either of us will be too worried by that. He clearly isn't a team player, sadly, as he does have a following of sorts.

Wednesday, 17 January

As anticipated, Anderson, Clarke-Smith [Deputy Chairman of the Conservative Party] and Jane Stevenson [Wolverhampton North East] resign or are sacked.

We meet the PM and rehash numbers based on a possible majority of 10 (way too close) but there's a long way to go yet. Most of the one-to-ones indicate abstention or support at a third reading even if not at committee. The rebels are wobbling again. I can smell uncertainty.

To the PM's Commons office for final summit to decide on whip removal or labelling the third reading vote as a 'confidence' vote. Full team on the pitch. LB-S, Rupert, James etc. We go round the room. On my advice we hold fire. The rebels are edging our way and I explain that issuing the threat now risks

creating a 'Spartacus moment'. This would create an excuse for the cantankerous to vote against us on principle alone. LB-S grins at me and mouths the word 'pussy'. It's a big gamble but sensing the direction of the tide is vital at moments like this. We must not panic.

So, we are heading for what looks like a 25 majority – ideal for now. However, the noise, clamour, tension (and bitterness) is palpable. Yet again, the pressure is as intense as anything I've known, but we cannot blink or give the slightest indication of nerves.

Mid-afternoon and we can see a landing place but just as we think we are safe we have a 'Houston we have a problem' moment.

At roughly 5.15, Philip Davies, ideally positioned in an 'enemy meeting' reports that they (Jenrick, Simon Clarke etc.) are colluding with Labour to collapse the debate early and trigger a standalone vote on 'clause 5 stand part'* – and if successful the Bill will be dead – and us with it. The No. 10 team joined us in the Whips' Office. There was a conspicuous lack of the usual banter. This was serious. We had a very short time, less than an hour, to put an operation in place and see them off. To be honest, we had no solution. We had not seen this, nor did we have a contingency. It was the first time I felt helpless and I was worried the whips team, already tired from weeks of emotional preparation, would feel as I did.

What a misjudgement it turned out to be. In the next 60 minutes I saw a side of my team that was nothing short of brilliant. There was no panic, no fluster, no doubts, just a desire to get the job done. Sixty rebels were called, reassessed and had quite a complex piece of legislative chicanery explained to them. And the clock was ticking. The rebels needed to know this was

---

*   The parliamentary expression that refers to a motion to retain a certain aspect (clause) of a Bill.

not just an ambush on the Rwanda Bill, but an attack on the PM and HMG. Lose this and we were in election territory.

Next door the civil service team worked out we needed to keep the debate going till 18.54 to ensure the standalone vote was avoided. Not a minute earlier, or later, would do.

I scampered over to the Chamber (trying to look suitably unflustered) to talk to the Bill Minister Michael Tomlinson and gave him emphatic orders to keep talking until 18.54. Often messages to ministers like this, part way through a debate, are misunderstood or ignored. His response – 'No problem, chief' – was as welcome as it was brief.

We then roped in speakers to pad out the time. Alun Cairns, former Welsh Secretary and good on his feet. Bob Seely [Isle of Wight], former military and safe under fire. Robert Goodwill [Scarborough], a fiercely loyal and effective Yorkshire farmer. Even Matt Hancock, still whipless but anxious to return, dropped what he was doing to help. And yet to the outside world the afternoon was simply playing out as planned.

On the dot of 18.54, Tomlinson concluded his wind-up speech. The Chairman Roger Gale (as this was a committee of the whole House) brought the House to order and the division bells rang out, signifying the moment of truth.

We had avoided the ambush and the crisis was not only averted but, as the rebel sixty came through the lobby with us, it seemed like it was all part of the plan.

And then the third reading. By now we knew we had them beaten. We contained the debates to keep the momentum and when the bell went only 11 voted against us. We won by a margin of 44.

The Home Sec, Michael Tomlinson (the hero of the hour), the Attorney General and the PM came over to a jubilant Whips' Office where the sense of relief was extraordinary. We all knew what this meant, and the price that we would have paid for failure.

None of this may change much. The polls will hardly notice,

and the threats and dangers remain largely undiminished – but it was still 'our finest hour'.

Monday, 22 January

Today is the day of the 'rebel army', minus Suella Braverman who is ill, coming in to see me, one by one. The script is not to remove the whip, but to assure them that our patience has worn out and that they are in last-chance saloon. It was civil (if frosty). I did feel a little guilty telling dear old Bill Cash that he was 'not a folk hero, but a pain in the arse'. The trouble with Bill (and others like him) is they are institutionalised. They just don't see their approach as being so fundamentally out of step with public expectation. He doesn't see that what they were doing damages colleagues and volunteers in particular.

The rest were sort of okay – but fundamentalist. Andrea Jenkyns arrived with her dog and her six-year-old son and then attempted to say that because she has ADHD, she 'couldn't be held accountable for what came out of her mouth'.

Jenrick suggested that 'Clarke is the problem' and that he was 'floppy and gutless'. He blamed Rishi for 'making unnecessary mistakes' without recognising the irony of his period of service under both Johnson and Truss, who he presumably now believes made no mistakes at all.

I doubt any of this dialogue will do much good but it does clear the way to finally axe someone. Rishi is rightly keen to set the bar high and not create martyrs. He sees them as needy, entitled and determined to achieve some degree of notoriety. We must resist the temptation to be goaded by them.

Tuesday, 23 January

I get a hand-wringing memo from Simon Clarke explaining why he is submitting a letter of no confidence to Brady, alongside a

Daily Telegraph opinion piece. We can't sack him for the former but colluding with the *Telegraph* raises an interesting question. We meet with LB-S and agree a response. I suppose I should be grateful that Simon has bothered to tell me in advance, although why he needed to 'go public' I'm not so sure. Many wouldn't have but he does have form when it comes to flapping. It wasn't many months ago that he was the first to break cover in Cabinet by calling for yet another Covid lockdown (with Gove in support). At least BoJo was having none of it.

As the story breaks (to accompany a questionable bit of polling) the whole Party gets stuck in – partly organised, partly spontaneous, but either way very effective. People are livid with Clarke. The pressure is on to 'deal with him'. We agreed to test the water on Wednesday morning.

Wednesday, 24 January

Extraordinary. By 9 a.m. the storm has blown through, the poll has been widely rubbished, PMQs goes rather well and Clarke has been made to look thoroughly out of step. So, we simply carry on. However, my guess is it's a temporary position. These people are still hell-bent on their kamikaze mission. They may dress it up as some kind of principled stand, but it becomes clearer and clearer to me that this is all driven by a desire to get rid of Rishi.

I see Brady just before the '22 photo. He drops a hint about the number of 'letters in' by telling me the press always 'double the numbers' and people tend to write to him as 'a last resort, not a first option'. Graham is the most discreet man I have ever met, annoyingly, but he exudes the demeanour of someone who isn't on the cusp of yet another execution.

Limping and bleeding, we fight on . . .

8

REALISATION

January–May 2024

Welcome to election year. If you are an MP, especially in a marginal seat, there is nothing on earth that occupies the mind more relentlessly than the realisation the public will soon be given the chance to kick you out. It fills every living moment of your time. For those who follow politics there were only really a few serious options for the election timing.

Although frequently reported as a possible option, May and June were complicated as they would overshadow the huge mayoral and council elections due on 5 May. August and September were out because of holidays and conferences, and there was little appetite to leave it until December. In other words, we had July, October and November to choose from.

As the weeks rolled by, the PM and others were less and less persuaded that 'things could only get better'. The chances of getting a flight off to Rwanda were slim. At some stage, the prison system would collapse, and we were facing vast payouts (quite rightly) to the victims of infected blood and Post Office Horizon scandals.

It was also the season for defections and conspiracies. The polls just weren't budging despite tax cuts, economic tranquillity and a raft of other (normally) important core election conditions.

We lost MPs Poulter and Elphicke to Labour in an extraordinary display of self-indulgence. The fact that they were

political 'nobodies' misses the point. We were damaged, every week there was another scandal or drama or honeytrap. Our majority was in reality less than 30, meaning our ability to get complex business through was compromised.

And we were picking up intelligence (of varying degrees of reliability) of leadership teams being formed around Mordaunt, Jenrick, Braverman, Badenoch et al. It had become a fight for survival.

Our job was to give no indication of fear or weakness. We chose our Commons business carefully to avoid creating any bizarre coalitions of the malevolent. We spread mixed information about reshuffles and potential election dates. The less certainty there was, the harder it would be for a well-organised attempt to defenestrate the PM to take hold. And we studiously avoided creating martyrs by resisting the temptation to hang them out to dry. There were plenty of colleagues lining up for their 'Spartacus moment'.

Some readers might spot the rather blatant absence of any reference to election date speculation, or the betting furore that followed during the campaign proper. Tempted though I am to correct the multiplicity of views, opinions and fiction that shaped the running commentary, it is still an unresolved legal matter. As such, the advice is to let the process follow its natural course. After that though, it is a different matter.

———— • ————

Saturday, 27 January to Sunday, 28 January 2024

It looks like a Stormont deal* is imminent. It will inflame the hardline Brexiteers, but then, doesn't everything? We must take

---

* The new arrangements under this deal allow Northern Ireland's businesses to access the same benefits and opportunities as the rest of the UK, while maintaining sufficient protection for farmers.

the win if we can although it all hinges on the DUP, Labour and a few of our Spartans. Multiple conference calls are required, most of which will be repeats of the one before and the one after.

Monday, 29 January

It seems no one much has the stomach for a fight. The DUP will support us and their deserters will be gagged. Labour will support as well and the SNP also, so victory (at least on this occasion) is ours. One of 'our chaps' has been approached by Reform to defect but is helpfully feeding all the relevant information back to us. The charismatic Richard Tice [Reform] continues to give the impression of an upper-middle-class tory landowner involved in a lifelong row with the neighbouring estate – in this case us. I haven't forgotten that twenty-five years ago he tried to do the same thing with the Countryside Alliance, which I was running at the time. He didn't like our approach to things so set up his own equivalent, 'The Real CA'. He tried to steal our members and champion more 'direct action' but in the end he got bored with not getting his way.

Cameron is in Israel again, but he has a tendency to give the impression of going off-piste on occasions which can spook the Conservative Friends of Israel [CFI]. Of course, what he is saying is sound and considered, but CFI are easily rattled at the moment by the risk of misinterpretation and who can blame them? Watching him at work reminds me that he is many leagues ahead of most colleagues when it comes to panache. He is made for this job.

Wednesday, 31 January

It was hard to concentrate on an okay PMQs or have a great deal of sympathy for yet another direct ask from one middle-ranking colleague about his knighthood. I mean the guy in question

is a decent bloke but I am not sure that he's yet met the PM's 'above and beyond' criteria. My already over-dangled carrot gets another airing.

Thursday, 1 February

Today we really are 'doing the honours'. Off we go to the usual rather nondescript room in the Treasury, accompanied by tea and biscuits and several dozen pages of well-written citation for four hours. We could do it in half the time, but we don't want to be accused of treating the process too lightly and Stephen [Lord Sherbourne] is an expert in soliciting everyone's view and nudging us to a conclusion that I suspect was largely settled before we even turned up.

It's a much feistier meeting than last time.

One prominent Labour MP seeking an upgrade to his knighthood gets defeated again – rightly. One of our chaps' CBE gets similar short shrift by the lay members. I really don't know what he's done but something he shouldn't have on a foreign trip by all accounts, so that's him done for.

But the rest eventually go through. Poor George Freeman [Mid Norfolk] has had a bad week. Somehow his very sound 'application' for a knighthood for 'services to science' got sent in error to 120 people on a public WhatsApp group along with an out of context reference to his being unable to afford his mortgage whilst on £118,000 p.a. Anybody who knows him will realise that he is a decent human being, but this irritates people, including the committee.

And then to the Londoner Hotel near Leicester Square for an 'awayday' session with Isaac Levido and his team. By and large these sessions are quite uplifting, but it was short notice and a Thursday so only 130 colleagues showed up. Lo and behold though, Tom Hunt, John Redwood and Adam Holloway were just three who gave the impression of a gradual thaw. Are they

at last accepting that we are not changing leaders? It's hard to tell with Redwood. I've hardly met anyone with such self-belief in his own economic and political expertise, but quite so little ability to exude the warmth needed to rally people to his side. Richard Drax thinks he [John] would be a brilliant CX, but not without some relationship coaching, in my view.

Overall morale was gratifyingly upbeat, especially after LBC's Nick Ferrari's speech. Apparently, we once tried to get him to stand as London Mayor but the salary cut would have been too great. Shame really as he is a 'character' even if his line in jokes failed to amuse two prominent leadership contenders, Penny Mordaunt and Kemi Badenoch.

I am told that Kemi is up to something, but then again, so is half the Cabinet.

Monday, 5 February

After much arguing as to which office we meet in, Gove and his extensive team come to see me about housing (so many in fact that Michael's top man Henry Newman ended up sitting on the floor). MG thinks we are backsliding on Renters Reform which we really aren't, at least not yet. MG doesn't really believe that our MPs hate it as much as we tell him they do and as a result he is reluctant to engage. His most ardent critics think he is a 'meddlesome leftie' and he enjoys poking the hornets' nest. Try as I might, I can never quite tell whether Michael is listening intently and respectfully, or just waiting for us all to lose interest so he can continue with his intellectual mission. I suspect it is the latter. The trouble is, he is also so charming and funny he gets away with the mischief and we always end up forgiving him.

Tuesday, 6 February

A rare moment with both Adam and Nell in town so fixed a tour of No. 10 (before it's all too late). Craig was the host and walked them through all the usual places – state rooms, Cabinet Room, etc. – and then grandly announced, 'And behind this door is where the PM sometimes works, take a look.'

Unknown to them this was one such occasion (he was in on the plan), so they were already in the room before the realisation that the PM was indeed at work dawned. Nell was especially taken aback, apologised and went to reverse out but RS would have none of it, and insisted on spending half an hour on the sofa, chatting about his kids, Nell's Loughborough course and Adam's book. The PM is so good in these situations. If only more people could see him like this.

Then to Raffles where two rounds of cocktails came to £260. Being Wetherspoons devotees, the kids were horrified.

Wednesday, 7 February

PMQs. Even before it started the atmosphere was flat. No reason really, just lacking in energy. The PM made a sort of overly scripted trans joke which he has done before at Keir Starmer's expense, but it didn't really land. So what? Unfortunately, the parents of murdered school kid Brianna Ghey were in the gallery. Labour and the Lib Dems went nuts and sanctimonious, and some of our people – Penny Mordaunt, Jamie Wallis, Alicia Kearns [Rutland and Stamford] – were not too keen either. And so, for 24 hours or so it became 'a thing'. I don't think it's a massive deal but it's background noise that we could do without. Luckily, Elliot Colburn [Carshalton and Wallington] rounded things off with a very poignant question about his own attempt at suicide, which concentrated everyone's minds on other topics.

Thursday, 8 February

Half-term recess coming up this week in which we could see a small inflation rise, two by-election defeats and a technical recession. What a time to be alive . . .

Sunday, 11 February

The cops tell Andrew Rosindell that after two and a half years of investigation they will not be submitting a file to the CPS following allegations of rape. So, all that time banned from the parliamentary estate and they don't even have enough evidence to consider.

Monday, 12 February to Sunday, 18 February

Recess week, although punctuated with 'events'.

Inflation figures are published and thank goodness remain unaltered. Then the OBR [Office for Budget Responsibility] announces a contraction in the fourth quarter of last year meaning we are now in a 'technical recession'. This is not as bad as a real one and is likely to correct itself quite quickly anyway. But it will get everyone jittery again as most people don't really know the difference and the media won't bother to explain.

Then the two by-elections, Wellingborough and Kingswood. We lose both of course, but even though turnout was crap, Reform did pretty badly with 13% so nowhere near well placed for a general election rout. Back in the days of UKIP by-elections they would have been at 30%+.

And as if that wasn't enough, in an act of shameless brutality, Putin reports the death of his rival Navalny in a Russian jail. He doesn't even pretend to be subtle any more . . .

Throughout all this, very little evidence of anarchy or panic in the ranks . . . Something must be up.

Tuesday, 20 February

Andrew Rosindell returns. He is an interesting character, and is at last officially innocent. Why it has taken the cops this long to reach this conclusion is anybody's guess but raises again the question as to why anyone would pursue a life in public service.

To the Lords bar for a drink with Kit Malthouse. I can't quite work him out. He is finding life outside the Cabinet intolerably hard and as a result is beginning to resent everything. That's not a good place to be as the chances of an imminent return to the centre seem pretty low. For his own sake I wish he would just make the most of his rock-solid seat and grind out his wilderness years.

Kemi popped in for a chat about trans stuff – I try, but I cannot find a mutually usable wavelength. She is another one who lives in a permanent state of outrage. It must be so tiring.

Wednesday, 21 February

The SNP is using their 'opposition day' to force a debate and vote on Israel. So far so good. Our position is reasonably united (for us) and Labour is split down the middle. However, the Speaker is being strangely indecisive and can't decide what to do. According to the Clerks' advice he has to accept a Government amendment to the SNP motion and that's that (Standing Order 31 to be precise).

Tensions rise dramatically as some pro-ceasefire Conservative colleagues align with Labour and the SNP to support the Labour amendment, which the Speaker now wants to take first.

The Speaker loses his nerve completely and starts protracted discussions with Starmer and the Labour Chief, without officials, in the Reasons Room, whilst their whips deliberately delay matters in the Chamber. The Reasons Room is a tiny windowless

office just behind the Chamber in which people mainly leave their baggage but which also gets used for urgent discussions on Chamber matters.

Our numbers are now far too close to call and getting worse by the minute as colleagues start to fret and desert – so we need excuses fast. Our only option is to contrive a walkout – Penny Mordaunt needs to come to the House, denounce the process and declare: 'His Majesty's Government will take no further part in proceedings.' She is at the Palace so we need her back pronto. To be fair she does this with considerable panache, to a packed and astonished House. It works a treat.

Chaos ensues. Will Wragg [Hazel Grove] moves that the 'House sits in private'; the SNP demands blood (everybody's) and then when the division occurs the Deputy Speaker Rosie Winterton refuses to allow the SNP to divide on their motion at all.

I've seldom seen a more heated Chamber – Speaker in, then out, then in to apologise. He's really screwed this up. But apart from him there are no actual losers. An innocuous opposition day has attracted headlines. The SNP has got its point across without being voted down; we have avoided a messy display of disunity and Labour has avoided another Israel-based drama.

However, the ramifications of this will run for ages and the Speaker's authority has hit a new low.

Friday, 23 February to Saturday, 24 February

McDonald's, Haverfordwest. Unwisely I was thinking how quiet things this weekend were, notwithstanding plenty of 'Speakergate' follow-up, when word reaches me from a colleague that Lee Anderson has, as he put it, 'escaped from his cage'. Apparently, he has made some comment about 'Sadiq Khan and his Islamist mates' or words to that effect, as part of a wider critique of the Mayor. Of course, most of what he has said is fine, if a little unsubtle, but the direct link between Khan and

terrorism is the wrong side of the red line, especially after we created such a recent fuss over Labour's Rochdale by-election candidate Azhar Ali. He made some off-the-scale comments about Israel and the attacks of 7 October. Labour thought an apology would do, but inevitably that fell apart after a week's bad publicity. It falls to me to speak to Lee and broker some sort of apology, retraction or clarification.

This being Lee, he is having none of it. I explain that he can stand by everything he has said about Khan but that he needs to rephrase that one sentence. Still nothing. He won't apologise because he says it is a matter of pride, even though there is an easy way out of this. He knows, and I know, that we are left with no option but to suspend the whip. In fact, he is quite decent about it, asks me to agree a form of words for a short statement and we make a plan to meet early next week to plot a way for him to rejoin the Party. Inevitably, our right-wingers moan like hell, but they were the first to call for action from Labour over anti-Semitism so we must at least try to be consistent.

The Speaker is now talking about an SO24 debate on Israel (a binding vote) for the SNP on Monday – is he mad?

Monday, 26 February

A *Times* journo is sniffing round a story from the North West in which one of our members (Mark Menzies [Fylde]) has allegedly managed to acquire thousands of pounds from a campaign account to pay for two dodgy blackmailers who were holding him hostage in the middle of the night (not another one?). The elderly lady who had control of the association's campaign account thinks it was a loan and the MP in question believes it to be a donation. Either way, it smells fishy. CCHQ start an investigation but almost immediately discover that several people (five or six we know of) have had similar approaches from Menzies. The pattern is always the same. Call in the middle of the night,

MP being held against will, send money for immediate release. Some fell for it, others didn't, but it involved a lot of money, and I am quite certain the intention of donors and members was not for the cash to be used like this.

Wednesday, 28 February

8.30 at No. 10. We laugh about the passage of the Pedicabs Bill that will crackdown on rogue rickshaws and which I describe as 'irrelevant to most of the nation'.

Dowden: 'Well, they get in the way between No. 10 and the Garrick.'

He can be very funny sometimes, even when he is deadly serious.

The *Express* describes me as the 'wokest Chief Whip ever' and Jonathan Gullis pledges full support for the Government. And it's not even 1 April.

And it's a by-election in Rochdale which follows the death of Labour veteran Tony Lloyd.

I represent David 'TC' Davies [SoS Wales] at the US Embassy in Wingfield House for a St David's Day event. It's the first time I have been let loose in public as Chief Whip so I have some wine, tell a few gags and hope for the best.

Friday, 1 March

Galloway [Workers Party] wins in Rochdale – simply extraordinary and all rather depressing. He is, in my view, such a revolting individual having praised the likes of Saddam Hussein for his 'courage' and 'indefatigability'. However, it does mean the PM speech is going ahead, which turns out better than anticipated. It is a thoughtful, well-argued piece but does stop a little short of saying exactly how we will avert the danger of religious extremism.

It pleases our troops although some ask me if Anderson can have the whip back as he only said what the PM said – which of course is bollocks. Lee's statement implied the Mayor was in the pocket of terrorist movements, the PM did not.

Monday, 4 March

Met with Lee Anderson to discuss 'the way back'. It grates a bit as he's totally unaware of the damage he is doing. There is a lot of northern 'speak as I find' rhetoric. (Plenty of our real northerners don't think Ashfield really counts as the 'north' but I don't tell him that.)

Drinks with the Chancellor, who hardly touches a drop, and the PM who doesn't drink at all. Thank goodness for Craig who drinks for both of them and makes everyone else feel marginally less guilty.

Tuesday, 5 March

Budget prep. We are all worried it will be unexciting in electoral terms, i.e. bad. However, it's sufficiently steady that nobody will think of it as a pre-election giveaway, so that will allay fears of anything happening soon. Jeremy [Hunt] is clearly a bit edgy too and feels cornered by the OBR who have managed away what little 'fiscal headroom' he had for more eye-catching tax cuts.

Wednesday, 6 March

Hunt was good at the pre-budget Cabinet. He is concise, neat and well organised. He has a good bedside manner with which it is hard to be angry. Everyone was content, in so far as no one raised concerns in the room.

The budget itself lived up (or down) to its expectations. A few tax cuts, a bit on child benefits and a few stealthy tax rises too.

Jeremy made it sound much better than it was and it indeed slayed talk of an early election. As ever with budgets, if it unravels it will be tomorrow.

Thursday, 7 March

After days of preparation, it's my turn to give evidence to the Covid-19 inquiry in Cardiff. The lawyers have managed to convert my limited role into several thousand pages of evidence, which takes up two three-inch-thick ring binders and all of which I am expected to learn for my one-hour slot in the witness box. We all decamp to a tired-looking conference hotel somewhere in a Cardiff suburb.

Mark Drakeford's written evidence (already a matter of record) tried to portray UK Government as either interfering or irrelevant (we surely can't be both?). But it was Vaughan Gething's hilarious attempts to explain why his WhatsApp messages had mysteriously disappeared that caused the most smirks. Although he wasn't in the room today, the recording of him blathering on about 'I sent my phone in for essential maintenance and when it came back all my Covid messages had gone' was fanciful. Who sends their phone in for essential maintenance? It's not a car, for goodness' sake. But Labour will form a defensive circle around him, and nothing will be done, as per usual.

Theresa May calls to say she is stepping down at the general election. Predictable really but she was very decent about it and wanted to choose a moment that suits us all. She has been such an exemplary post-premiership backbench colleague.

Monday, 11 March

There is suddenly fever-pitch media speculation over the possibility of a 2 May general election. I am not sure where this is coming from as it really isn't true. It will spook people though,

as no one is really wising up to the reality that it does have to be this year, and we really do need to be ready.

Lee Anderson defects to Reform – despite personal assurances that he wouldn't. I have tried to avoid the conclusion that he is a total knob, but he has made it nearly impossible. No manners, no nerve, no loyalty to the Party that provided him the platform from which to launch his career. It's the ultimate act of selfishness and obstinacy to chuck your mates under the nearest bus and perpetuate this 'I'm from the north' narrative as if that is some sort of legitimate excuse. My only regret is that it didn't happen sooner or that we were seduced by him in the first place. Reform claims to be in discussion with others but I have my doubts. Frankly, if people are susceptible to their charms I would rather they went now. I have a list they could choose from.

News breaks that Tory mega-donor Frank Hester, also in the 'speak as I find' category of Tory, was recorded saying he thinks Diane Abbott [Labour] should be shot, and that looking at her made him 'dislike all black women'. I despair. I have met him once and whilst he was interesting and unquestionably generous, he did remind me a bit of Harry Enfield's 'Yorkshireman'.

We seem to get paralysed with fear when it comes to responding, resulting in a delayed and flat-footed reaction to both this and the election date story. I feel sorry for Nissy [Chesterfield, Director of Comms at No. 10] who seems to have been outvoted on the best response. The heat has risen sharply and burnt even more of our capital and credibility. We find ourselves in a mortal battle for survival. The troops will panic – it doesn't take much these days – and the press go nuts. I used to talk to Swinford, [Olly] Wright, Kuenssberg but now find myself ignoring their calls rather than having to openly lie to them.

Wednesday, 13 March

PMQs and Starmer homes in on the Hester story, but rather fluffs it. It's a score draw at best when it should have been four-nil thrashing. Anderson cuts a lonely figure on the opposition benches next to George Galloway. A lesson in why defections never end happily.

Thursday, 14 March

Coffee at the Athenaeum with former colleague and podcaster extraordinaire Rory Stewart which we had been planning for a while. I like Rory, although he outplays me at every level. We have common ground on most issues, and our journeys have taken us to the same centre ground in politics. He is nattily dressed, a zip-up cardigan under his suit. He is at ease with himself and is greeted by club members and staff with fondness. As expected, we agree on almost everything, especially the grim state of politics, which is the theme of his latest book, which he tells me has sold more than 450,000 copies in hardback. It seems mad we lost him from our ranks. After coffee we walk back over St James's Park where he is stopped by numerous members of the public to comment on his podcast. It's a remarkable star quality for someone who is a 'voice' rather than a 'face'.

Penny Mordaunt calls. There is a breaking story (which she denies all involvement with) that both left and right are now coalescing around her as a possible leadership contender and there is an operation to oust RS.

I head for her office where we have a pleasant late-night chat, but I'm not sure either of us totally believes that the other's intentions are entirely innocent. I doubt she believes me when I explain that I am not there at the request of No. 10 and I am unconvinced that she wouldn't make a move if the stars aligned.

What I do believe is that she is not ready to trigger anything yet and that she is not driven by malice.

Penny does have great qualities of presence and a good instinct, possibly too good, for comms and publicity. I just can never be 100% sure she is fully committed to the Sunak project. We agree to keep talking and that another leadership bid this side of an election would be crazy.

Saturday, 16 March

The election and leadership stories persist into the weekend.

Monday, 18 March

The usual whips meeting over in No. 11. The team is pretty resilient, but the endless backchat is wearing thin and becoming emotionally exhausting. Every weekend they speak to 20–30 colleagues who just sick up all their baggage, frustration, concern and criticism in one massive smelly heap. Our job must be to remain positive, and never, ever let them or the opposition smell weakness, but it gets harder.

On the contrary though, I caught up with Ian Levy [Blythe]. What a great man. He's been on the receiving end of relentless intimidation, his kids included, by some nasty local nutter, but he refuses to give an inch. Why aren't more people like Ian? I remembered the moment he won against all the odds in 2019 and how brilliant, humble and respectful his acceptance speech was.

Tuesday, 19 March

Cabinet quite good but the PM is clearly exasperated in private and I can't blame him. He is doing the right things in the right way, but we just can't get a run of luck. The polls remain

stubbornly welded to the same 20-point deficit that we inherited from Liz, and although there is the odd more positive outlier, it is a depressing-looking pattern.

The Rwanda Bill will be defeated in the Lords tomorrow and the No. 10 plan is to bring it back after Easter. A few people sense a suspicious and deliberate delay although we will get Royal Assent on or around 18 April roughly as planned.

The real reason is that the Home Office is not quite ready, and we want to observe all of the usual requirements necessary to achieve Royal Assent.

Robert Roberts [Ind., Delyn] wants the whip back which he lost a few years ago for a sexual misdemeanour. He has a good case, but very few in the Whips' Office think we should. Matt Hancock is also agitating. Both cases expose the weakness of the system. Their two offences are fundamentally different yet the only sanction we have is the same. The collective view of the Whips' Office (and which will form advice to the PM) is that restoring the whip to Roberts will be a signal that we don't take his type of misbehaviour seriously enough. However, if the punishment for these offences is a ban for the duration of a Parliament at least, then we should make it clear to MPs at the start.

Wednesday, 20 March

PMQs. We suggest to the prep team that the PM 'comes down the wicket and attacks'. He did and it went quite well. There was noise and approval and his mood lifted a little. The Speaker now appears to have given up trying to exert any Chamber authority at all.

The PM and I do the '22 at 5 p.m. I read out the business and nobody seems to raise the Rwanda delays issue so we will stick to Plan A. Anyway, the meeting was well attended and the reception for the PM was genuinely warm and prolonged. His

speech was fine and well argued, but unlike some of his prede-
cessors, he believes every word of what he says. It is authentic
and thoughtful rather than flamboyant. As ever with Rishi, his
Q and A is always 100%. It's like he moves into a different gear.

There were especially great contributors from floor too. Liam
Fox shared the full horrors of life in opposition. I think he
served on the opposition front bench for the entirety of our
last spell on that side of the House. Almost no one on our side
is old enough to remember that but the old saying, 'your worst
day in Government is better than your best day in opposition', springs to mind. Richard Fuller made a rare contribution,
word perfect and stressing the importance of integrity, and from
nowhere came Jonathan Gullis. He may not have the same gift of
eloquence as the others, but he spoke with passion and captured
the room more effectively than usual. It didn't feel like the eve
of a revolution, but I've been here before.

Monday, 25 March

Dinner with *House of Cards* author Michael Dobbs and Jesse
Norman in Members where we are joined by former Chief
[Whip] Patrick McLoughlin. As ever with that lot it was a jolly
and irreverent affair, sadly interrupted by numerous votes on the
Investigatory Powers Bill.

No. 10 has now agreed that a short Honours List will be
announced on or around Thursday. It will include knighthoods
for Mark Spencer and Philip Davies and DBEs for Harriet
Baldwin [West Worcestershire] and Tracey Crouch [Chatham
and Aylesford]. You would think such moments would result in
universally warm tributes from colleagues but, in reality, it is
bound to trigger a few people who consider themselves more
deserving. We share out a list of those who might need handling.
Craig is dispatched to speak to Nusrat Ghani, whose issues with
Mark Spencer show little sign of fading with the passing years.

When Mark did my job he made the mistake, as did Nusrat, of having a meeting to resolve a complicated and unpleasant issue of racism without a third-party being present to take notes. They both had conflicting recollections about who said what, leading to lasting acrimony.

Thursday, 28 March

It's recess, so we are off to mid Wales for a 'simulated game shoot' with Spencer, Young [Redcar], Sambrook [Birmingham Northfield], Anderson [S], Craig and me. It's all very grand and 'MPs on tour' is always revealing. The plan was that the PM would ring the lucky honours recipients early today so we would be able to greet Sir Mark and Lady Spencer at the breakfast table (and, more importantly, so they can celebrate their new title on their daughter's upcoming wedding invite).

The PM makes the calls. Philip apparently delighted, Harriet over the moon, Tracey the upper end of pleased, and Mark – deadpan, Rishi tells us. Classic Spencer. We prised it out of him in the end, and forced some champagne down him, but he said he had been sworn to secrecy and in Mark's world that is that.

Friday, 29 March

To everyone's amazement the DUP's Sir Jeffrey Donaldson and his wife are arrested and charged with historic sex offences. It seems unbelievable. He is the quietest, most softly spoken, reasonable of all the people I deal with, which only goes to show – if he is guilty – how impressions can be very misleading.

Sunday, 31 March, Easter Sunday

More dire polling in the *Sunday Times*. In the old days there would have been a violent reaction and a loud running commentary

from disgruntled colleagues. Now there is almost no reaction at all. The nation is clearly not listening, not interested or not bothered. Either that or the polls are somehow miscalculating the undecideds.

Thursday, 4 April

The *Daily Mail* tells us that it is running a story about a honeytrap involving MPs, seemingly of gay colleagues but not exclusively. We have heard rumours for a bit, but had neither names of victims or perpetrators. The only hard fact we know is that Dr Luke Evans [Bosworth] received flirtatious messages, complete with photos from someone purporting to be 'Charlie Miller' and, a week later, from an 'Abigail Marsh'. These messages were nearly identical but also separately attempting to entrap people both gay and straight, which is what raised his suspicions.

As the story unfolds several things emerge. 1) Will Wragg admits to *The Times* that he was passing phone numbers of MPs to 'Charlie' after feeling compromised by a photographic Grindr exchange. 2) Up to twelve MPs of both parties plus a journalist or two have been approached but that none we know of so far has fallen for it.

As expected, when *The Times* story breaks other colleagues join the commentary. Sarah Dines and Andrea Jenkyns are especially barbed about Wragg, the latter claiming that her number had also been passed on, despite offering no evidence at all to support her claim.

But for us we have a whip's dilemma. Despite everything – the salacious nature of the story, the Pincher history and the fact that Will is a classic Marmite colleague – he is still a vulnerable human being. He has multiple frailties, and we are genuinely worried about his welfare. By early Saturday morning he admits himself to hospital for his own safety. We speak and he realises his issues have caught up with him and that he is painfully aware

of the impact on himself and others. He is broken emotionally and professionally. This won't end here, and it won't end well for anyone either.

Monday, 8 April

The Wragg saga continues. He is clearly in a terrible place and reports to the welfare whip, and friends ensure that we put him firmly on watch. MP for Great Grimsby Lia Nici joins the small chorus of former Boris Johnson acolytes who want his head on a plate. After some discussion Wragg agrees to resign the whip and his Party membership, two things that mean more to him than probably most people. The Party is his life. I could have sacked him myself, and plenty of people would have relished that, but one day a Chief will respond to the noise rather than the facts and we will end up with a suicide. I don't want it to be me.

Tuesday, 9 April

I speak to Wragg again who is in a fragile state. I reassure him as best I can, and we laugh about the hypocrisy of some of our colleagues. He has resigned from his committees so we gently reach a position where he is happy to surrender the whip in addition to his membership, and we agree words and timings accordingly.

Thursday, 11 April

Time to replace Graham Stuart as Energy Minister who has decided to resign. He really doesn't get on with Secretary of State Claire Coutinho and I suspect wants a job in the private sector. I wouldn't be surprised if he also wants to agitate within a leadership team. I quite like Graham but he has never really

forgiven us for dumping him from his 'attending Cabinet' role, meaningless though it was, and it feels like he still hankers after the old Boris regime.

So we prep up Justin Tomlinson for Energy Minister and Mims Davies to get her old Minister of State position and, slightly against my mean-spirited instincts, agree to give Andrew Mitchell the title of Deputy Foreign Secretary. It's not that Andrew isn't very good at his brief and handles all the tricky stuff in the Commons rather well, it's just that he has a terrible voting record and I hate giving people things they ask for. I will be over-ruled. Justin is both amazed and pleased and will love being back in Government, for however long it might be.

A reflective lunch with Rupert, Nissy and Julian at Gordon's by Embankment Station. We sat out in the sun, dealt with some rather nice Chablis and several plates of cheese, laughed a lot about what fun we have had and how lucky we have been. They are exceptional people and should be proud of what they have done to keep the rusty old ship afloat. There seems to be an unwritten acceptance that we are nearing the endgame now. I hope we will stay in touch.

Saturday, 13 April

Overnight, Iran launches 300 drones at Israel, 99% of which are intercepted by a combo of forces including the Brits. An expensive failure by Iran but a hugely significant moment in Middle Eastern hostilities. The question, as always, will be whether this will escalate, who will it involve – Russia? And how does it end? Cameron deployed to maintain peace. At least we have in David someone, possibly the only one, with the international gravitas needed to succeed.

Monday, 15 April

Drink with Mitchell and then Tugendhat. Neither short of self-confidence but both remaining loyal, although Tom feeling rather unloved. He is probably underrated but he is 'but a boy' and will resurface at some future stage.

Tuesday, 16 April

Political cabinet and then full Cabinet. The former brief and perfunctory, the latter more interesting than usual. Just like under Boris it's amazing how quickly Cabinet goes from being the most exciting, meaningful occasion of the week to a tedious distraction. Not this time though.

Cameron gives a brief and thorough sitrep, for which he gets full marks. He is in his element and the Cabinet is enthralled by him.

RS and I have a late night one-to-one. He confesses to being fed up on occasions but still determined. He is not certain how, or even whether, he would contest a confidence vote, for reasons of pride, I guess. We talked about what we might have done differently, who we wished we had sacked earlier, but neither of us are sure anything would have made much difference in the end. We are nearly fifteen years in and on our fifth PM. We have lived through a pandemic and a war in mainland Europe. It's a miracle we are still standing at all.

Today we vote on the PM's smoking and vaping proposals. Our Party has become very pompous about 'personal freedoms' recently, so I recount in the whips meeting my dad's attitude to seatbelts, which he resolutely refused to wear, as well as surprise our younger office colleagues by telling them that we always used to smoke in our offices, trains, planes and cinemas. They were equally dumbfounded to learn that we were allowed to

keep shotguns when I was at Radley. Mind you, I did get shot by a fellow pupil but that's another story . . .

Wednesday, 17 April

After weeks of speculation, it looks like the Mark Menzies story is eventually breaking, thanks to having been leaked by CCHQ in all its gory detail. The CCHQ investigation is frankly rubbish and ends up recommending (in draft luckily) that the elderly and loyal complainant is the one who gets sacked not Menzies. Holden clears up the mess quickly and effectively.

The waves of crap feel never-ending. Between dinner at White's and getting home I speak to Menzies, suspend the whip, extend the inquiry and learn yet more about the bizarre lifestyles some of our MPs lead. How do they ever get on the candidates list?

It is the new season of Ks and peerages. Requests (demands more like) pour in. Some people are delusional about their personal status, but not as delusional as former PM Elizabeth Truss who publishes her book this week. A trip (literally) through the strange world in which she feels genuinely hard done by and misunderstood. She has zero self-awareness sometimes, literally none. Every conversation I have with constituents, especially Conservatives, includes an expression of exasperation as to how we managed to destroy the one remaining attribute we had, namely our reputation for economic competence.

Thursday, 18 April

We argue all day about Rwanda, now deciding that we should ignore [Lords leader] Nick True's advice to conclude in the Lords on Tuesday next week, instead opting for Monday when half our peers are not on site. He may well resign over this I fear, so Rupert

is tasked with talking him down. If only this level of urgency was shown before Easter when it could have been concluded.

Drink with Rishi and others in the Spy Bar at Raffles, where the Glenfiddich 50-year-old malt comes in at £10,000 a glass (not that we order one). It's a great location, down in the cellar somewhere, with a real Aston Martin behind the bar. He doesn't stay long, but it's a boost for us knackered soldiers.

Monday, 22 April

Rwanda Bill comes back from the Lords for what could be a long night. Nick True is still incandescent (with some reason) but it looks like he has extracted a verbal concession to get Labour to call off the dogs, meaning it will be done and dusted today. PM gives a press brief in which he makes it clear that we will sit until it is done.

There is no sense of fight as far as the 'Dirty Dozen' is concerned so we grind our way through the night. At 11.30 a few of us go over to the Lords and see the final, quite graceful, capitulation. Against all the odds and at considerable political cost the Rwanda Bill will now receive Royal Assent. We still haven't got to the hard bit, as the Attorney General still predicts choppy legal waters ahead.

I have the last bit of chicken off the shelf in the Chicken Palace Lambeth. Home at 2 a.m.

Tuesday, 23 April

PM, CX and Shapps in Poland to announce that defence spending will rise to 2.5% of GDP by 2030, a commitment that receives a warm response from the people we need on board. I can't help but think it's all a bit arbitrary. Why not 2.4 or 2.6? Surely it should all hinge on assessment of threat, and emerging technology. Anyway, the punters love it and it's one of those totemic

Conservative things we should be doing if only for the message rather than the actual impact. We used to own anything to do with Law and Order, Agriculture and Defence, but now voters are not quite so sure.

Wednesday, 24 April

Dowden does PMQs. He has a style all of his own but Rayner is characteristically poor so it all went okay. Oliver spends hours on prep so his answers are technically perfect and his jokes just about land. He is likeable too, and that matters in the Chamber. Like me, Penny hates PMQs and we both grimace a little too visibly.

Gove's Renters Reform is today's headache. Labour miss a huge trick by not aligning with Anthony Magnall [Totnes] to vote it down at third reading. We would have almost certainly lost without a major concession and rapidly undone all the good of the prior two days. But some good whipping (and disingenuous promises . . .) land us in a good place and the Bill passes with no rebels and comfortable majority, hopefully never to be seen again.

Sunday, 28 April

Cabinet Room – PM, me, LB-S, Olive, James F, Will Tanner, Isaac Levido (and two Levido underlings), RY and Nissy on Zoom, and Craig. Being a Sunday, everybody is 'casual' which always feels a bit odd in a room so steeped in formality. The purpose is for Levido to provide a résumé of expectations for the imminent local elections and what happens next. He estimates, roughly, this: we lose 450 council seats; mixed results on the Police and Crime Commissioners which we all agree is the least of our concerns; we retain the Teesside mayoralty with Ben Houchen but on a reduced majority; it's too close to call with

Andy Street in the West Midlands; we come second in London but narrow the 20-point gap.

Our challenge – to avoid a confidence vote by carrying out a standard 'cascade' plan of sensible and measured 'grandee' reaction as results come in. We agree we need one, preferably two, mayoral wins to be sure of this and to be clear of immediate danger. And then the key bit. If we succeed, then he's minded to call the GE on 13 or 20 May for 4 July, but with important significant caveats.

This will astound most people who think and hope we are still looking at November, but he seems increasingly convinced there is a compelling strategic advantage.

Given all this, the mood is okay. Whichever date he goes for we are only talking about the difference of a matter of months. In 2017, we went two years early and nearly lost because of it. Surprise is a potent political weapon, so long as everyone keeps schtum.

Tuesday, 30 April

Met with one of our 2019 colleagues who resides in a safe seat. They want to trade the seat for the House of Lords. 'Give me a peerage and I will give up my safe seat,' they say.

Me: 'Sorry, that's not really on the table. If I do it for you then there will be dozens of potential retirees making the same pitch.'

'Well, you are all bastards and this is unfair.' I explain the Lords is not a right, especially for people who have made a rather modest impression over their four-and-a-half-year stint.

Another example of the sense of entitlement that has crept into our world and for which we are now paying a heavy price.

Wednesday, 1 May

Chat with Danny Kruger about New Cons [his and Miriam Cates's splinter group] which he claims has rather fizzled out. Again, he

is a curious character. Son of TV chef Prue Leith, he can clearly woo a crowd as he won the nomination for one of the UK's safest seats of Devizes. Yet, the notion of teamwork is still a problem for him. In the old days, if colleagues disagreed with the leadership it was resolved, hopefully, behind closed doors and with awareness about the damage visible divisions can do. These days, the pattern seems to be hire a room, write an alternative manifesto, brief the media that the Government is crap, and then express surprise when opinion polls reflect what you have just said.

Friday, 3 May into Saturday, 4 May

Polling Day. There is always a sense of relief when it actually comes. No more speculation, no more time to doubt. In fact, the news coming in shows an inexplicably varied range of outcomes. Some tremendous results in certain areas and dreadful ones in others. Perhaps this is more of a reflection of the local candidates than previously?

The counts were partially Thursday night, some Friday and the larger mayoralties not until well into Saturday. So, with each twist, the media would launch into yet another round of speculation. By dawn, we were getting a feel for where this was going. A mixed result but roughly as expected. By lunchtime, it felt like there was no real impetus to oust the PM (which is frankly the only thing I care about any more). For a serious attempt to succeed by now there would have needed to be a clear statement of intent from a serious contender with the numbers to prove it. There isn't.

Saturday, 4 May

Win a few Police Commissioners, lose a bunch of councillors. Win Teesside, but it's neck-and-neck in the West Mids. Andrew Mitchell and Michael Fabricant [Andy Street's partner] provide

live updates from the count and it really does look like it will be down to just a handful of votes in what is a huge electorate. We worry about how Andy will react. If he blames the PM we will have an issue, but he has given every indication it would never be his style.

Looks like we will lose London (that was never really in doubt) but by a lot less than the pollsters said. It shows what an impact a live local issue (in this case ULEZ [Ultra Low Emission Zones]) can have on the process.

Sunday, 5 May

The local election post-mortem rumbles on. People (like Andrea Jenkyns again) just can't help but provide a running commentary when the classier option is to stand back. We ignore her as usual, which I suspect she finds infuriating.

Panic sets in as Rehman Chishti [Gillingham and Rainham] makes a strange X announcement. 'Personal statement coming soon,' he says.

Given his first position in politics was as a Labour councillor we all assume another defection is on the cards. So, we press all of the usual panic buttons.

Emma starts to prep the hostile questions document. His whip is tasked with tracking him down. CCHQ does a quick by-election prep plan and we brief the PM's team. The media is all over us so we prepare and issue a holding line. And then we wait.

Turns out he's announcing his engagement. Twat. Until this moment, I was unaware that Reh had such a sense of humour.

Tuesday, 7 May

Chat with Penny Mordaunt. She's clearly very unhappy with the position we are in and is thinking hard about the future (there are

others in the same place). In some ways I don't blame her. All the leadership hopefuls will be doing the same and she has as much credibility as they do. She remains resolute in her rejection of media reports that she is engineering an outcome soon though. Whatever happens, I won't be playing much of a part.

Wednesday, 8 May

Political cabinet. Slightly out of the blue Gove makes quite a 'centrist' speech and gets immediately hosed down by Chris Heaton-Harris and Alister. He is up to something, as he always is, we just don't know what.

Nadhim Zahawi is going to announce he is standing down (sort of expected) and David Duguid [Banff and Buchan] remains on life support in Scotland. He has had a severe stroke of the spine.

The mood is extremely fragile but moves against Rishi don't seem to have gathered much pace.

Thursday, 9 May

Arrive at PMQs to the sight of Natalie Elphicke sitting behind Starmer on the opposition benches. No warning at all. Defected. Our side bemused and baffled and of course infuriated. Her whip reported a chat they had earlier this morning in which she said she would be in and supporting the Government. It's hard to tell with Natalie whether her facial expression is one of pleasure or regret as, for whatever reason, she has such a limited range of visible emotional expressions. Apart from being one of the least engaging people you will ever meet, with a very compli-cated past even by our standards, she is also way to the right of almost all the Labour Party. Whilst we really are well rid of her, the effect will be debilitating to our side. It's a very cynical (and brave) move by Labour too and may yet backfire. I am told

the defection was all handled by Starmer's office and not by the Labour whips. She's yet another example of someone wholly ill-equipped to be an MP, but who slipped through our candidate recruitment system unnoticed.

It triggered Emma into reminding me of a previous Commons Labour defection which the handler in question (a Labour whip) put down to the magnetism of her 'magic pussy'. The mind boggles.

Tuesday, 14 May

Routine (which means boring) Cabinet, followed by the 'Farm to Fork' summit in the No. 10 garden. Everyone who's anyone in farming and food production is there. These are such simple events, and so productive, I don't know why we don't do a different critical sector a week. Being straight after Cabinet works too as the whole 'machine' can look in and forge relationships.

The delightful 'Cheerful Charlie' (Charlie Ireland) from *Clarkson's Farm* was there. What a sound man he is. The series has done more for farming than anything I can remember. By magic and great skill Clarkson has created a new audience of many millions who now understand just a little more about the importance of farming and what a struggle, and delight, it can be.

Wednesday, 15 May

All parties are summoned to meet the Speaker, his plan being to draw up a code of practice for the behaviour of candidates and activists during the GE campaign – Labour whips and their Chief of Staff, SNP, Lib Dems and a few officials too.

His idea is sensible in fact, if a few years behind where we should be. It just won't happen this time, and even if it does, I hold out low expectation of widespread compliance. The hardcore

Labour activists, especially the remnants of Momentum, view Conservatives as beneath contempt and therefore no abuse is considered out of order. And the Lib Dems invented dirty campaign techniques but conceal them quite well under the cover of dull and sanctimonious candidate selection.

One nice call – and there aren't many of those these days – was to alert James Morris [Halesowen] of his incoming OBE. He's such a decent man and has been dealt a tough hand, missing out in reshuffles through no fault of his own. I remind him his efforts have not been in vain after all.

Monday, 20 May

Bids for a seat in the House of Lords come rolling in. Most will come to nothing. MPs are divided on the 'go early or go late' question. I suspect the majority of 'go lates' would rather not go at all.

Off to Chelsea Flower Show as a guest of Ben Brogan at Lloyds. It's definitely one of the best perks we get and well worth the usual Lib Dem sanctimony that will pop up when it appears in my Register of Interests. What a week, what a day, to be doing it.

Plenty of friends and celebs about to make it interesting (Richard E Grant, Joanna Lumley) and the usual spattering of Labour MPs including, inevitably, Jess Phillips. And, of course, Starmer's Chief of Staff Sue Gray covering all bases. I think I am expected to dislike Sue, but it's impossible. She is the opposite in real life to the persona the press has assigned to her. Not the brutal executioner, but rather someone fighting a losing battle against a strong tide of crap. We are united in that place and both partial to some of Lloyds' finest Chablis.

Tuesday, 21 May

The final plans are signed off. The speech. The Q and A, the Cabinet handling sequence et al. James Forsyth leading on the words. Ben Riley-Smith at the *Daily Telegraph* is desperate to stand the story up (we assume the Cabinet Office has leaked) but everyone remains mostly calm. Chris Evans [*Daily Telegraph* editor] was on my table at Chelsea last night but we never spoke!

The PM is to discuss it with Cameron later, then the rest of us are to bring trusted colleagues into the loop. In my case that will be TC, the Whips' Office, Alister and others. Everyone is tired.

We know this is a huge gamble and we know it will take a miracle. The public seem to have stopped listening some months ago and become susceptible to the 'time for a change' narrative we too have used to great effect over the years. The PM increasingly believes that the only way we can break the silence is to force the date on people and force the choice in the process. In other words, we have to set a deadline for the undecideds to decide, to choose between Starmer and Sunak.

9

CAPITULATION

May–July 2024

Back in 2010, the year I was elected, we feverishly repeated the message that it was 'time for a change'. Now it was Labour's turn to use the same old, but effective, trope. Bolt on a 'nothing really works any more' narrative and it can be hard to get a worthy policy commitment heard above the noise.

In the first few days of the campaign, I sat on the committee that made the final candidate appointments (150 of them!). We ploughed through reams of very good people but in only a few instances were we ever able to ascertain if they would make good MPs. They were experts in their fields, but we never found out if they could work as a team, build consensus, handle disappointment or rejection. We reap what we sow. It became a running joke, of sorts, in the Whips' Office that I attributed almost every challenge we faced to poor candidate identification, selection or training. During my period in office, I have met some of the finest people I have encountered anywhere, in any role. Decent, kind, competent and effective. Yet I have experienced the opposite too, and that's a problem we need to resolve if we are to succeed in Government again.

In my seat in west Wales the voters' message was not a critique of ideas, or even achievements, but one of boredom and exasperation with the endless Conservative soap opera and psychodrama. People just wanted an alternative, even if they knew it would come at a price. By supporting Reform, Conservative voters

knew they would be helping shepherd in a Labour Government with an even bigger majority, but they were past caring.

I deal with the hidden formalities of winding up what's left of Government business, the tearful farewells, especially with Palace of Westminster staff who had looked after us so well all these years.

Rishi Sunak is a man whose ability to study, learn, absorb and analyse is in a league of its own. Throughout his premiership I would see him every day, often alone, as he wrestled with a reluctant Government machine, juggling the egos and expectations of MPs. He always took decisions for the right reasons and yet even that – eventually – wasn't enough to unite our own colleagues, let alone the wider nation.

———•———

Wednesday, 22 May 2024

GE announcement day. We have made it, just about. We are wounded, but still alive. But RS's desire to manage this to a time of his own choosing, on his own terms, has been achieved. No confidence motion, no men in grey suits, no resignation, none of the things that have unfairly beset his leadership since day one. Messages of speculation pour in. Some say we are insane (Crouch, Tolhurst [Rochester and Strood]), others that we have no option, even others in support (Eddie Hughes, Richard Graham).

It's pissing down by the time Cabinet arrive. We pre-brief a few key players. TC is emotional and kind. We hug, which is a new experience for us both, I think. I speak to Vic so we can at least be ready to go with wash-up. We will need to agree a chunk of legislation by Friday when the House will rise for recess (and prorogation).

Cabinet (minus Penny Mordaunt who is chairing a Privy Council meeting over at the Palace and could not get back in

time) was measurably better than I thought. Solid opening knock from the PM and then warm comments from DC, Cleverly, AJ, TC, Harper. In fact, the only two dissenting voices – and they were heavily qualified – were from Esther [McVey] and CH-H. Cameron was especially good, given he has as much to lose as anyone. Bill Clinton once said the world divides into two sorts of people: 'big people' and 'little people'. The former never lose sight of the goal, the latter always get distracted by meaningless drivel. He said this in the context of the NI peace process but it applies to every political dilemma we have ever had. David is a 'big' person.

By now the news was out, journos descending on No. 10, the lectern (minus the Government logo) in position and despite the now steady, heavy rain RS ready to go.

The rest of us stood nervously in the Cabinet Room huddled around the big screen. The speech itself was sound, decent and respectful but the rain hammered down, turning RS's suit into a shiny sodden mess (I'm not sure what happened to the wet-weather plan we discussed only yesterday but the metaphors started pouring in as fast as the rain poured down). He held on, even when the world's greatest moron – Steve Bray – attempted to drown it all out with his music blasted out by the gates. It takes a very special level of idiot to think public support for your cause is boosted by that. Forsyth (in the room with us lot) had his legendary patience stretched sufficiently far that he took Simon Case on one side to suggest that at a moment of significance like this the Met might just step in and ensure the public could hear?

And now the reaction of MPs. As I mentioned, the whole range of responses was on offer: fear, surprise, delight, concern. Let's not forget we are 4.5 years in (to a 5-year term) so I am hardly sympathetic to those who thought it was ages off yet or it could be delayed much further. Classic heart vs head stuff and many people who hate the idea, just don't want to confront reality. The

embracing and crying has started too, but we mustn't forget that we now have two intense days of business to conclude.

Thursday, 23 May, Election Campaign Day One

RS choppers off on a UK-wide tour (very sensibly) starting in Wales, to a brewery (not so sensibly), where the 'piss up' jokes wrote themselves. It was sort of fine, he was well received, had a minor hiccup about the Euros but as starts go, so far so good. I'm sure Jack Sellers [formerly my SpAd in the Wales Office, now working in No. 10] and TC will keep the peace.

Back in the curious world of the Whips' Office, the impending election has flushed out all the honours hopefuls, yet again. God they are persistent. Do they actually think multiple WhatsApps are what is needed to get into contention? We pass half the wash-up measures with ease as Labour are keen to get on with it too.

Friday, 24 May

Exchanges between the Lords and Commons carry on all day as we mop up the remaining bits and pieces. Vic and the team do a brilliant job as the rest of us pack our bags, confident that whatever the GE throws up we are unlikely to be back in the Whips' Office. Even if we win, I would take some persuading to stay on. It's the most brilliant job, but the goodwill evaporates quite quickly and a fresh pair of legs is needed.

Friends do a lot of handshaking and embracing. For many this will be their last time here and for all its strangeness it has become our home and our way of life. A special place in our affections is kept for doorkeepers and bar staff and the officialdom that quietly keeps the place afloat. Wayne, the head doorkeeper, has seen it all before of course. He is a bit like the Regimental Sergeant Major at Sandhurst, treating each eager

new entry and outgoing cohort with the same degree of respect. It's why former police officers and service personnel are so good in the role.

Craig, Rupert and myself pay a final visit to Sheekey's for lunch – I will definitely miss that place. And then back for the final act, prorogation. By now, around 8 p.m., the place had emptied, bar the final fifty or so. We drank champagne in the Whips' Office, there was a little thank you speech from me, and then to the Chamber where we processed, semi-formally, to the Lords for a little ancient ceremony, complete with Norman French to conclude.

It was harder, more emotional and felt more final than I had anticipated. Back in the Chamber we bid our goodbyes to the Speaker, and a tearful Helen Wood [the Speaker's Chief of Staff]. We cleared the office which has been such a nerve centre for so long, and that was that.

On the UK tour, the PM was in Northern Ireland, where in Belfast some bright spark decided the Titanic Quarter was just the place to go for a photo op. Who is commonsense-checking this stuff?

And so, to the first big political announcement. National Service for kids divided into a voluntary military element or 24 days a year for institutions like the RNLI [Royal National Lifeboat Institution]. It's quite sensible but easily misrepresented. The older generation likes it and it does generate some noises.

Thursday, 30 May

Our first 'wanker' moment. Mark Logan, formerly the MP for Bolton North East, has decided to endorse Labour. It's not really a defection as he is not standing, but it is an act of someone unfit for the role he had enjoyed thanks to us. If only people knew about the various meetings he insisted on having with me over the last few months. Meetings at which he demanded,

not requested, to be given an ambassadorial role, preferably Japan, purely on the basis of his language skills. Or the threats to defect or revolt on the back of our Gaza position unless we gave him a job in government. His attitude was neither appropriate nor compelling. I guess Labour may offer him something if they win, but they would be mad to sign him up. Once a shit always a shit.

CCHQ is in candidate overdrive. We have roughly 160 seats to fill by 7 June, the close of nominations. Winnable seats are treated very differently from unwinnable seats, and there is a long list of MPs displaced by the boundary changes (Stuart Andrew, Neil Hudson, Kieran Mullin and even Party Chair Richard Holden, for example). Then there is the cream of the SpAd team to try and find homes for, including Will Tanner, Declan Lyons and Henry Newman.

Each day we join the Zoom committee where Matt Lane [CCHQ candidates department] sets out the rules and the details. How many applied and who they have shortlisted. Our job is to get the list down to three who then go to the local association for their final pick.

Then it's off to the research department for a propriety check. We do thirty a day at least. Some good, some awful and inevitably a fair few fail the vetting process. Dick pictures mainly, but also inappropriate comments on X and a few dodgy financials. In one assessment, poor James Forsyth and Rupert Yorke were required to judge whether a candidate's defence, that a photo of his penis had been sent in error to a contact rather than his doctor as intended, was enough to allow him to apply for seats. It wasn't. Associations respond to our work with scepticism. They don't really like being given shortlists, especially containing what are clearly hopefuls with no real affinity or knowledge of the area they themselves have spent so much time nurturing.

We get Tanner into Bury St Edmunds, but Declan and Henry narrowly miss out to displaced MPs Chris Clarkson and Kieran

Mullin. Neil Hudson gets Epping Forest and everyone's favourite Stuart Andrew slips into Daventry nice and comfortably.

Monday, 3 June

Having previously said he would not stand, Nigel Farage has now decided to stand in Clacton, once held for a short while by UKIP. It's naked opportunism and ego obviously but whether and how voters will react is another matter. Colleagues suggest we do a deal, but what does he want that we haven't already delivered? Farage is the sort of pub bore who stands at the bar shouting about foreigners and picks up the support of around 25% of the angriest voters and the opposition of everyone else [Reform is unlike other political parties, it is a business of which Farage is the major shareholder so there is a commercial incentive at play too]. He has worked out that the harder of the 'right-wing' British voters didn't have a home any more so with a subtle rebrand and more nuanced language he can stir up a similar amount of hatred and division. His only impact will be to deny a few Conservatives a seat by eating into their vote, so it will be Keir cracking open the largest bottle of socialist champagne this evening.

But it's not all going Sir Keir's way. A row has emerged as to whether Diane Abbott, who is plainly unwell, can stand as a Labour candidate. Keir's office says no, then there is a leftist outcry, which results in an immediate U-turn.

And so, the first of the TV debates, hosted by ITV's Julia Etchingham in Manchester. Our team is RY, Nissy, Craig, Gove, Mercer, Coutinho, Brett, Isaac. It goes especially well. RS is sharp and impressive; Keir vague and dithering. The gap we wanted to expose – that Keir simply saying 'we will stop illegal immigration' is not actually a plan for how to do it – is there for all to see. So too is the tax bombshell Labour has been trying to keep well buried. RS lands the punch that Labour will

cost you £2k per annum so Labour then tries to report him for a breach of the ministerial code. Colleagues are delighted, as it has extinguished any doubts they may have had about his hunger to win or his ability to outmanoeuvre Keir on every topic. Will it change the polls? Doubtful, but if we can keep it up, who knows?

Thursday, 6 June to Friday, 7 June

The PM is in Normandy for the commemoration of the D-Day Landings. It's quite a big deal with a gaggle of world leaders in attendance. Later that evening Rupert calls, concerned there is a story emerging Rishi returned early, possibly too early, from the commemorations, missing out on the final international bit involving Biden, Macron et al. Even Starmer had hung around. Cameron was there for us but the accusation, gathering pace, is Rishi has shown disdain for the Normandy Veterans.

To be fair, the itinerary would have been agreed prior to the election being called and he had been present for all the UK parts of the event. But the media and opponents sense a story brewing. Social media and others are now in full cry. What was supposed to have been a great example of RS comfortable on the world stage has become a huge PR gaffe, and on a topic we should claim as ours and ours alone. RS immediately issues an apology, risky but probably inevitable, to quell the noise.

Candidates are besieged and angry. They take it out on RY, Nissy, Craig and I. RS critics are in open revolt and some even describe it as the turning point of the campaign and suggest he should consider his position. Everything we have done so far has now been compromised. Reform accuses us of being unpatriotic. In many ways it could not be worse – but is that actually true? Where I am I have received no emails on the topic. Canvassing in Carmarthen produces no comment and in a two-hour Q and A with voters in Llandovery this evening, nobody raised it either.

Of course it's a gaffe, of course it shouldn't have happened, but I just wonder if the public is quite as outraged by what is clearly a mistake as the media would like us to be. We have four weeks to go, so we just cannot risk these errors.

Sunday, 9 June

Our candidate for Southend [Gavin Haran] has made an inappropriate aside on X about coconuts. The *Guardian* has the story so we will insist on an apology and withdraw support.

Monday, 10 June

The campaign is in full swing. Considering the surprise nature of it, Labour is in gear quickly – some would say sharper off the mark than we were. Pollsters Redfield and Wilton give Labour a 26-point lead, us at 19 points and Reform at 17 points. Things don't feel good around the constituency, but they don't feel that bad either. There is pity out there rather than anger.

Tuesday, 11 June

We are discreetly summoned to a 'location near Towcester' for the manifesto launch. No surprise it turns out to be Silverstone, causing a fit of the jitters for those fearing yet more 'car crash' headlines. The launch is further compromised by Brad Pitt and a film crew attempting to blow up a car at the same location on the same day. What chance Brad giving us a word of support?

Our slogan, 'Clear plan, bold action, secure future', would be compelling if it weren't for the fact we are fourteen years in. As expected, there was lots on tax cuts (including another bash at NI), NHS spending, immigration, defence and the environment. In other words, strong and stable. But who will be on the edge of their seats? RS greets us all in the green room first, lots of fist

bumping and a decent, positive vibe followed by a decent, positive speech and a Q and A which is always his strongest feature.

The Lib Dems launch their manifesto containing – as usual – a whole load of stuff about 'saving the NHS' and new tax measures. I do envy parties who can say what they like on the basis they will never be put in a position to fulfil their promises. 'Right-wing' Tories (who the press unsurprisingly name as Braverman and Jenrick) are threatening to publish a 'rebel manifesto' if ours doesn't meet their requirements. This is another example of wilful mischief, the fallout from which is just a public reminder we cannot agree with each other on anything. Seasoned campaigners know manifestos make no polling difference anyway, whereas divisions do.

Starmer and Sunak go head-to-head on the ITV debates and whilst unexciting in terms of TV viewing the consensus was our man comfortably won the day. At least we have something to cheer about.

Thursday, 13 June

It's Labour's manifesto slot. If I was them, I would publish a blank piece of paper. There is no point handing out reasons to question or doubt them when they are 20+ points ahead.

As it is, he [Starmer] goes for a business-friendly agenda, designed to cast further doubt in the minds of our traditional core supporters. Shapps is on the airwaves openly talking about trying to 'minimise the Labour majority'. Apart from on tax, we seem to have all but given up.

Friday, 14 June

With far too much glee the *Telegraph* splashes that Reform has overtaken us in polling terms for the first time ever. I guess it is too much to ask the *Telegraph* to recognise that their infatuation

with Farage will be celebrated most by Starmer? Conservative votes will be diluted by Reform where it really matters and deliver Labour not one but two terms. Ironically, it will be *Telegraph* readers who suffer the most.

Saturday, 15 June

St Clears [Agricultural] Show, where my small team of Havard, Tara, Charlie and the indefatigable octogenarian Neil Davies sit under a gazebo trying to give the impression that victory awaits us. They are a remarkable bunch, replicated across every constituency in the land. It was different doing this for the first time fourteen years ago. Then it was in the wake of expenses scandals, but in those days a doorstep dressing down was an exciting challenge not another kick in the nuts.

And then the 'show bore' turns up, plastic carrier bag in hand, and the look of someone with plenty of opinions. 'Give me one good reason I should vote Tory then,' he opens with. I wearily outline our successes and a few of our plans. Much eye-rolling followed by a lecture on 'how anybody with half a brain could have solved the boats crisis' and 'only an idiot could have cocked up Covid like we did'.

Back in 2010, I would have sat him down, made a coffee, taken his details and followed up with a thoughtful letter. But it's 2024, so I said, 'Here's an idea, why don't you find someone else to vote for, and leave me to finish my coffee with my friends?', to which Neil helpfully added, 'Yes, bugger off.' I'm now feeling a great deal better.

Monday, 17 June

The papers are waking up to the fact Labour has the wind behind them and there is little we can say or do to dent their progress. On the doorsteps there is little love for Starmer but

there's also a feeling nothing really works in the UK any more. We have had a long time in charge and it's tricky to refute. Percy reports that canvass returns (and early postal votes) err towards a tighter margin than the polls predict, but also a lower turnout. We don't know who that really favours.

Tuesday, 18 June

Boris comes out with some helpful comments about Farage and Reform, but one intervention from him is nowhere near enough. There needs to be a relentless repeat of the risk of tactical voting and Labour cleaning up on the back of it.

Thursday, 20 June

Akin to a messy orgasm, the *Telegraph* splashes with 'Tory Wipeout' which inevitably gets picked up everywhere. Our own colleagues are conditioned to it now and there is nothing they can do anyway. The paper predicts we will end up with just 53 seats, Labour 516 and Reform a reassuringly miserable zero. This may get voters thinking more seriously about being flippant with their votes. We can but hope. What we must now recognise, though, is the underlying polling conclusion that we are fucked, the only argument is by what degree.

Friday, 21 June

Former MP, and friend for that matter, Chris Skidmore has said he will vote Labour. Self-indulgent and unnecessary, Chris. Do what you have to do but show some respect to your colleagues who haven't slunk off to some well-paid private sector climate job. As my dad would have said, 'second-rate behaviour'.

Saturday, 22 June

We soldier on with the door-to-door campaign. Some of this is in person, but much is online. Making personal contact with 75,000 people distributed around 40,000 households would take years. Recognition is good, support measured and blame largely heaped on others. 'You have been a good MP, Simon, but it's time for a change.'

Monday, 24 June

Rowing oddball and Conservative candidate James Cracknell describes the Party as a 'Shower of Shit'. I think he's talking on the back of the betting scandal, clearly oblivious to a) the law and b) basic rules of electioneering. He may be right of course, but posting a reminder will not help him or us. Tobias Ellwood [Bournemouth East] and IDS also weigh in, neither of whom will stimulate the nation into reversing its current voting intentions.

Wednesday, 26 June

RS trounces Starmer in the BBC debate. It's an almost embarrassingly dominant performance. But we all know nothing will change. The nation decided long ago (probably over two years, if we are honest) and nothing will alter that now. What remains important is to salvage what we can, behave with honour and integrity, form a decent opposition, elect a sensible and sane new leader, and start again.

Thursday, 27 June

A Labour member involved in their election campaign is arrested for allegedly being the brains behind the honeytrap scandal that sunk Will Wragg. Is there a huge public outcry? Don't hold

your breath. It barely makes the BBC news app. Wragg will feel aggrieved and upset, but there is little he can do.

Pollsters Redfield and Wilton show the Labour lead has shrunk from 26 to 23 points. Victory is ours!

Having sworn to refuse all hustings on the basis that the audience's voting intentions are set in concrete before they even enter the room, I end up doing a double-header in the Ivy Bush, Carmarthen, firstly with the NFU [National Farmers' Union] and FUW [Farmers' Union of Wales] and then soon after, the local Chamber of Trade. Both went on far too long and, in the end, I had to cut short the 'closing remarks' for a much-needed piss. The candidates had by then been on the go for four and a half hours, addressing about 40 out of our electorate of 75,000. The Labour candidate was a very competent and friendly local lady, Plaid (the race favourite) a larger-than-life farmer's wife who kept claiming that she would 'take Westminster by storm'. At one stage I told her that Parties of three people soon sink beneath the waves, which was greeted by much outrage in the audience. And then there was the Workers Party of Wales, represented by a man who never once removed his hat, and inevitably Reform, who obsessed about migrants, not an issue that has any direct effect on this area.

Friday, 28 June

Farage goes head-to-head with Penny Mordaunt and surprisingly is her match in terms of combat (if not in terms of class). Reform is under pressure for a member making derogatory and racist comments about RS.

Saturday, 29 June

Elton John comes out for Labour along with a few other celebrities determined to do something to publicly appease their

consciences, but the most grating is the sanctimonious Deborah Meaden. She is so grand these days.

Wednesday, 3 July

In election news we are all now stumbling to what we know will be an inevitable drubbing tomorrow. Absolutely nothing we have done, good or bad, during this campaign or even over the last two years, has moved the dial an inch in any direction. We started 20 points behind when Rishi took over and it looks horribly like that is where we will end up.

Thursday, 4 July to Friday, 5 July

Polling day, the highlight of which is taking the core team to lunch in Carmarthen. How amazing they've been in face of it all. Of course, staff lose their jobs as well but nobody cares much about the collateral damage they become. Many will have served with great distinction for many years and will be the true champions of their constituencies. Then the chef surprises us by instead of coming to berate, coming to say thanks for a well-done letter I had sent him many years earlier.

So we end up where we began back on the night of 19 December, staring at a TV screen as the seconds pass in slow-motion in the direction of the BBC exit poll. In just a few minutes history will be made, careers launched and service concluded. Polling predictions will be borne out or become the subject of ridicule. It's almost certainly going to be another 'fuck me' moment.

Postscript

It's around 4 a.m. and it's raining hard in the car park of Llanelli Leisure Centre where 'the count' nears its conclusion. Early indications from the tabletop counting suggest that I should comfortably maintain the third position that was anticipated when the election was called just a few weeks ago. Determined to avoid spending several hours pretending to enjoy myself and drinking disgusting tepid tea, I sit out the final moments of my Commons career in my friend John Kilcoyne's Range Rover watching the news reports of a Labour landslide as each return is declared. It is brutal, but we all know how this goes. The exit poll gives us around 125 seats, so just enough to form an opposition and start the long march back to Government. But we have been punished rather than Starmer rewarded. It is as someone has already said, a 'loveless landslide'.

With formalities concluded and as the early morning light starts to show, John and I head for London, for there is one important task still to complete. At around 9.00, we congregate in the hall of No. 10 to 'clap out' Rishi and Akshata. Everyone is there, officials, civil servants, support staff, catering and housekeeping, as they make their way from the Cabinet Room to the front door through which Rishi will shortly go to make his final comments. It's a strangely uplifting moment too, despite the tears of some of his oldest friends and colleagues. I am stood by the front door next to Cabinet Secretary Simon Case and with a

good view of the approaching couple. Perhaps the best was saved to last as he reached Comms SpAd Jack Sellers, who had been with him every yard of the campaign and whose job it was to keep him focused, briefed and upbeat. And with that it was my turn, a hug, some words of thanks from me to him and that he had much to be proud of. And with that we were instructed to place our passes in the cardboard box and leave the building.

Acknowledgments

It might sound strange, but if it wasn't for Boris Johnson, this book, and my career, might have been a great deal more boring. He gave me the ringside seat from which I ended up seeing more of the action than either of us bargained for. Less surprising is the thanks I owe Rishi Sunak for entrusting the Whips' Office to the hands of someone untried in that department, at one of the most volatile times in recent political history. It was a brave move, and he never failed to support me and the team thereafter.

In listing those to whom I owe so much, I am also conscious that books like this need to tread a careful line between being an accurate, no-holds-barred account of what happened at the time, and a breach of custom or confidence.

As such, I am also going to risk even greater ridicule by devoting a few sentences of tribute to the Special Advisers (SpAds) and civil servants who have quietly ensured that the roles I have undertaken throughout government were as trouble-free as possible. Jack Sellers and Emma Pryor in particular became quickly adept at second guessing my next move or comment to the extent that they managed to avert numerous opportunities for me to humiliate myself in public.

I quickly learnt that the pressures of life in No. 10 are unlike anything else I have experienced in my professional life. If it wasn't for the remarkable resilience (and humour) of people like Rupert Yorke, James Forsyth, Nissi Chesterfield, Will Tanner,

James Nation and Cass Horowitz, I dread to think how we would have coped. Our most valued friend, PPS Craig Williams, discovered in the most painful way how quickly things can go badly wrong.

It is with sadness that I am bound by convention not to mention by name the numerous civil servants in the Cabinet Office, Wales Office and in No. 10, who fulfilled a similar uphill task at the same time as resolving complex and confidential challenges without ever giving away what they must have really been thinking about our latest venture. They – you – are brilliant people.

As a newcomer to this book-writing process I have been amazed by the number of (very patient) people who are vital to its completion. In the same way that a surgeon gets all the credit for a successful operation, I doubt very much they could have achieved the same outcome on their own. At different stages in the process some quite young but very talented people put all the pieces together, smoothed egos and mopped up tears. They would make brilliant whips! I'd especially like to flag a couple of those who went above and beyond. Checkie Hamilton and Tom Lloyd-Williams at Aevitas, and more recently Alex Osmond at Apple Tree Literary.

I have loved working with the team at Pan Macmillan. Whether it was James Annal for coming up with the cover design, Kim Nyamhondera for managing publicity, Kate Tolley, Meg Le Huquet and Lydia Ramah for project editing, Holly Sheldrake for getting us to print or the Macmillan lawyers for being brave enough to leave some of the manuscript intact, it has been a delightfully pleasant journey. My thanks to everyone there!

And of course, leading that team with such calm authority was my publisher, Sara Cywinski, structural editor, James Nightingale, and the undisputed owner of this project, my indefatigable and indestructible agent, Max Edwards.

Back in 2010 I started writing a diary as a light-hearted record

of my lifestyle, as something my then-young children could laugh at in years to come. It was a good while later that the reality of what it's like to be the family of an MP dawned. There are some incredible upsides, unfettered access to places and occasions that most can only dream of. But there are also costs to bear too, and that results in the greatest gratitude being reserved for Abi, Adam and Nell whose patience and understanding were regularly put to the test, but who never allowed that to impact on the unpredictable journey upon which I had surprisingly embarked.

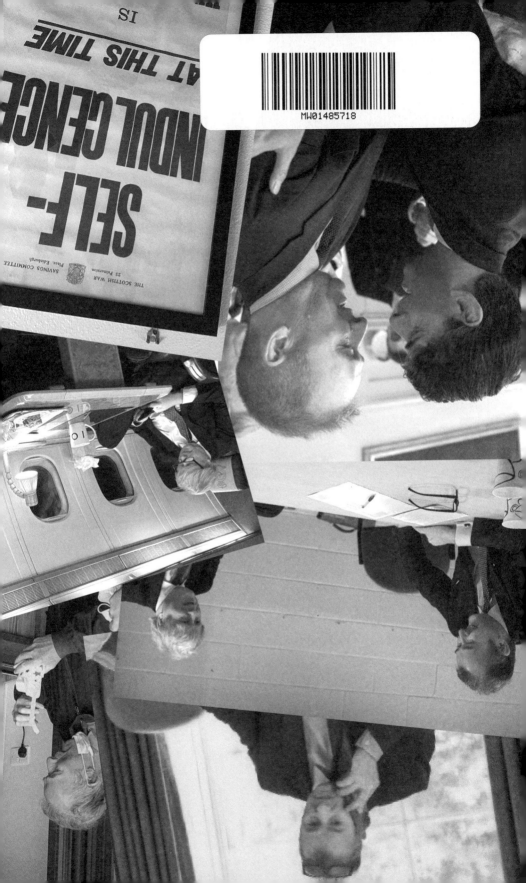